was born in 525 B.C. at Eleusis, the scene of the ancient Mysteries, and died in the new Greek world of Sicily in 456, yet he was a complete fifth-century Athenian— an aristocrat by birth, a democrat by commitment. He fought at Marathon, Athens's proudest victory. And he was the creator of her proudest artistic achievement, tragedy—thanks to his introduction of the second actor, the originality of his style, somber and sublime, and his dramatization of fundamental tragic questions: what is our inheritance of brutality? what is the bond between our suffering and our self-awareness? between our willpower and the dictates of the gods?

Only seven plays remain of perhaps ninety written during Aeschylus's career. Of these the ORESTEIA—composed of AGAMEMNON, THE LIBATION BEARERS, and THE EUMENIDES—is his undisputed masterpiece. The only complete trilogy that has come down to us from antiquity, its spirit of struggle and renewal is eternal.

"The present scholarly and sensitive translation could almost stand as an education in itself."
—Kenneth Burke

"Much the best translation of THE ORESTEIA I've ever seen."
—Rex Warner

"A majesterial translation of THE ORESTEIA."
—Joyce Carol Oates

"The best translations, it strikes me, are like trees: they have their roots down deep in the original culture, but their tops glisten with the sun and rain of our own speech. This translation obviously belongs to that rare class."

—Maynard Mack

"I have been reading the Fagles ORESTEIA gratefully, with excited rummaging in the Greek text. The translation is in living English, and actable, but close to Aeschylus and never free, I feel, but in his behalf. One has the sweep of the trilogy interpreted in a consistent style, high but easy, folding in the colloquial where appropriate, rising to the occasion in visionary passages.... All in all it's an impressive work."

—Robert Fitzgerald

"Professor Fagles conveys more vividly and powerfully than any of the ten competitors I have consulted the eternal power of this masterpiece.... A triumph; I yearn to see it acted."

—Bernard Levin,
The Observer Review

"It is Fagles' remarkable power as a translator to produce an English style that is willing to subdue itself in favor of the original Greek, without, in fact, incurring the fate of being subdued: that is to say, his English is mindful of its responsibility but not intimidated by it."

—Denis Donoghue,
The Southern Review

"Justly acknowledged as one of the most admirable English translations of a classical text."

—Dennis Kratz,
The Translation Review

Aeschylus
THE ORESTEIA

Translated by
Robert Fagles

Introductory Essay,
Notes and Glossary
with W. B. Stanford

BANTAM BOOKS
TORONTO · NEW YORK · LONDON · SYDNEY

*This low-priced Bantam Book
has been completely reset in a type face
designed for easy reading, and was printed
from new plates. It contains the complete
text of the original hard-cover edition.*
NOT ONE WORD HAS BEEN OMITTED.

RL 11, IL age 16 and up

THE ORESTEIA
*A Bantam Book / published by arrangement with
The Viking Press*

PRINTING HISTORY
*Viking edition published October 1975
First Bantam edition / January 1977
Bantam Classic edition / February 1982*

ACKNOWLEDGMENTS

Harcourt Brace Jovanovich, Inc., and Faber and Faber Ltd.: From "The Dry Salvages" and "East Coker" from *Four Quartets* by T. S. Eliot.

Liveright Publishing Corp.: From "The Dance" from *The Collected Poems and Selected Letters and Prose of Hart Crane* by Hart Crane. Copyright © 1933, 1958, 1966 by Liveright Publishing Corp. Reprinted by permission of Liveright Publishing, New York.

Macmillan Publishing Co., Inc., M. B. Yeats and the Macmillan Company of London & Basingstoke, and the Macmillan Company of Canada: From "To Dorothy Wellesley" from *Collected Poems* by William Butler Yeats. Copyright 1940 Georgie Yeats, renewed 1968 by Bertha Georgia Yeats, Michael Butler Yeats and Anne Yeats. From "Two Songs from a Play" from *Collected Poems* by William Butler Yeats. Copyright 1928 by Macmillan Publishing Co., Inc., renewed 1956 by Georgie Yeats.

The New American Library, Inc.: From *Lucretius: On the Nature of Things*, translated by Palmer Bovie and published by The New American Library. Reprinted by permission of The New American Library.

The Viking Press, Inc.: From *The Collected Letters of D. H. Lawrence*, edited by Harry T. Moore. Copyright © 1962 by Angelo Ravagli and C. Montague Weekley. All rights reserved. Reprinted by permission of The Viking Press, Inc.

Yale University Press: From *The Earth, the Temple, and the Gods: Greek Sacred Architecture* by Vincent Scully (New Haven and London, 1962).

CONTENTS

FOREWORD

My thanks to Aeschylus for his companionship, his rigors and his kindness. I found him a burly, eloquent ghost, with more human decency and strength than I could hope to equal. As I tried to approach him, I remembered what they said of the ghost of Hamlet's father: "We do it wrong, being so majestical, To offer it the show of violence." Translation has its violent moments, and I suppose it must. It begins with attraction, then a kind of attack, and it ends, if you are lucky, with a strong impersonation of your author. Whatever the end, at any rate, it is meant to be a thing of love and homage. So in thanking that proud old spirit, I would also ask for his forbearance, if he should ever hear what I have written in his name.

Now it is time to let this version of the *Oresteia* speak for itself, without apologies or statements of principle (petards that will probably hoist the writing later). A translator's best hope, I think, and still the hardest to achieve, is Dryden's hope that his author will speak the living language of the day. And not in a way that caters to its limits, one might add, but that gives its life and fibre something of a stretching in the process. In translating Aeschylus I have also tried to suggest the responsion of his choral poetry—the paired, isometric stanzas that form the dialectic dance and singing of his plays in Greek—but I have done so flexibly, and using English rhythms. The translation has its leanings too, yet they are loyal to Aeschylus, at least as I perceive him, and loyal to the modern grain as well. There is a kinship between the *Oresteia* and ourselves; a mutual need to recognize the fragility of our culture, to restore some reverence for the Great Mother and her works, and especially to embrace the Furies within ourselves, persuading them to invigorate our lives. I hope this kinship can be felt in the English text and supported by the introductory essay.

The essay begins and ends with broader, general sections; in between come more detailed descriptions of each play. The final version of the introduction is my own, particularly the freer conjectures about images and symbols, the moral power of the Furies, and the psychological and religious dimensions of the *Oresteia*. My collaborator, W. B. Stanford, has supplied accounts of the dramatic action and a good deal of historical and linguistic material—the discussion of the watchman, Clytaemnestra's third speech, and her crucial exchanges with Agamemnon and the elders. The passages on technique owe much to him, to what he has written for the purpose, and his books on Greek metaphor, ambiguity, and *Aeschylus in His Style*. As we will indicate later, we have shared the writing of the notes. We have relied on Fraenkel's edition of *Agamemnon* with few exceptions, on Murray's of *The Libation Bearers* and *The Eumenides* with help from other scholars. (Unfortunately Denys Page's new edition of Aeschylus arrived too late for us to use.) Our line numbers refer to the English text throughout and not the Greek; and we have kept the English or Latin forms of the most familiar proper names, but have transliterated the rest.

I could not have done my part without the help of many people. Bedell Stanford first, of course. He offered me what I have needed most, Ionic tolerance and Doric discipline. So much patience with my questions, so many cautions to revise—he has been the brake to my locomotive, in his phrase, and the conscience of Aeschylus in mine. Before they met their deaths in June, 1971, my friends Anne and Adam Parry often came to my rescue with their knowledge, comradeship and warmth. Robert Fitzgerald helped me on many points, even as late as the galleys of the first edition, with his Homeric magnanimity and tact. Kenneth Burke taught me that *The*

Eumenides is less tragic than I had thought, and less transcendental than he would like. And the one who led me to translate the *Oresteia* gave me his painstaking, strenuous criticism of the opening play, its notes and introduction. He would rather not be named; I owe him more than I can say.

Others have helped as well, with advice or encouragement or both. The list is long because the work was long, and they were very generous. Some are gone now—Alan Downer, Dudley Fitts, Erich Kahler, Robert Murray, Jr., and Fred Wieck. But many more remain: Donald Carne-Ross and the staff of *Arion*, where parts of the translation first appeared; Patricia Purcell Chappell, Julius Cohen, Robert Connor, Mark Davies, Francis Fergusson, Joseph Frank, Georgine and Ralph Freedman, Caroline Gordon, Edmund Keeley, Bernard Knox, Hanna Loewy, Maynard Mack, Mary Renault, Erich Segal, George Steiner, Dorothy Thompson, Kathryn Walker, Rex Warner, Theodore Weiss, and Theodore Ziolkowski.

My students ought to know how much I have learned about tragedy from them. I think of William Abernathy, Louis Bell, Kathleen Costello, James Donlan, Ruth Gais, Katherine Callen King, Kathleen Komar, David Lenson, James McGregor, Robert Scanlan, Celeste Schenck, Janet Levarie Smarr, and Macklin Smith. And I remember the brave actors who performed an early version of *Agamemnon* at McCarter Theatre in 1966, Angela Wood, and George and Susan Hearn. Princeton University granted me leaves of absence to work on Aeschylus, and the Research Committee freely saw to my expenses.

This is a new edition of the book, and I want to thank the ones who made it possible. Especially my editor, Toni Burbank, for her precision, her care in preserving the original design, and her sheer affection for the writing; and the good people at Bantam Books for their belief that Aeschylus should have a broad appeal. Once again Georges Borchardt poured the wine and sped the work, and Alan Williams cared for this *Oresteia* as if it were his own; without their kindness it might never have seen the light.

Thanks above all to Lynne, abiding thanks and more—

... ἔστι γὰρ ἡμῖν
σήμαθ', ἅ δὴ καὶ νῶϊ κεκρυμμένα ἴδμεν ἀπ' ἄλλων.

R. F.
Princeton, New Jersey
September 1976

A READING OF THE Oresteia

THE SERPENT AND THE EAGLE

Now is the strong prayer folded in thine arms,
The serpent with the eagle in the boughs.

—HART CRANE, *"The Dance"*

Aeschylus was forty-five in 480 B.C. when the Persians sacked Athens and destroyed the shrines of the gods on the Acropolis. Soon afterward he fought in the forces which defeated the Persians at Salamis and Plataea, as he had fought in the Greek victory at Marathon ten years before. The Greeks in general, and the Athenians in particular, because they had played the major part in the triumph of Hellas, saw these victories as a triumph of right over might, courage over fear, freedom over servitude, moderation over arrogance. After their struggle the people of Athens entered upon a spectacular era of energy and prosperity, one of the great flowering periods of Western civilization. Physically the two noblest monuments of that age were the Parthenon of Ictinos and Pheidias, and the Oresteian trilogy of Aeschylus. Paradoxically, when one considers the contrast between the durability of marble and the fragility of papyrus, the *Oresteia* is better preserved by far. But both were expressions of optimism as well as of artistic genius. Out of the savagery of past wars and feuds a new harmony—religious, political, and personal—might be created. Perhaps Athens would achieve what public-spirited men and women have always longed for, a peaceful, lawful community, a city of benevolent gods and beneficent men. Within fifty years of the Persian defeat the dream had faded, and before the end of the century Athens, overextended abroad and overconfident at home, lay defeated at the mercy of her enemies, a Spartan garrison posted on the Acropolis and democracy in ruins. Much in the intervening years had been magnificent, it is true, but so it might have remained if the Athenians had heeded Aeschylus. As early as *The Persians* he had portrayed the Greek victory as a triumph over the barbarian latent in themselves, the *hubris* that united the invader and the native tyrant as targets of the gods. Their downfall, like the downfall of Agamemnon, called not only for exultation but for compassion and lasting self-control.

The *Oresteia* perfects this vision of warning and reward. Athenian exhilaration still ran strong in 458 when Aeschylus, at the age of sixty-seven, produced his trilogy. It breathes the buoyant spirit of his city. Its dominant symbolism is that of light after darkness. Beginning in the darkness-before-dawn of a Mycenaean citadel benighted by curses and crimes, it ends with a triumphant torchlit procession in an Athens radiant with civic faith and justice. The entire drama is one long procession, and each step brings us closer to the light. Originally the *Oresteia* consisted of four plays—*Agamemnon, The Libation Bearers, The Eumenides,* and *Proteus.* The last was a satyr-play, completing the full "tetralogy" dramatists composed. It would have presented gods and heroes in a comic situation that relieved the tensions of the tragedies while illuminating them with fresh perspectives. The *Proteus* has not survived, but the three tragedies form a unity in themselves, the only complete Greek trilogy we have, and its scope is as expansive as an epic. Aeschylus referred to his work as "slices from the banquet of Homer," but his powers of assimilation were impressive. His trilogy sweeps from the *Iliad* to the *Odyssey,* from war to peace. Yet it was the darker events of the *Odyssey*—the murder of Agamemnon by his wife and the vengeance of his son, Orestes—that inspired Aeschylus to produce a great tale of the tribe. He deepened Homer with even older, darker legends and lifted him to a later, more enlightened stage of culture.

Let us recall the outlines of the tale. The house of Atreus is the embodiment of savagery. No other Greek family can rival it for accumulated atrocities. The founder of the line was Tantalus of Lydia, a barbarian whose spirit haunts the *Oresteia*. He offended the gods by feasting them on his son's flesh, and they condemned him to starve in Hades, "tantalized" by the drink and luscious fruits they dangled out of reach. But they restored his victim, Pelops, to a new, resplendent life. Later he went to western Greece, where he won the hand of Hippodameia by a ruse which killed her father—a murderous chariot race which may have been the origin of the Olympic games. Pelops had two sons, Atreus and Thyestes. When Thyestes seduced his brother's wife and contested his right to the throne, Atreus banished him and then, luring him back for a reconciliation, feasted him on his children's flesh. Horrified, Thyestes cursed Atreus and his descendants and fled into exile once again, accompanied by his one remaining son, Aegisthus. Atreus had two sons, Agamemnon and Menelaus, who jointly inherited the realm of Argos and married two daughters of Tyndareos, Clytaemnestra and Helen. Agamemnon became the commander-in-chief of the Greek forces that attacked Troy to avenge the seduction of Helen by Paris, son of Priam. At the outset of the expedition, however, Agamemnon had to sacrifice his and Clytaemnestra's daughter Iphigeneia—a fact that Homer had omitted, perhaps to exonerate the king for an aristocratic audience—and so he becomes an agent of the curse upon his house.

The action of the *Oresteia* begins more than nine years later, just after the fall of Troy and Agamemnon's seizure of Cassandra, the daughter of Priam and priestess of Apollo, whom he abducts to Argos as his mistress. The *Agamemnon* describes how Clytaemnestra kills her husband for the death of their daughter and the insult of Cassandra, and establishes herself and Aegisthus, her paramour and also the avenger of his father, as rulers over Argos. It is not a case of right against wrong as it is in Homer; it demonstrates Nietzsche's motto for Aeschylean tragedy: "All that exists is just and unjust and equally justified in both" (in Walter Kaufmann's translation). And its sequel erupts into a moral struggle never told by Homer. In *The Libation Bearers* the only son of Agamemnon and Clytaemnestra, Orestes, obeys the command of Apollo and kills the murderers in revenge; but his mother's Furies drive him mad and in the final play, *The Eumenides*, pursue him to Apollo's shrine at Delphi. The god can purify Orestes of bloodguilt but cannot release him from the Furies and refers him to Athens and Athena for their judgment. There the goddess appoints a group of men to conduct a trial for manslaughter and so establishes the Areopagus, her famous court of law. Orestes is acquitted and restored to his fathers' lands in Argos, while Athena persuades the Furies, the demons of the primitive vendetta-law, to become benevolent patrons, changing their names to "Eumenides," the Kindly Ones of Athens. The final choruses are in the mood of Beethoven's Hymn to Joy: let us rejoice, the spirit of man has triumphed over the harsher elements of life—a new order has been born.

What Aeschylus builds upon the house of Atreus is "a grand parable of progress," as Richmond Lattimore has described it, that celebrates our emergence from the darkness to the light, from the tribe to the aristocracy to the democratic state. At the same time Aeschylus celebrates man's capacity for suffering, his courage to endure hereditary guilt and ethical conflicts, his battle for freedom in the teeth of fate, and his strenuous collaboration with his gods to create a better world. The tragic burden of the *Iliad* is magnified, then channeled into the battle of the *Odyssey*, the battle to win home. Aeschylus is optimistic, but he would agree with Hardy: "if way to the Better there be, it exacts a full look at the Worst." How had we come so far? he asks. Through struggle, and through struggle we will advance. Zeus, as the old men of Argos tell us, "lays it down as law/that we must suffer, suffer into truth." Perhaps no paradox inspired Aeschylus more than the bond that might exist between *pathos* and *mathos*, suffering and its significance. That bond is life itself. Reflect on the house of Atreus, what's more, on Pelops' regeneration from the caldron, on the rise of the Olympic games from an act of murder, on the establishment of the Areopagus in response to Orestes' matricide, and that bond produces our achievements—pain becomes a stimulus and a gift. This commitment to suffering not only as the hallmark of the human condition but as the very stuff of human victory lends the *Oresteia* its perennial appeal. But it does not speak to certain later, more spiritual ages which sublimate our anguish into "the blest Kingdoms meek of joy and love." Aeschylus speaks to a world more secular, to some more dangerous, more exhilarating, more real. He would say with Keats, "Do you not see how necessary a World of Pain and troubles is . . . ? A Place where the heart must feel and suffer in a thousand diverse ways! . . . thus does God make individual beings, Souls, Identical Souls of the sparks of his own essence—This appears to me a faint sketch of a system of Salvation which does not affront our reason and humanity."

The suffering of Atreus and his sons is a very old and yet a very modern matter. They are less removed from us than we might like to think. They are cursed, their lives are an inherited disease, a miasma that threatens the health of their community and forces them, relentlessly, to commit their fathers' crimes. It is as if crime were contagious—and perhaps it is—the dead pursued the living for revenge, and revenge could only breed more guilt. For such guilt is more than criminal; it is a psychological guilt that modern men have felt and tried to probe. Every crime in the house of Atreus, whether children kill their parents or parents kill their children and feed upon their flesh, is a crime against the filial bond itself. So dominant is the pattern, in fact, that E. R. Dodds and others say that such mythology reflects the pathology of a culture ridden by its guilt. This is a subject that psychohistorians may explain; we can only allude to its vaguest generalities here. What the members of that culture may have fantasized and repressed, creating a pressure of recrimination in themselves, the sons of Atreus, their surrogates, have acted out with relish and abandon. They have heard Blake's Proverb of Hell: "Sooner murder an infant in its cradle than nurse unacted desires." Those desires rose to a fever pitch, some surmise, between Homer and the age of tragedy. Whatèver conflicts caused them—the miseries of existence that might seem to set the dead against the living; or historical upheavals, the economic crisis of the seventh century that unleashed the class warfare of the sixth; or emotional tensions bred by the breaking-up of family solidarity—a people felt themselves in the grip of an angry father-god. His injustice was their fate; his judgment was the measure of their guilt.

They sought escape in the purges of Apollo, a god of self-restraint. They appealed to his opposite, Dionysos, a god of ecstasy who may have promised more. We will never be certain of his nature—what follows is sheer conjecture—but our intimations point to a god of paradox. Dionysos, son of Zeus and a mortal woman, Semele, was born of the earth and yet is always striving for the sky. Originally he was a god of fertility, even of life in all its contradictions, blasting us and blessing us at once. He was the menace of existence turning fruitful and, as the god of wine, leading us to joy. His spirit well might rule the house of Atreus, its atrocities and its achievements. For the rites of Dionysos could include the rending of living creatures and feeding on their flesh; yet his rites were horrible and holy too, as Dodds suggests, and through them his communicants could absorb his vital gifts. He is the god who dies, the hunter who is hunted, the render who is rent—but all to be reborn. According to one legend Hera was enraged that Semele had borne the child-god by Zeus; she commanded the Titans to tear him limb from limb and eat him raw. So they did, and Zeus consumed them with lightning and Dionysos with them. But he was restored, and from the Titans' ashes with their residue of his blood the race of man sprang forth, part Titan and part god, rage and immortal aspiration fused.

Through Dionysos, in other words, men might be restored, not by escaping their nature but by embracing it, not by expiating their guilt but by exercising it constructively. Here was a father, an authority who challenged us to challenge him. Only by acting out our fantasies against him—by ritualistically dismembering his body and partaking of his strength—could we become ourselves, human, seasoned, strong. Perhaps that is why he lashed a guilty age into a dance of life as irresistible as St. Vitus' dance in time of plague. He was health and more; his euphoria led to better realms of being. By the time of Aeschylus, some believe, Dionysos had become the god of the senses straining toward a religious affirmation. His worship was a return to nature led by sensible, sophisticated men who reached for the world in its primitive aspect—its innocence, its terror, its powers of renewal—not as a cue for madness but as an incentive for their culture. The ecstasy of Dionysos became ennobling. He became Olympian; he shared Apollo's shrine at Delphi. The suffering god was transformed into a savior, but not in the way of later martyrs who reject this life. Dying into life, into more coherent, vibrant forms of life was the way of Dionysos and his people.

They communed through tragedy, "a terrible sacrament of the god," as Yeats imagined it. Tragedy was created for Dionysos' rites of spring in Athens and was performed in his theater on the southern slopes of the Acropolis. The ritual origins of tragedy are totally in doubt, often hotly contested. We will merely suggest how certain rites may still exist within the *Oresteia*, not as rituals in themselves, religiously observed, but freely adapted to the point of sacred parody, re-created and recast by Aeschylus' distinctive tragic vision. For while these rituals may reflect the growth of Dionysos from a spirit of the year to the spirit of human culture, they dramatize, continually, his tragic spirit of suffering and regeneration. Throughout the trilogy we may feel the sunrise breaking from the night or the seasons wheeling in their rounds, the winter yielding to the spring that leads again to harvest. Even more deeply, we may sense what the early tribe inferred from the making of the year: the making of a man, his rites of passage. Such rituals are ordeals, painful strides from loss to gain that mark a person at the crises of his life—puberty, marriage, death—and unite him with a larger set of values, his mate, his society, the ancestral dead. Yet the *Oresteia* far exceeds the customary trilogy of tribal rites of passage. The *Agamemnon* is like the rite of separation; the king is cut off from his society. *The Libation Bearers* is like the rite of transition; the son is at the threshold of maturity. But *The Eumenides*, the rite of aggregation, celebrates Orestes' initiation into Argos and our initiation into Athens.

The *Oresteia* is our rite of passage from savagery to civilization. What strengthens this impression are the specific rituals that may stir within the trilogy. In debates about the origins of tragedy, they are among the main contenders: the rituals of the dying god, the hero cult and the legal trial. Consider each in turn. The Athenians who gathered in the Theater of Dionysos may have assembled for a passion play, as a congregation assembles at Easter, to worship the god whose death releases vital energies; to see, in Yeats's words,

> *a staring virgin stand*
> *Where holy Dionysus died,*
> *And tear the heart out of his side,*
> *And lay the heart upon her hand*
> *And bear that beating heart away;*
> *And then did all the Muses sing*
> *Of Magnus Annus at the spring,*
> *As though God's death were but a play.*

And the Athenians may have come as patriots to honor his incarnation in a more historical hero, in *his* achievements and their heavy moral price. And when they watched his acquittal before his judges, they may have renewed their dedication to Athenian justice as they witnessed its creation by Athena. Or they may have beheld one rite emerging from another in one continuous drama, from the trial at the altar to the trial at the oracle and the hearth, to the trial at the high tribunal. Like Dionysos struggling into higher forms of life, the trilogy bodies forth each form of trial in turn. More than a rite of passage unrefined, the *Oresteia* dramatizes our growth from primitive ritual itself to civilized institution.

Aeschylus transforms ritual into art, a symbolic action at once more individual and universal. "All human actions which are worked out to the end," as Francis Fergusson observes, "passing through the unforeseeable contingencies of a 'world we never made,' follow a similar course: the conscious purpose with which they start is redefined after each unforeseen contingency is suffered; and at the end, in the light of hindsight, we see the truth of what we have been doing." The way is hard but bracing. Aeschylus presents our lives not only as a painful series of recognitions but as an initiation into stronger states of consciousness. Perhaps most great tragedy conveys this double thrust of shattering and confirmation. Tragedy is a challenge and a trap, a vehicle for our character and our fate. It was Apollo, as Oedipus tells his friends, who multiplied his pains, "but the hand that struck my eyes was mine and mine alone" (in the Bernard Knox translation). The momentum of tragedy threatens to crush us—it is some terrible engine of the gods, yet it also summons the insurgence of the human will, the power of the proud and self-aware.

In the work of Aeschylus, moreover, our self-awareness may revise the "world we never made." Through the *Oresteia* we may recognize a god within ourselves, transform Dionysos into a spirit of morality and say, "Thou art indeed just, Lord, if I contend with thee." For only if we contend with Dionysos will he stimulate our hopes for human victory; and Aeschylus, his celebrant, translates those hopes into clear dramatic forms. He would personify the god in many guises, from a king dismembered physically, to his son, whose mind disintegrates as he strains to reform society. Dionysos is a god; Orestes is a revolutionary hero. He labors under his fathers' curse, he must re-enact its cruelty, but his conscience spurs a sense of responsibility to his people, and he leads them to the city of the rights. His guilt becomes the basis of Athens' greatness. His story, the *Oresteia*, resounds with national purpose. It is the concerted triumph of all that Peisistratos envisioned a hundred years before, when he instituted the Festival of Dionysos, the public recitations of Homer and the competitions of the tragic poets. The genius of that protodemocratic tyrant saw that if ritual, epic and tragedy could fuse—if tragedy could harness the collective force of Dionysos to the willfulness of Homer's heroes, all might be enlarged. The chorus might support the leader, the leader steer the chorus, and the drama urge a nation onward, potent in unity and individual freedom. Tragedy, in Aeschylus' hands, might empower the young democracy.

The *Oresteia* revolutionizes the archaic world. Homer and Hesiod had an earlier parable of progress. Hesiod in his *Theogony* traced the gods themselves from savagery to civilization, or rather to a peak of absolute control. The *Theogony* is a story less of succession than of suppression, of fantasies acted out in filial brutality. Kronos suppressed his father, Ouranos, by castrating him. Zeus suppressed his father, Kronos, blasted him and the Titans with lightning and shackled them in Tartarus. Zeus ruled on high, not because he was good but because he was beyond good and evil, too strong for the law of retaliation that consumed his forebears. He was the invincible masculine will, the Father who triumphed over Mother Earth. His justice, his *Dikê*, was the way of Might Makes Right. His way toward men was the way things are—not in the golden age when men and gods were equal but in this iron age where we grind out a subsistence, sons and fathers at each other's necks, belabored by the gods with massing hardships. Such was Zeus's reign in the third generation of his house, and Aeschylus compares him with Orestes in the third generation of his house, not only to buttress Orestes' victory but to humanize the gods. Aeschylus reopens the *Theogony*, not on a battleground but on a moral plane, the rocky and rewarding soil of the guilt-culture itself. Here Zeus's lightning bolts are of little value. He must use the forces of recrimination he had suppressed, the matriarchal Furies, yet he must contend with them as well, and he plays with a fire somehow equal to himself. The Furies will help to temper Zeus, and *Dikê* will be tempered in the process.

Dikê must evolve from the blood vendetta of the tribe to the social justice of our hopes. Potentially *Dikê* is the force of right and orderly relations, but because of acts of recklessness it has remained a force of vengeance, cursing offenders and their heirs with endless acts of violence— the punishments of the Furies. Paris' rape of Helen is an international violation of *Dikê* that deploys the Greeks against the Trojans, with Agamemnon as the minister of Zeus's Fury. But to accomplish his mission he must violate *Dikê* on an internecine level, sacrifice his daughter and arouse Clytaemnestra in return. The Fury of the Father collides in Argos with the Fury of the Mother, and the Mother wins a battle to the death. But these forces reappear and concentrate within the son, Orestes; they begin to wage a dialectic struggle, straining toward a crucial resolution. Civilization, as Aeschylus sees it, hangs on their success. This *Theogony* is a battle on which the house of Atreus, the house of the gods, and all our houses stand or fall. Aeschylus insists that each generation create a new alliance between the forces in contention for its world; and he presents their conflict in a range of ways, from cosmic to intensely personal. From a theological conflict between Will and Necessity, or Zeus and the Fates—the gods of the Sky and the powers of the Earth; to a social, political conflict between the state with its patriarchal bias and the family with its matriarchal roots; to a psychological conflict between our intellect and our hunger for release, our darker, vengeful drives that can invigorate our dreams of ideality, equity, and balance. For while these forces strive against each other, they are ultimately allies as well. They are as complementary as Dionysos and Apollo, or their partisans who strive to explain the tragic vision—Nietzsche versus Hegel, Cambridge anthropologists versus literary historians, ritualists versus rationalists, fatalists versus spokesmen for the tragic flaw. Like Dionysos in Nietzsche's final vision of him, the *Oresteia* would invite the adversaries to embrace. The trilogy ends with a union of energy and order, the way of nature and the way of man. The shackles of the primitive vendetta lend their rigor to the lasting bonds of law. Society takes what Freud has called "the decisive step of civilization"—*Dikê* turns to justice.

Many powers work toward this end, but none is more essential than the Furies. As they evolve in the *Oresteia*, so they may have evolved in Greek religion, progressing from curses to righteous causes, the ministers of justice who, as Heracleitos saw them, would detect the sun if it should overstep its limits. The Furies are a paradox of violence and potential. Snakes in their hair and black robes swarming, they represent a real, objective law—blood will have blood—yet that is a law of human nature too, and the Furies become the pangs of conscience that can lead to self-fulfillment. This is a paradox that modern psychology has prepared us to accept, especially the psychology of aggression that discovers ties between our powers of destruction and our powers of survival. Their symbiosis, in fact, may have given rise to the Furies if, as legend tells, they sprang to life from the blood of Ouranos' genitals when Kronos lopped and flung them in the sea. For the Furies are the spirits of the avenging dead that can also bring regeneration. They are the paradox of woman, Clytaemnestra first of all, murderous in defense of those she nurtures. They are the potency of creation, now consuming, now empowering, and so their transformation into the kind Eumenides may have been latent in their nature from the start. To another age they would seem the archetype of evil—"these wasteful Furies," in Milton's words. But Aeschylus saw them as the force of love-in-hate that impels our rude beginnings toward our latter-day achievements.

The fire of the Furies is Promethean. "The former age of the Titans [is] brought back from Tartarus once more, restored to the light of day," as Nietzsche says, yet the new divinity that Aeschylus confers upon them is both primordial and perfected too, a merger of the Furies and Athena. And the closing scene of the *Oresteia* rings with joy as well as tumult. A final procession forms, vivid with red cloaks and bright with torches, to escort the Furies to their new homes. The bloody robes of Agamemnon and his murderers have become the robes of law-abiding citizens and their guests. The torches that heralded assassination blaze in honor of a harmonious settlement of ancient wrongs. Athens has suffered; Athens will now go forward under the guidance of her goddess who embodies justice and compassion, the equity of Heaven and the energies of the Earth.

AGAMEMNON

First the king must die. It is Argos, the tenth year of the Trojan War, the year the prophets say that Troy will fall. A watchman has been posted on the roofs, waiting for a beacon that will signal Agamemnon's victory and alert Clytaemnestra for his assassination. The second meaning, unknown to the servant, is reflected in his moods. Despite the impending triumph he is restless, he wavers between sleep and wakefulness, love for his master and servitude to his queen, devotion to the gods— the stately patriarchal stars—and dread of the shooting star this mannish woman may release. Things are moving toward some strange eruption. Suddenly the beacon flames from a nearby mountaintop. He cries for joy, to welcome the king and rouse the queen, and the note of foreboding rushes back. The rhythm of the trilogy has been set. We begin in dark suspense: we are waiting for the light, and it no sooner dispels anxiety than a shadow falls again. The light and the darkness, hope and fear, triumph and defeat contend in all three plays, and the light will not prevail until the last. The day of Athens' glory begins in the "dawn of the darkness," the warlord in eclipse. The very stones of the house would cry it out, but terror chokes the watchman into silence. His closing words—"I speak to those who know; to those who don't/ my mind's a blank"—are the watchword for the play. *Agamemnon* speaks to those who sense the secrets of the house. That façade with its history of cannibalism, adultery, and murder soon will rise and tell its story.

A chorus of elders enters as the watchman leaves. They have not heard of the victory, they are still the voice of the home front anguished by the war, and the war itself appears a dubious battle. It is a mission of Zeus, but its leaders resemble vultures whose stolen offspring, Helen, may not be worth recovering. "Many-manned," she has brought the Greeks and Trojans to a costly stalemate. The old men are helpless as children to resist their fears or the conspiracy that surrounds them. Ironically they turn for reassurance to Clytaemnestra—who has entered silently, ominously to burn her grateful sacrifices; but while they told of the Fury sent to punish Troy, they seem to have summoned the queen whose sacrificial fires spread through Argos now. Dubious as the war itself, she kindles hope on one hand, terror on the other. The old men beg to know what her fires mean. She ignores them. So they turn to the security of a sacrifice conducted in the past.

They break into a rolling epic song—they are charged with the fighting strength of song, *Peitho* or Persuasion— and the *Iliad* begins again, in effect, with the omen sent to Aulis. When the Argives marshaled under Agamemnon and Menelaus, two eagles swooped down on a pregnant hare and devoured it with its unborn young. Calchas, the prophet of Apollo, gave the omen an Olympian interpretation: the Atreidae are avenging eagle-kings of Zeus who will triumph over Troy. But they are child-murderers too, and Artemis the goddess of childbirth, outraged at the sacrifice of innocents at Troy, may demand an innocent of Argos in advance. That is the double force of Calchas' reading of the sign: the kings must "slaughter a suffering, trembling female creature together with its young before coming to the birth" *and* "sacrifice a suffering, trembling female creature, their own offspring, in front of [or on behalf of] the armies." The sacrifice of Troy and Iphigeneia, the justice of Zeus and the appeasement of Artemis clash. And Agamemnon is pinned between them, the man whose justice leads to further crime. Calchas prays that Artemis may work with Zeus, but she will fulfill the Father's murderous will by making Agamemnon fulfill *his* murderous nature. The curse is where the war begins and ends, overshadowed by the internecine warfare that surrounds it. The precondition of victory, Iphigeneia, "another victim" like the children of Thyestes, is the pretext for her mother's vengeance ten years later—"Memory womb of Fury child-avenging Fury." Clytaemnestra will kill Agamemnon to avenge their daughter, then avenge herself upon her son. Calchas' vision is the mainspring of the *Oresteia*. He not only sets the Aeschylean forces against each other, male against female, gods of the Sky against the powers of the Earth; here at the outset he consigns his people to the Furies.

"Cry, cry for death, but good win out in glory in the end." The ominous refrain beats drumlike through the opening stanzas. What glory can be wrung from so much grief? Nothing less than a cosmic union, a new and better world. But the old men strain to praise it here and now, celebrating the only god who can create it—Zeus. They appeal to his vast, incomprehensible power, and they are uplifted by recalling his victory in the *Theogony* which, through savage strife and atrocities like those at Troy and Argos, brought glory out of grief. Yet it also brought the iron age of man, and the old men's hope is undermined by what they offer as its basis: Zeus's law "that we must suffer, suffer into truth." His law may look ahead to the suffering that leads to wisdom, to the restorative power of staid, reasoned judgment; but suffering in *Agamemnon* leads to knowledge that is sorrow. "Pain comes from the darkness," in the words of Randall Jarrell, "and we call it wisdom. It is pain." Our only consolation is that we may suffer into *sôphrosunê* too, the knowledge of our mortal limits—readiness in the Shakespearean sense that "men must endure / Their going hence, even as their coming hither; / Ripeness is all." In Aeschylus the truth is never neutral; it is a gift of the gods, and they have made it vivid. And for that kindness, certain thanks, the old men seem to say, as if they could foresee with Keats that "faint sketch of a system of Salvation which does not affront our reason and humanity" because its basis is suffering itself.

But at this point in the *Oresteia* such salvation is a dream. The elders' hymn is a leap of faith; it heightens the pain of men because it yokes them to the harshness of their gods. Before the hymn Agamemnon's murder of Iphigeneia seemed ordained, but the hymn implicitly evokes his power of choice. He is torn for a moment—how to choose between child-murder and dereliction of duty? "Pain both ways and what is worse?" It is the tragic choice of evils. And it may be predetermined supernaturally by the gods and genetically by Agamemnon's nature—being his father's son, he is bound to choose the worst. But more than a victim of his fate, he is its agent with a vengeance. The more piously he reacts against this outrage, the more he can perform it with impunity, with his own outspoken sense of justice. As Aeschylus says in a famous fragment, "god plants an *aitia* [responsibility] in a man when he wants to destroy a house entirely; nevertheless a man must not be reckless with his words." Agamemnon and his gods are *metaitioi*, co-responsible, yet there is something in this man that may rival his gods for murderous self-righteousness. It is his *Atê*, his frenzy and his ruin, his crime and punishment in one—"the madness of doom" in Werner Jaeger's phrase, and Agamemnon's ruling spirit. He not only conspires with the storm that strikes the fleets, he excels it with the violence of the curse.

Agamemnon's sacrifice of Iphigeneia, now described in superb, swift strokes, is a brutal parody of the Olympian ritual of marriage. According to legend Iphigeneia was brought to Aulis on the pretense of marriage, and here she appears the bride in saffron robes; but the robes become her winding-sheet—her slaughter becomes the *proteleia*, the sacrifice preliminary to the bloody wedding of the armies, a symbol of all our fruitful unions torn by war. She actually consecrates the lethal brides to come, Helen and Clytaemnestra, for her sacrifice is a genuine chthonic rite. It seems to soothe the winds, the spirits of the dead, but it will only bring the dead to life. The chorus cannot bear to describe the deathstroke—"What comes next? I cannot see it, cannot say." Iphigeneia remains a still life, the knife still poised at her throat, the fountainhead of *Agamemnon* still about to burst. The old men try to drown her cries with Zeus's law, a moot reassurance now. They had turned away from Clytaemnestra, but the past is worse and they return to her. She is their only hope, yet she is the very fear they have unleashed—*Dikê* with her sword.

Clytaemnestra approaches. For a moment she seems lost in grateful prayer to the Night, the mother of this day and of the Furies too. For when she reveals the Greeks have taken Troy, the old men challenge her for proof, and her passion overwhelms them. How could the news come overnight? By fire, she replies, and launches out with "tiger-leaps" of imagination, her surging, fiery temper racing the fires like one tremendous torch relayed west along the peaks from Troy to Argos. As the torch announces her husband's victory abroad, however, it predicts her own approaching victory at home. As her beacons leave behind the mountains ruled by the gods, they kindle up a symbolic geography of peril to Agamemnon, building a conflagration of his guilt and Clytaemnestra's superhuman power to avenge it. She is binding him, as Knox suggests, with the burning chains of crime and punishment that bound his fathers. And as she seizes command from the warlord, she is seizing fire from heaven—not only do her beacons rival the relay race of torches run for Hephaistos and Athena; they mark the end of a heroic, Olympian age and the dawn of an age primordial, matriarchal, ever-present.

Zeus's eagles began the war; Clytaemnestra's flaming omen ends it and begins its repercussions, since she is a prophet too. She reads her sign with such immediacy that Troy and Argos seem to merge as cities struck by war. She is here and there, ranging through the streets like the winning general, but more sensitive than Agamemnon, she can see the victims are so pitiful, the victors so pitiless that their victory may recoil,

If only they are revering the city's gods,
the shrines of the gods who love the conquered land,
no plunderer will be plundered in return. . . .
And even if the men come back with no offense
to the gods, the avenging dead may never rest—
Oh let no new disaster strike!

Prophetic warnings that incriminate the king. He *will* desecrate the Trojan shrines and commandeer a priestess, adding the gods to Clytaemnestra's stronger motive, "the avenging dead" themselves. But now, conscious that she may have started suspicions, she breaks off with some conventional womanly phrases (not without their muffled warnings) and goes inside to prepare for Agamemnon.

And so the trap begins to close at the first approach of Agamemnon in his triumph. The old men begin a hymn of thanks for the victory and its lesson: the Trojans repeat their fathers' crimes and so are cursed with *Peitho* in its compulsive aspect, the beautiful, blinding lightning of Helen. She is the bride whose dowry is death for Troy, but death for Greece as well. She plunges both sides into grief, a demon of retaliation who, with Ares the "gold-broker of corpses," leads the people of Argos against the "defenders" who led them into war. Now those who died in victory demand vengeance as surely as those who died in defeat. "Poor exchange, poor return" pervades this chorus; its six stanzas form six turns in a vicious circle of revenge. The guilt that incriminated Paris incriminates Agamemnon—Zeus and the Furies await the murderer of Greece. And the victory hymn becomes a moan of fear, as the old men fall back on a muted prayer for peace; they try to reject Clytaemnestra's message (women are gullible, they murmur, oversanguine) but it is too late. The leader sees a herald fresh from Troy. A victorious spray of olive "shades" his face, and he tells a double story: though the Greeks have won the day, the king has desecrated Troy. There is little reason to rejoice. Argos and the armies longed for each other, but as the leader hints, the citizens needed the men to save them from repression. In his joy the herald fails to understand, yet as he recollects the miseries that the army has escaped abroad, he contributes them, like echoes from another country under siege, to the growing miseries of Argos. The more he revels in the spoils of Troy, the more he provokes the envy of the queen, absent but listening, or so her triumphant entrance would suggest.

She taunts the old men with their doubts. She meant what she said, and she gives the herald a message for the king that means the opposite of all it seems to say. She rushes to welcome him in "the best possible way," to "open wide the gates"—her husband has been saved by the Saving God, whom she will identify with Death. She has heard "no joy or blame from another man" as surely as "dye will not stain bronze"—a proverb for the impossible, but you can dye bronze with blood, as she intends to do. She all but tells the herald so. Her closing words would seem to mean "Such is my boast, filled with truth and not disgraceful for a noble woman to utter," but their more sinister meaning is "I am not just twisting the truth; I am proclaiming my determination to take revenge on Agamemnon." These ironies acquit her of telling blatant lies in public. Her scorn of dull conventionality forbids that, and so does her demonic nature. She is no loyal Penelope; she is a female Odysseus waiting at home to murder her husband and marry the suitor—a grim travesty of epic events, cloaked in all the warped familiarities of a nightmare. The loving wife's words mask hideous infidelities; the pious prayer becomes a witches' Sabbath; the palace gates become the Gates of Hell; "the best possible way" to welcome a husband is to kill him in the name of Artemis and the Furies. Clytaemnestra's ironies, more than strong deceptions, conjure up the supernatural—she becomes infernal, the terror that walks in darkness, and what speeds her husband home is the tempest she releases in effect.

A storm, the herald admits, has struck the returning fleets, "and not without the anger of the gods." Not only does it carry off Menelaus, leaving his brother less protected; it makes Agamemnon seem the lone survivor of the victory. Worse, the north wind has come howling for another victim, ten years later; but now the storm is Clytaemnestra's spirit, as lethal as the spirit of her sister. The old men sing of Helen who has "realized" the meaning of her name, fatal to the Greeks (*Helena* from *hele*, implying "to destroy," *-na*, implying ships) but far more fatal to the Trojans. Her marriage is a *kêdos*, both a tie-by-marriage and a grief that ravages their city. For it leads to a birth as painful as that of the lion cub in the parable, "adopted by the house to lend it warmth" until the savagery in its blood broke out and it massacred its hosts. So Helen was captivating at first and then a Fury to the Trojans in their pride. And the moral of the story is a fundamental of early Greek ethics. In all prosperity there is a seed of insolence that matures and leads to ruin, or so the common man believes, oppressed by a sense of guilt for every kind of gain. But the old men stress the importance of responsibility; it is not opulence alone but outrageous acts that breed disaster. And they foresee that righteous acts bring justice shining through the darkness—the paramount message of the *Oresteia*.

The elders are prophetic but premature. They have overrated Zeus from the start, forgetting his alliance with the Furies in the Furies' first, vindictive form. To rationalize the storm above their heads they have sublimated Helen into a principle of justice, but the revenge she takes on Priam reminds us that her sister waits to take revenge on Agamemnon. In fact the cue for his entrance at this moment, laden with plunder, may be their warning against the riches got in excess. The first half of the play, an *Iliad* of the king's triumph, is all an ominous prologue to his *Odyssey*, his reunion with the queen. He is driving toward his "destined end"—his death at the hands of Fury.

This conflict between justice and the Furies builds to the clash between the king and queen at the center of the play. Agamemnon is a mass of contradictions. The old men salute him as the scourge of Troy and the savior of Argos, and despite his excesses in the past, they see him as the hero of the Mean who can distinguish enemies from friends—he will have to now, they warn him—and they praise him as the shepherd of his flock. As an Athenian audience would have known however, he is a brave but reckless king in the *Iliad*, and Aeschylus presents him here as majestic in his power but inhuman. His destruction of Troy is a sacrilege equal to Xerxes' desecration of the Acropolis. Worse, he may even be the archetype of the native tyrant so recently expelled from Greece. More than the justice of the gods, he has become a law to himself. He reduces his gods to *metaitioi*, now lieutenants who must insure his lasting triumph—and so, in less than an hour, they insure his death. His royal We unites him with his fathers—"our bloody lion lapped its fill, / gorging on the blood of kings"—while he exceeds his fathers' fatal pride and downfall. Certain he can restore his city as conclusively as he demolished Priam's, he calls for a trial to test his people, appealing to Victory to "speed [him] to the last." And Clytaemnestra *will*.

She is the far more potent force—like Milton's Satan in her ingeniousness, her arrogance, though Milton gradually undermines Satan's heroic energies while Aeschylus is building Clytaemnestra's. Not only does she have the right of retaliation on her side; she is one of the towering figures in European drama, diabolic yet strangely touching as her ironies portray her here. In self-defense she testifies to "how she loves the man," and the man must be Aegisthus, unless it is also Agamemnon, for she reveals an embattled love for him. It is the war she fights at home, within herself, and has been losing. For all her resistance to solitude, her love for Agamemnon has yielded to infidelity, then to resentment, but it has not ceased to be a kind of love as well. It lingers between her lines like one of the old men's memories that bring delight and pain:

> I'd watch till late at night, my eyes still burn,
> I sobbed by the torch I lit for you alone.
> I never let it die . . . but in my dreams
> the high thin wail of a gnat would rouse me,
> piercing like a trumpet—I could see you

suffer more than all
the hours that slept with me could ever bear.

The torch goes to the heart of Clytaemnestra's darkness, flickering like her feeling for her husband—now the lamp beside their bed, now the light for her paramour, now the beacon burning for revenge.

In dreams begin the queen's responsibilities and a vision of their price. Again she means what she says, but now her meanings multiply and blend. "If he took one wound for each report / to penetrate these walls, he's gashed like a dragnet, / more, if he had only died..." Her extravagant pity becomes a death threat and, as if just breathed in a half-line, the wish that he had died at Troy and she were spared the dreadful work at home. Through her war she gains what he has lost through his: sympathy for the victim and something even deeper. Empowered by a love that makes her hatred stronger—by an admiration for his prowess that makes her prove "that heaven had made her such a man"—she manipulates her husband, the elders, and ourselves:

> And so
> *our child is gone, not standing by our side,*
> *the bond of our dearest pledges, mine and yours;*
> *by all rights our child should be here...*
> Orestes.

In defending herself for the absence of their son, she suspends his name until we recall their daughter Iphigeneia too, and so she indicts the king for murder. He is the victim of irony, she is the master. She "would salute" him as a public defender, but he is indefensible, and he is standing trial in her court.

Clytaemnestra's welcome, the tapestries she spreads before him, are the grounds for his incrimination. These were fabrics sacred to the gods; to walk on them would be an Oriental excess and, to a man like Agamemnon, a strong temptation. They glitter with silver embroidery; they are also dyed with the red dye from the Murex snail, "sea-purple" dark as blood—a visual paradox of deadliness and richness. At first Agamemnon rejects the queen's temptation. He knows *hubris* when he sees it, he reveres the gods. He protests too much. Clytaemnestra knows hypocrisy when she sees it. Turn that piety inward, you have self-destructive pride. She overpowers him in a tense, brusque dialogue—less than a minute in performance—that seals Agamemnon's doom.

She begins by challenging him as the man who knows his limits. She asks him if he will speak his mind frankly. "You may be sure," he replies indignantly, "I shall not destroy [or 'violate': the Greek could carry a military or a sexual metaphor] the principles I have just expressed." By gaining this promise—Agamemnon is too vain to refuse it—Clytaemnestra makes his mind as vulnerable to her verbal thrusts as his body soon will be to her weapon. "Suppose you had been afraid of some disaster," she continues, "would you have sworn to the gods to do the kind of thing that I am asking?" Agamemnon admits he would, if a person skilled in such matters prescribed such a ritual—as Calchas had, we remember, to appease Artemis at Aulis. Clytaemnestra then attacks on another front, turning adroitly to the war itself, and asks, "What would Priam have done if he had had your success?" Certainly, Agamemnon thinks, almost with a trace of envy, *he* would have walked on the tapestries. Clytaemnestra is too skillful to draw the obvious conclusion— "Why not you, then?" She draws things out, eager for him to excel his enemy in hypocrisy as well. He seems to fear popular condemnation, she insinuates, but would Priam? Agamemnon is superior to Priam, isn't he? Indeed he is, as he replies. He is morally superior, and he stands his ground in good democratic style. He respects the *vox populi*. "Well, the man who won't risk envy will never be enviable." Here she strikes a nerve: Agamemnon did risk public criticism for glory in the past; argue the point, and the pose of the democrat may collapse, so he resorts to other platitudes. "A woman shouldn't want to fight this way." He is losing his grip on the first issue and playing into Clytaemnestra's "man-designing" hands.

Now she takes the offensive, as only a woman can. A victorious soldier can quite properly yield to a woman, she insists, and her appeal from apparent weakness to apparent strength makes him waver: "Do you really value victory in this contest of ours?" "Do be persuaded," she replies, and then with brilliant insight—since Agamemnon was always the man to have it both ways—she adds, "because if you willingly yield you are really the victor." How irresistible for him to satisfy her whims and at the same time, by her own admission, to be the true superior! The shifts of the queen's attack have outwitted him. The victor of the ten-year siege of Troy is defeated in a moment of psychological warfare with his wife.

It is all so swift, so simple. Yet behind the king's clichés we hear his sacrifice of Iphigeneia and his own imminent death, more terrible than Priam's. Behind the queen's cajolery we hear the great impersonator play the prophet Calchas, while dominating this struggle between male and female, justice and the Furies. As her final imperative suggests (*pithou*—"be persuaded!"), she personifies *Peitho*, but not in the manner of her sister Helen; she is not compulsion but temptation, deft, insinuating, luring Agamemnon to expose himself in all his guilt. As he consents, idly hoping to appease the gods by taking off his boots before he treads their vestments, he demonstrates his moral blindness once again. Yet at Aulis he had to choose between two acts of outrage, both fatal to himself, as well he knew, and so the choice was torment. At Argos, ten years later, he *may* choose an act of abstinence. It will not save him, but it will not incriminate him either. Instead he chooses outrage because it seems so innocent—a scrap of ceremony, not the flash and stab of a knife. This outrage, thanks to the insight of the queen, can appear as superficial as the conscience of the king has actually become. The war has deified the man. His potential as a tragic hero is defeated. With his first step on the fabrics he displays Cassandra as the model of his piety, unaware that her abduction is a sacrilege and her presence is an insult to the queen. The "flower and pride of all the wealth [he] won," Cassandra epitomizes what he always does with wealth. He triumphs over it, lending it fatal power over himself, and he does so of his own free will.

Only after he consents does Clytaemnestra rise, in a wild, whirling speech, and speed him to the last:

> There is the sea
> and who will drain it dry? Precious as silver,
> inexhaustible, ever-new, it breeds the more we reap it—
> tides on tides of crimson dye our robes blood-red.

The sea is both the reservoir of their riches and the incarnation of their never-ending strife, a harvest and a grisly reaping both. Thus the sea reflects the tapestries and Clytaemnestra's victim, the deadliness beneath the surface grandeur of the fabrics and the man. The sinuous red line they form is in the vein of Agamemnon—they fuse his slaughters and his bloodline, his will and his hereditary guilt. And at every step he takes upon them he exceeds his limits and retraces his descent: an Olympian outrage to be punished by the forces of the Earth. For as he tramples on the gods he re-enacts his trampling on the innocents of Troy and on his daughter—just as his forebear trampled on the banquet of his children—and so the king reactivates the curse. As if caught in a slow-motion camera, all his murderous acts dissolve into a single act, deliberate and majestic and profane, that accelerates toward the murder that awaits him.

An entire history of violence marches toward its violent but valid retribution. Clytaemnestra has created a theatrical triumph that is also a solemn moral judgment. Through her words and tapestries the assassination of her husband becomes an execution, a sacrifice. She is the great artist of ritual. And this ritual not only incriminates her victim; it exhilarates herself with sacramental power—whipping the priestess into fury, even yoking the gods beneath her fury as she drives her husband toward his destination. "Arrival" is her theme. She hails him as a sun-king whose arrival ushers in a greater darkness. He is a prodigy like Zeus, when Zeus

*tramples the bitter virgin grape for new wine
and the welcome chill steals through the halls, at last
the master moves among the shadows of his house, fulfilled.*

Zeus-Agamemnon has arrived to trample out the vintage where the grapes of wrath are stored. Agamemnon is *teleios* or fulfilled, "arrived at perfection" and also "ripe for sacrifice." Zeus is *Teleios* too, as we hear in the queen's closing prayer, the lord of fulfillment who will consummate her rites.

Now for the agony of that event. The king and queen go in, the doors close—the sense of disaster is electric, and the old men cry out as never before. They had made deeper and deeper sweeps into the past; now there is no escaping from the present. Their hopes for justice have collided with the Fury that is "real, true, no fantasy," and their song is torn in half. First an explosive dirge the Furies thrust upon them, then a manual of Olympian platitudes. They cling to their old safeguards, the virtue of moderation, the doctrine of the Mean—if only it were asserted now, Agamemnon might be saved. But he has trampled on the Mean, he must pay the price, and so must they. The more they try to exceed their limits, to pour out words that match their feelings, the more they choke and mutter through the nights, while the "burning" in their hearts goes unexpressed. Struck dumb by the gods on one hand, powerless to sing without the Furies on the other, they are at the threshold of a new awareness.

At this point in a Greek tragedy the audience would expect to hear the death-cry ringing out, but Aeschylus will delay it for more than three hundred lines, building its suspense and its significance through Cassandra. Clytaemnestra enters, unctuously invites her to share the sacrifices of thanksgiving for a husband's safe return—offered to Zeus *Ktêsios* who guards the possessions of the house—though of course she means the murder of Agamemnon and his mistress. Cassandra remains impassive, and Clytaemnestra goes inside, exasperated. In this brief clash of wills the silence of Cassandra seems to defeat her argumentative opponent. But she is impervious to outside events, in the grip of a higher power and entranced, like a medium on the verge of vision.

Cassandra breaks her silence with a scream that turns the house of Atreus into an echoing torture-chamber—a scream for Apollo, the god of enlightenment and prophecy, that makes his very name Destruction. And through his seer there flows—in language that could be clear only to "those who know"—a pageant of disaster. The collective, curse-ridden past of the house is streaming into Thyestes' murdered children, streaming into the murder of Agamemnon, streaming into the murder of Cassandra, into Argos are streaming all the murders done at Troy. At the core of her vision stands the king's death, and each event that rushes toward it rises in stylistic violence, from the floating wreckage of the house, "kinsmen / torturing kinsmen, severed heads," to a *tableau vivant* surfacing into the light like ghosts from a cavern half seen, half moving, "babies / wailing . . . their flesh charred, the father gorging on their parts," then to the murder of Agamemnon breaking out of the swirling mists of prophecy, breaking off in horror—Cassandra's outcries stabbing into the darkness like the wounds that pierce the king. Apollo's vision is a crescendo of shattering impressions. For all its seeming order of events, each stands out in isolation, unrelated in human terms, unmotivated, unbearable. Through the eyes of Apollo, history is a chronic nightmare, and Cassandra is at the mercy of the god, forced to endure his piling impositions. Her vision breaks apart. She is wrenched from Agamemnon's death to prophesy her own. And although she subsides into an elegy, her suffering only grows. First Apollo exploits her as his medium, then he destroys her, "treads [her] down"—his service is a rape.

But there is a counterforce at work. At first the chorus is confused, as Aeschylus increases the pathos of Cassandra: Apollo gave her the gift of prophecy but added, "No one will believe you." The old men begin to, however, as the violence of her language forces them to live out the horror she foresees in broken flashes. They turn from terse disclaimers to a more coherent, lyric form of protest, and they do so when Apollo's seer invokes another power. "Let the insatiate discord in the race / rear up and shriek 'Avenge the victim—stone them dead!' " It is her first self-motivated utterance; it forces the old men to identify the Furies, the Furies shock them into song and new awareness, and Cassandra answers with a sudden, lucid pause: "There's stealth and murder in that caldron, do you hear?" One mention of the Furies brings unusual clarity and more, Cassandra's vision of the murder of the king. "Drag the great bull from the mate! / . . . black horn glints, twists—*she gores him through!*" Man is brutalized into beast, and the beast's sex is perverted. A phrase from the *Odyssey*, Agamemnon "cut down like an ox at the trough," erupts into a kind of religious, mythological upheaval. At the core of Apollo's vision may stand the shattering of the god himself and his original triumph over Mother Earth: she rises up again, in effect, to claim her sacramental bull. And Apollo's perspective shatters into tragedy and deeper human feeling. The old men reach toward Cassandra, they cry out to her, silent and about to die, to live and sing a more prophetic song.

Now she repeats her declarations, with a difference. The old men ask for clarity, so she engages them in discourse, iambics and normal syntax, much as at Delphi the interpreters turned the outcries of the Pythia into conventional language. But Cassandra does not lose intensity; she gains. She has been like a bride who hides behind a veil, a song of innocence. Now she calls for a song of experience and the only force that can inspire it:

> These roofs—look up—there is a dancing troupe
> that never leaves. And they have their harmony

> but it is harsh, their words are harsh, they drink
> beyond the limit. Flushed on the blood of men
> their spirit grows and none can turn away
> their revel breeding in the veins—the Furies!
> They cling to the house for life. They sing,
> sing of the frenzy that began it all,
> strain rising on strain, showering curses
> on the man who tramples on his brother's bed.

A brutal irony and a brutal truth. The Furies' revel, passing through the house, becomes as permanent as the roaring in the blood. They offer a form of re-creation, which re-creates our pain and makes it inescapable. "Evil is unspectacular and always human," they might say with Auden, and they reveal what lies behind the traditional, sensational version of Thyestes' banquet and the curse—a simple breach of faith. That is the curse, so human it is a perennial menace and, as we shall see, a wellspring of compassion. It is mortality itself that can, at any time, consume one's offspring and one's future, but it may provide a kind of sustenance as well. Live with the curse and with the Furies, and we may live intensely, even perhaps invigorated by their force. Apollo is oblivious to our origins; the Furies *are* our origins. Through them we may articulate ourselves, if we can bear to sing their song and take Cassandra's lead.

The old men are struck by her knowledge. She has passed the customary test of seers; she can report events she never witnessed. And she owes her vision to Apollo but not its credibility. She committed a breach of faith herself, she explains; she deceived the god, and that is why he aborted his gift of prophecy. What added pathos to her lyrics, in other words, now gives her kinship with the story of fallibility she is telling, and increases her effect. Again she approaches Agamemnon's murder, but now she begins at its source, Thyestes' children,

> holding out their entrails . . . now it's clear,
> I can see the armfuls of compassion, see the father
> reach to taste and—
>   For so much suffering,
> I tell you, someone plots revenge.

Here she assembles her own vision, basing it on insight, not the lightning of the god. In her eyes history becomes a living force, a continuum of movement and motivation. The suffering children, more than victims, have a new potential; it is less the macabre crime of Atreus than their grief and the grief of Thyestes, even of his insensitive son, that breeds the murder of Agamemnon. And Cassandra sees other human factors too. There is the blindness of the king who, by obliterating Troy, destroys his own perception. Above all, there is the queen's manipulation of appearances. Detest her as she may, Cassandra sees as Clytaemnestra sees, and brings to light her terrifying powers. There is a relationship between the murderess and the victim, as if Cassandra's vision might inspire the queen's revenge, the queen's revenge fulfill Cassandra's vision.

The old men cannot accept the murder of the king. Hoping against hope, they look for a man to do the work and cannot see the woman, but this is a matter for the matriarchal hearth, as Cassandra's third, climactic speech implies. Indignant at Apollo's cruel indifference, she revolts against the god. She rips off his regalia, stamps it into the ground—an act of trampling that is the opposite of Agamemnon's. She is not surrendering to her destiny, she is struggling to create it; not committing an outrage but decrying the abuses of the god. As she tramples on his robes she re-enacts his trampling out her credibility at Troy and now her life in Argos. And by implicating Apollo so severely, she may strip him of his power in this play. Not until she has revolted against the Prophet can she prophesy what is to come. Not until she bares herself to the Furies can she foresee the coming of Orestes— the promise of the future rising from the torment of the present:

> We will die,
> but not without some honor from the gods.
> There will come another to avenge us,
> born to kill his mother, born

his father's champion. A wanderer, a fugitive
driven off his native land, he will come home
to cope the stones of hate that menace all he loves.
The gods have sworn a monumental oath: as his father lies
upon the ground he draws him home with power like a
  prayer.

This is Cassandra's first constructive prophecy, her first to be believed, and through it she herself becomes empowered. Now her death fulfills her with a strength she offers to the elders. She approaches the door, she smells the reek of blood and cries, but she turns her cry into evidence that can convict her murderers in a later court of law, like the Areopagus toward which the *Oresteia* turns. Cassandra has a genius for conversions. She converts destructive images into their opposites: she is a bride of death like Iphigeneia, but she bears a prophecy that lives. In her closing lines she turns her personal misery into a vision of the human condition. She has suffered into truth. Under Apollo she is the *Peitho* that is *pathos*; under the Furies she acquires *mathos* too, the *Peitho* of compassion. She has turned the Furies' harsh incriminations into kindness—a prophetic turning-point indeed. Through Cassandra we turn from the eagles killing the mother hare, the father killing the daughter, and the warlord razing Aphrodite's Troy, to the queen who kills the king, and the mother's vengeance that pursues the son until this clash between male and female is resolved in the union of Athena and the Eumenides, Zeus and Fate. It is a turn, in short, that is creative as well as destructive, like Cassandra's growing kinship with the queen. Both are destined to be murdered, yet as they die they may predict a crucial balance. Cassandra sees that Orestes must be "born to kill his mother"—her Fury must impel him in his mission. That will be the crux of the trilogy, yet even at this point, while summoning Clytaemnestra's vengeance, Cassandra surrounds it with the aura of its offspring, justice. She is both the victim of the queen and her vitality, the Eumenides in

Clytaemnestra's Fury. Cassandra is the redemptive heart of the *Oresteia*. She is the agony of vision. She is the tragic muse.

Throughout the trilogy Aeschylus will dramatize her power. As she goes to her death, the chorus can finally accept Agamemnon's murder and its cause: his excess, and his place in a great triad of murders, his father's, his own, and soon his wife's, "a threefold hammer blow" like the three blows about to be dealt by Clytaemnestra. When the death-cries of the king ring out, the old men are terrified; they scatter into individual voices—daring, cautious, or disengaged—but a majority favors what Cassandra would have urged. They storm the doors to "see how it stands with Agamemnon," and what they see unites them once and for all.

Rising over the bodies of the king and the seer, Clytaemnestra speaks the truth at last, magnificent in her defiance as she reveals what lay behind her ironies: a murder as climactic as any in the *Iliad*, a welcome more perverse than any in the *Odyssey*. As she re-enacts the trapping and the killing of the king, she impersonates Artemis the Huntress in effect, but she rebels against her fellow Olympians, she devotes her victim to Zeus, whom she demotes to the God of Death, and triumphs over Agamemnon:

> So he goes down, and the life is bursting out of him—
> great sprays of blood, and the murderous shower
> wounds me, dyes me black and I, I revel
> like the Earth when the spring rains come down,
> the blessed gifts of god, and the new green spear
> splits the sheath and rips to birth in glory!

Clytaemnestra represents the Earth, and behind her words we may hear a famous Aeschylean fragment:

> The clear pure Heaven yearns to wound the Earth
> and yearning seizes the Earth to wed the Heaven—
> rain comes down from the throbbing skies
> and pierces the Earth, she teems with flocks
> and Demeter's full rich life that strengthens men,

and from that drenching marriage-rite the woods,
the spring bursts forth in bloom. And I, I cause it all.

Aphrodite is defending Hypermnestra, the one daughter of Danaos who refused to murder her husband, acting in the name of love that weds the Heaven and the Earth each spring. Without the echo of Aphrodite, Clytaemnestra is a grim perversion of nature—the joy of the cornfields in the gift of rain, so precious in parched Argos, is twisted into the euphoria of a wife drenched with her husband's blood. The echo makes her all the more terrifying and universal, but it has a further resonance, however distant, that may lend the queen a measure of the goddess' fruitfulness as well.

By the end of the *Oresteia* we may see Clytaemnestra yield to the spirit of Hypermnestra, vengeance yield to justice, Earth and Heaven join in bonds of marriage. The legends say that from the bloody wounds of Ouranos, god of the Sky, came both the Furies and Aphrodite, vengefulness and love. And the more demonic Clytaemnestra grows, the more she will become a mother, human, vulnerable. Even now she labors with the spear at spring, the son who will destroy her. Even before the end of *Agamemnon* we may sense her creativity, the Great Mother within the Terrible Mother—love-in-hate personified—but for the present, of course, the Terrible Mother that Calchas first invoked and Cassandra just envisioned has come rushing to the fore—"the womb of Fury child-avenging Fury."

She appalls the chorus. The old men rise in outrage—poison has made her criminally insane—and sentence her to exile. For a moment she makes a rational self-defense; she indicts the king for murder and the old men for criminal neglect in failing to pursue him. But she revels in the carnage of her husband and his lover—she is sadistic, as oblivious as Agamemnon to the meaning of her actions. And so far we have a mistrial; she is lost in self-indulgence, the jury is reduced to threats. We need a change of venue, and the interchange that follows takes us to a higher court. It is not an easy form to grasp by reading; performed, it has increasing impact. Gradually the chorus realizes that the queen's act is another manifestation of the curse, but like Agamemnon's decision to kill Iphigeneia, her act involves both free will and predestination. At the end, the chorus and Clytaemnestra seem to reach a deadlock: how can curses be reconciled with prayers, blood feuds with communal justice, the Olympian theology with the Furies? How can a family that "has been welded to its ruin" be redeemed? Certain answers come to light in the course of the trial, but it is not a cold debate. Its music builds operatically, in a series of emotional crises, shocks of recognition.

We begin in the depths. The old men pray for a painless death, lamenting, almost appealing to Helen, the spirit of destruction. Seeing a chance to deflect blame from herself, Clytaemnestra rises to her sister's defense in sudden lyric power, as if they were in league. Their kinship, in fact, forces the chorus to recognize the kindred spirit working here—the curse that has impelled the sisters from the start, and counteracts the initial omen sent by Zeus. Now the old men see the spirit in command and not the gods, twin Furies and not twin kings, a raven, not an eagle, with its victim. Clytaemnestra seizes on their vision, since it exonerates herself and Helen too. They can be nothing more than carriers of the spirit raging through the generations of the house. Yet the spirit seems amoral, and the next stage of the trial changes that. The old men return, *de profundis*, to their faith in Zeus: "What comes to birth that is not Zeus? / Our lives are pain, what part not come from god?" Full circle from the opening hymn, Zeus *is* the anguish in their hearts; and as they mourn their king they may even mourn the death of faith itself, but Clytaemnestra gives them something to believe in. She declares the spirit lives within her body; more, he is the spirit of revenge and he is right—he has murdered Agamemnon for the murder of their daughter, indeed for an enormous legacy of murders. The conspiracy between the queen and her spirit, her freedom and her fate, is just as total as that between the king and the winds at Aulis, but her conspiracy is more deeply, more lastingly self-aware. And the chorus finds it so retributive that its moral impact cannot be denied: "revenge will stride, / clots will mass for the young who were devoured." Clytaemnestra glories in her work. All can see it now for what it is: homicide justified by the law of retaliation.

But her Fury is a staggering moral force. "The heavy rains of blood will crush the house." The old men pray to Mother Earth for their own oblivion and burial for the king, and Clytaemnestra will conduct the rites of death, hand Agamemnon back to their daughter waiting in Hades to embrace her father's ghost. And the chorus breaks into a hymn for even more destructive unions: the law of Zeus reverts to the *lex talionis*, the prayer to Zeus becomes an invocation of the curse. It is a bold verdict. Zeus can be the arbitrary king no longer; if he wants to be *panergetos*, all-achieving, he must be *panaitios*, all-responsible too. He cannot use the Furies without suffering their recriminations, the Titanic law he had suppressed, yet his complicity here will mark his first step toward a more conscientious, communal form of justice. And the verdict is not without some credit to the judges. Brought face to face with the hopelessness of trying to foresee—much less effect—an end to the chain reaction of murder, the old men also suffer into truth. It is the Furies however, not the gods and the cautious precepts of Olympus, that have inspired them. Through Cassandra they have seen that history is a process; through the queen that process shatters them yet serves to make them whole. For her private crime has become a tremendous public burden, yet as they accept it the elders voice their greatest lyric outburst in the play. They "sing of human unsuccess / in a rapture of distress," in Auden's words, and they end the trial by insisting on their own complicity in the misery of the race. "Broken husks of men" at first, they could only narrate Calchas' prophecy—now they are the prophets.

Clytaemnestra commends them for their vision, then acts to save them all from ruin. Her confidence leads her to strike a pact with the spirit; a lavish sacrifice should persuade him to depart, "once I have purged / our fury to destroy each other— / purged it from our halls." What she tries to form, in short, is a marriage contract with the curse. And all the blood-weddings that went before— of Iphigeneia, Helen and Troy, even Agamemnon and herself—become *proteleia* like the slaughter of the suitors in the *Odyssey* that consecrates the reunion of Odysseus and Penelope. But here the king is murdered, the suitor weds the queen, and the queen assumes command; and here the crux of *Agamemnon* lies. The master of irony has become its target—Clytaemnestra's "marriage" is a death pact. She is locked within the chain, another instrument of revenge who must become a victim in return. That is what it means to dedicate oneself to vengeance. The queen is a repetition of Agamemnon, as Kitto sees her; she vainly hopes "that the *Dikê* now achieved shall be final," provided only that she lives a pious life. Yet there is a difference too. As she accepts her yoke she may also express a premonition of the Fury that will end her life and purge the house at last. Standing in her husband's steps, she may repeat his weakness less than she enacts her own potential. Witness the moral power she generates in the chorus, and her position in the closing scene.

We have reached a vision almost too intense, as if we were looking at the sun in its eclipse. We must come down to earth, and in a later Greek tragedy a *deus ex machina*, a god swung down from Olympus to resolve the future, might have intervened. But Aeschylus is composing on a larger scale than Sophocles or Euripides. The curse has far to go before it is laid to rest, and here he introduces a prologue to a new play. Called forth, it seems, by Clytaemnestra's evocation of the spirit, Aegisthus enters with his bodyguard, praising the gods because they bring him glory, gloating over Agamemnon's body as a product of the curse. We have never heard its history told so fully, not because Aeschylus has been saving it for last but because Cassandra, Agamemnon, and Clytaemnestra have embodied it so uniquely. Aegisthus relies on the common version of its origins—Thyestes' feast—and it reflects his vulgarity. What a confusion it is. He tells it to indict the Atreidae and justify himself, but he seems to relish both the virtuoso cookery and his father's vomiting and trampling on the children's flesh. He is trampling on his father, degrading the curse, the human complexity of Thyestes who was both abusing and abused.

History is cannibalism to Aegisthus, and he tramples on his victim too. He and Agamemnon are related in their excess, yet Aegisthus is mere front: he claims to have planned the murder, then he claims the throne, but he has *done* precisely nothing. He is a parody of the traditional Aegisthus, the hardy swordsman who shares the killing of the king with Clytaemnestra, and his recital of the curse is finally self-defeating: "Now I could die gladly, even I—" Yet his entrance marks the dawn of a mediocre present that is hard to limit; when he says, "Let me make this clear" (and the Greek made this translation almost irresistible), we may hear our own political leaders too and run for cover. When he alludes to culture, he is reaching for the knife. He speaks political language in Orwell's sense; it is "designed to make lies sound truthful and murder respectable," and it may usurp the place of poetry itself. The chorus is speechless for a moment, but the elders are so revolted by Aegisthus' cowardice they quickly rise against him. Troy left them behind, not this conflict. Now they seize on the coming of Orestes like a weapon—fighting, in their old age, with the courage of the liberator.

What keeps them from striking out against Aegisthus is the queen, for as he declines in power she increases. Contrary to legend, she is the single-handed executioner of her husband, and she alone suspends hostilities at the end, girding for a conflict that will rage around herself. She has tried to form a liaison with the spirit of the house. Her lover makes a mockery of that spirit, yet he may also represent how low the queen has had to stoop. To lash herself into an act of murder may have required valid rage and guilty passion, Fury and the curse. Now she accepts her union with Aegisthus for what it is, a coupling of righteousness and degradation. Without him she is a self-deluded victim like her husband. With him she becomes a combatant struggling to transform her guilt into a kind of strength:

> If we could end the suffering, how we would rejoice.
> The spirit's brutal hoof has struck our heart.
> And that is what a woman has to say.
> Can you accept the truth?

She cannot end the suffering, she knows that she must suffer most, and she rises to a majesty of endurance. Her language has become as clear as what awaits her, and her clarity is a legitimate source of pride. Clytaemnestra is at last no more conciliatory than Oedipus or Lear. She undergoes a change in awareness, not a change of heart. True to herself, she blazes out against the chorus calling for Orestes, and together they bring the play to its grating but prophetic close. Orestes will arise from the clash between his fatherland that cries for justice and the Fury of his mother, and hers may be the greater force. She alone can generate her destiny in the person of her son. That will be her achievement years from now, but we may sense it here as she embraces her fate. From that union comes her death, from her death the liberation of the race. The play is named for Agamemnon, but the tragic hero is the queen.

All that now remains of the *Oresteia* is the written word. We should remember that the text leaves much unsaid about the total impression of a Greek dramatic work. Its religious, social, and theatrical impact greatly increased its power. The Athenians who attended the *Oresteia* came to worship Dionysos and receive the sensuous fulness of the performance—perhaps to be overwhelmed, as Yeats was overwhelmed, as if he were present at "a terrible sacrament of the god." The Greeks used every medium they had. And now so much is irretrievably lost—the music, the choreography, the scenery, the timbre of the actors' voices, what must have been their memorable gestures. But we have not lost the essence. Our text, Aristotle encourages us to believe, is not a thin libretto. The words alone may hold the life of the thing itself. The music they create, the scenery, the acting, the complete consort dancing together in the theater of our minds may well be all we need. Perhaps—but this may be too daring—a performance of the *Oresteia* in the mind of a twentieth-century reader may be even more moving than it was in that crowded, often restive Theater of Dionysos at the first performance. At least we can do with the written words what no Athenian could do when they were spoken on the stage; we can stop and wonder and look back and tease apart the subtleties and pregnancies of Aeschylus' style, so that while we lose theatrically we gain in imaginative power. As Keats has said about a different *genre* of Greek art, "Heard melodies are sweet, but those unheard / Are sweeter." And perhaps with Greek drama, richer, too.

But in justice to Aeschylus, no summary of his tragedy, or translation, can convey the sensuous impact of his language, the superbly rich and flexible language of fifth-century Greece which he employed with a power few other languages could achieve. It is the flesh and blood in which his meaning lives. We cannot forget its vitality any more than we can hope to reproduce it. It threatens, always, to make our reactions to his work as lifeless as a paraphrase of *The Wreck of the Deutschland* or *The Bridge*. Hart Crane found the substance of Aeschylus "so verbally quickened and delivered with such soul-shivering economy that one realizes there is none in the English language to compare him with." He is so far from us, and further from our ingrained, often cramped and icy standards of classicism than almost all of his successors. He is as far from the lucid control of Sophocles as a Gothic cathedral from a Doric temple, Michelangelo from Leonardo. There is reason for his eccentricities, to be sure; he uses archaisms to root his action in the past, and neologisms that serve to make it new. But he uses them so freely that at times he is bizarre, his metaphors grotesque. At times he gives the impression of finding the Greek language, despite its richness, inadequate to the flood of his characters' feeling in a crisis. Poets have felt this inadequacy before and since—Homer, Virgil, and Tennyson, for instance—but they generally speak of it in terms of calm regret. The old men of Argos (probably speaking for Aeschylus in his later years) feel it viscerally, like a woman in childbirth. They fill with terror, they strain to give it voice, but their cries erupt in silence at the last, "never to ravel out a hope in time / and the brain is swarming, burning—"

The language is explosive, volcanic. It is giving birth to a new drama and a new poetic voice. The *Oresteia* is not a restatement of a tale of murder and revenge; it is a *mimesis*, a re-enactment, a re-creation of it in a new mode that concentrates *and* builds its older epic power, that requires "soul-shivering economy" *and* elevation, or what Longinus called "the reverberation of the grandeur of the soul." Aeschylus created tragedy, but he also used it to express himself. And between his public mission and his urge for personal release, his style bears all the marks of struggle—the far-fetched plays on words, the muscle-bound constructions, the breakings-off before a sentence is completed that led most classical critics to call him "incoherent."

Perhaps, but there is a distinction between the rudeness of a new convention and the rudeness which a poet chooses for himself. When Aeschylus strains for grandeur and it turns to grandiosity, there may have been a failure of technique. Greek tragedy had far to go before it reached a flawless classicism; Aeschylus was a pioneer, and like Schliemann at Troy, he could be faulted by the next generation for the occasional roughness of his methods. But again like Schliemann, he was the first to give his *métier* a universal status. When Aeschylus strains for self-expression and it turns to baffling obscurity, there may be a lack of technique, though more likely there is too much "self." Aeschylus is proud to grapple with concepts that are new, inchoate, mystical, tremendous—

like the mind of Zeus, as he tried to penetrate it, "tangled, thickly shadowed stretch the paths of Zeus's mind, blinding to the power of our words." But arrogance and magnificence, *authadeia* and *megaloprepeia*, are the two thrusts of Aeschylus' style, and what is essential is how his arrogance may magnify his work. He is continually turning the dangers of his language into strengths, its roughness into power, its cries of inadequacy into copiousness and song, an exultation he must struggle to control. Few, if any, poets can rival him in this. Again and again he re-creates the world of appearances—the animal world, the world of storms and calms, the sunrise on the ocean rolling with a glistening bloom of corpses—by some sudden flash of imagery that utterly recasts its meaning.

Aeschylus creates a world of violent paradox. We see this in his most intense expressions: in his "desperate" compounds as perplexing as his characters; in his mixed metaphors that grope toward the ineffable and reflect just how remote it is; in his oxymora that are acts of reverence in themselves, containing a mystery without explaining it away. Aeschylus transforms his genius for obscurity into an indispensable factor in his *Oresteia*. He is dramatizing passions and fears beyond analysis, even psychoanalysis, wrestling with problems whose roots go deeper than logical formulation can go—the conflict of family loyalties with state loyalties, the tortured relationship between our freedom and our fate. A century or so later Plato and Aristotle would give these matters philosophical solutions, yet as history has shown too clearly, the problems remained unsolved, perhaps because they had been immunized, for a time, by the cures of rationality. But Aeschylus *embodies* the problems in the problems of his style. He does not diagnose our illness and prescribe a cure. He uses homeopathy: he re-creates the symptoms in a newly created world; he compels his audience to relive their lives in that fresh light, and in the end, like a god in his own creation, he can establish a resounding, final harmony. Aeschylus is not simply a religious poet. He is a willful, headstrong visionary poet. He does not belong with the more self-effacing Sophocles and Spenser. He breathes the air of Pindar, Milton, and Isaiah—men who sing with arrogance to magnify the glory of their gods. He exults in the service that is perfect freedom. He is the Dionysiac artist, possessed by *divinus furor*.

But *Agamemnon* is possessed by a diabolic Fury. In style and theme the play represents a static, claustrophobic world, "a huddling together of fierce extremes," in Hazlitt's description of *Macbeth*. Still, the ferocity of action may seem obscured. Memory takes its place and renders action inescapable but frozen. Aeschylus may evoke a lost, primordial ritual, the sacramental killing of the king, but here the king has small potential to release, and his death may generate a deadlock in the future. Yet there is a movement too, a choking coil of image and event. It is the poetic justice of the play that every good must seek its opposite and be destroyed, the health that turns to sickness, the beauty that blinds, the theodicy that is a ministry of fear. And things more often go from bad to worse, the wound that breeds more wounds, the hunter who is hunted down and killed. There is a *lex talionis*, a law of retaliation working in the style as in the action—in the bond between Agamemnon's cruelty and his fate, in the double blow they deal to Troy and Greece, and all to strike against the double-bladed law that the killer must be killed, the law of Zeus that incriminates himself, binding him over to the Furies as they weld the race to ruin.

In fact there is a momentum in the Furies, "the terror raging back and back in the future / the stealth, the law of the hearth, the mother." These menacing phrases, like monolithic, unmovable building-blocks, are actually set in motion by the Fury who will construct her edifice, the house of Atreus or all our houses, where the elements of Aeschylus are clashing for control. There is an auditory struggle that intensifies the prophecies of Calchas with his cries. A stylistic struggle in which images of oozing and dyeing yield to Agamemnon's blood, spurting out to stain the ground and shower Clytaemnestra like the rain. And a dramatic struggle that, from the storm at Aulis lyrically remembered, releases the storm that sweeps the ships at Troy, breaking out of heroic narrative to overpower Argos in the person of the queen. As Agamemnon says, "The storms of ruin live!"

These are the dynamics of destruction. Nowhere do they work with greater force than in the symbol of the net and its companion, the symbol of the robes. Together they exemplify all the binding, recoiling, retaliating, revenging in the play, though they enter *pianissimo*. In the opening chorus Agamemnon is associated both with the hunt that captures Troy and with its first extension, the bridal robes his attendants wind around his daughter as he kills her. The robes of ceremony and the nets of capture: the chorus stresses the second in its hymn of triumph; the nets of the Night have trapped the prize of Troy. But soon the nets of Clytaemnestra trap the king—"if he took one wound for each report / to penetrate these walls, he's gashed like a dragnet." And as "she winds about him coil after coil of her glittering rhetoric" (Herbert Weir Smyth's description), her words materialize in the gorgeous tapestries that lure him to his death.

Cassandra sees this clearly. She is caught in the nets of doom while she perceives the nets that trap the king. They are things of nightmare that, like objects in surreal pictures, are themselves and inextricably something else. First she sees unattached hands reaching out, "hand over hand," to haul in things unseen, like nets perhaps, and so they are, she can see them clearly now, hellish nets— and no, not simply nets but a part of the one who casts them, a woman, in fact the woman *is* the net, "the snare, / the bedmate, deathmate, murder's strong right arm!" the queen who invests the king in robes, entangling him before she takes his life. But these are only flashes as Apollo sends them through his seer. Cassandra cannot see their pattern until she has trampled the vestments of the god and taken on, if only symbolically, the mantle of the Furies. Then she sees the tie between the violent nets of capture and the violated robes of ceremony, between Agamemnon's bloodlust and the majestic vengeance that it looses. The Furies also bind Cassandra to her death while they release her prophecy of Orestes, rising from the painful implications she has seen.

Her vision is enacted by the queen. Clytaemnestra murders Agamemnon, and as she unfurls the robes around his body—"he had no way to flee or fight his destiny— / our never-ending, all-embracing net"—the running weave of her words extends the nets into the murderous heirloom of the house, the curse itself. And as the elders mourn the king they meditate: This queen with her net, is she not a spider, the "black widow" with her fatal web?—the spirit of the Spider Mountain raining havoc down on Argos. Yet she is a Fury that can spin as well as kill. As her trial unfolds, she and the chorus expand the curse into an inescapable moral network of complicity, so large that it includes us all, so incriminating that it cries for justice, so dominated by the Furies they alone can give that justice power. The two forces will be bound together in Orestes, and when he is acquitted all the reticulations of evil decisions and evil destinies will be resolved at last by Athena's master hand.

But we begin in the darkness-before-dawn. In our nightmares the terror often comes most strongly when it emerges slowly from the background, or worse still, when a harmless, familiar object slowly grows more sinister, the commonplace becoming the macabre. That is the atmosphere of *Agamemnon*, and nothing makes it bristle more than the metaphor that comes to life, then passes into metaphor and into life again, one stage exceeded by the next in terror. "Present fears / Are less than horrible imaginings." But the forward thrust of *Agamemnon* brings us back to the beginnings, the first gods, the elements bursting from the night to bring the first barbaric dawn. The terror of *Agamemnon* transcends the terror of most tragedy, the terror that is "unspectacular and always human," or even that we may wake to find the roof come down upon our heads. It is all that and more.

It is what Eliot calls "the backward half-look / Over the shoulder, towards the primitive terror." It is chaos.

But, as in the chaos of mythology, there is a potential here that would be harnessed. Clearly the great weight of the play is destructive. It coils inward toward the killing of the king, then outward toward its most disastrous meanings. Yet it also turns the murder into justifiable homicide, as if the vengeance of the Furies might, on a later day, radiate toward the justice of the gods. An *Iliad* converges into an even bloodier *Odyssey*. Clearly the pain comes first—*pathei mathos*—but the pain will reverberate with meaning. For all the retaliation in the play, there are relations that may balance "great good blessings mixed with doom." There is the *charis biaios* of the gods, their violent kindness that breaks us into pieces but may leave us open, sentient, and prepared. There are the aging voices of the chorus rising into ringing social conscience. Behind all there is the poet, like Cassandra, venturing into the very dark and danger of Clytaemnestra to evoke her deep maternal power. There is the original paradox of Fury, the memory that must avenge her children, and the matrix of her children who avenge themselves on her—Fury, the muse of vengeance that will generate the future.

There is Orestes. There is a dialectic just begun to work. We are simply at the first, negative extreme. "Where there is a reconciliation," as Stephen Dedalus says, "there must first have been a sundering." Dionysos is dismembered, as prologue to the act of his rebirth. Here is an antigenesis with all the elements intact, waiting to be built into a world. That is the challenge of *Agamemnon*, and Aeschylus suggests it should be met with the tragic spirit of Cassandra and the queen who know that "all things fall and are built again, / And those that build them again are gay." Aeschylus is often swept off his feet by his own creative exultation, but he never loses grip on his faith that "good wins out in glory in the end." His exultation and his faith combine with enormous impact. We must surrender to him, let him sweep us on like a storm at sea, often violating our intellectual bent for precision and lucidity, often baffling when his genius seems to burst upon the majestic flow of his dramatic theme. At the end his violence will have brought us to a time and place of brightness and resilient peace, "gaiety transfiguring all that dread."

THE LIBATION BEARERS

The Libation Bearers is the crux of the *Oresteia*. After the killing of the king we have a rite of spring, like the Anthesteria sacred to Dionysos and performed when the god is struggling for rebirth, when winter yields to March. Memory and desire, dread and expectation mix, and the Anthesteria celebrates them both. It was a festival of libations which summoned the spring by summoning the great ancestral dead as the source of all new life. It was a festival of reincarnation, and to dramatize it Aeschylus re-created Agamemnon's son. In the *Odyssey* Orestes hungers for his patrimony, he travels home from exile, kills his father's assassins—his mother and her lover— and without a qualm of conscience "proclaim[s] the funeral day," as Robert Fitzgerald translates it, "a festal day for all the Argive people." Orestes is completely successful and completely in the right. But in *The Libation Bearers* he is right and wrong, his father's avenger and a guilty matricide and more, the vortex where the Furies and the gods converge with fresh intensity and effect.

If the *Oresteia* is a rite of passage from savagery to civilization, Orestes' step from youth to maturity is the rite of transition in the trilogy. Because of its inwardness, its privacy, this ritual often excludes the anthropologist in the field, but it may inspire the dramatist, especially if he wants to probe the relationship between suffering and regeneration. For what happens in the secret chamber or the wilderness, or the grave to which Orestes is exposed, may be some sort of creative agony, some radical humanization of the ruder past, as preparation for the more communal life that awaits the young initiate. Somewhere within him, we may say, his innocence dies and his experience is born, and he must be deeply wounded in the process. *The Libation Bearers* allows us to feel that wounding as only drama can—as an ordeal of recognition. And Orestes' ordeal will carry us through torment toward awareness and renewal and the light.

After years of his mother's usurpation he has broken out of exile and returned to avenge his father. That is Apollo's command, as we shall learn, though here at the outset, as Orestes takes his stand at Agamemnon's grave, what stirs him seems more personal, a deep tie between the living and the dead, reflected in his words that weave between the shadows and a sense of exhilaration. He prays to Hermes, the Escort of the Dead, to be his living comrade, then he drifts to thoughts of mourning. He combines two separate rites; he lays two locks of hair on the grave, one for his father's death and one for a local stream that gave him manhood. There may be ties between mourning and maturity, the debts he owes his father and his mother. No sooner does he place the locks than a procession of her women appears, and they are dressed in black, and bear libations. Like the watchman he prays for help and sees a sign, but Orestes' sign is human, and either way he interprets the women—as mourning a new wound to the house or appeasing his father's spirit—he is right and he is strengthened. He sees his sister Electra, and her sorrow makes him cry to Zeus for revenge, intensifying his first appeal to Hermes. There may be ties among the living, among men and women, vengeance and affection. Orestes' prologue ends with the watchword for his play: "We must see clearly what these women and their supplications mean." We must look beyond the libations to their source, and as he steps behind the tomb, the women introduce him to their mission.

Clytaemnestra has had a nightmare. The interpreters say the dead are crying for revenge, so she sends the women to appease them with libations. The women consider this hypocrisy and instead they mourn her reign of terror as relentless as the curse. Not only must Orestes avenge his father, he must avenge his father's world, and that will involve his mother. For her dream will coincide with the orders of Apollo, in fact her dream will prove as prophetic as the eagles in *Agamemnon*; but there is no prophet here, and people must unravel this omen slowly, painfully. Only its surface can be seen, yet it has brought the women, and they may help Orestes. Their mourning is a form of resistance; they beat the linen on their breasts like weavers, they set a work-beat throbbing, a pulsing of the blood in early spring, and in their knowledge of Clytaemnestra's dream they hold a cure. As they mourn the father, they will stimulate the son. All is latent for the moment. Behind their suffering lies their past; they are slaves from the wars, but they can match their hatred for their masters with loyalty to their mistress. Behind their veils they weep for her. "Sorrow turns the secret heart to ice." Now the thaw begins.

Electra asks what she should say as she pours her mother's libations on her father's grave. Like Orestes she must reconcile her parents' claims, yet everything she says will bring their claims into clearer opposition. She rejects the common formulas for mourning, one that tells of a woman's love for husband (that would be grotesque), another that answers gifts with further gifts—give her mother grief for grief instead. Nor can she adopt the silence that accompanies rites of purging. Freed from Clytaemnestra, she and the women can express their grief at last, renew the shock of Agamemnon's death until it seems a recent crime that calls for action now. Only his avenger can overhear, and what the women say must warm his heart, for in their hands the cups become a tonic for Electra and poison for the queen. Bless the ones who love you, they advise, and curse the ones you hate. Remember Orestes, then summon an avenger. This is a formula that indoctrinates Electra into the cruelty and the fondness of the world, and she is more than ready. Her questions seem designed to cue the leader in, even to cue her waiting brother in. Like him she prays to

Hermes, now to take her prayers to Mother Earth where they can bloom in twin emotions—longing for her brother, longing for her father's avenger still unknown. "So in the midst of prayers for good I place / this curse for them." For once a curse in the house is warmed by a hope for human improvement, and Electra prays to be purer than Clytaemnestra. She is an altered version of her mother, at the same time she anticipates her mother's new maternal power in this play.

Or so we infer as Electra pours her cup on the grave and invites her living brother from the dead. She sees the locks, she trembles and she turns her catechism with the leader into a dialogue of breathless recognition— the locks belong to Orestes. Yes, but he must have *sent* them, he is banished. Their joy is dashed; Electra sees how desolate they are, yet in her desperation she animates the locks—she gives them breath and voice, she sees them as the seed of their entire line and begs the gods for guidance. They comply at once. Here are Orestes' tracks, and the tracks relate the children still more closely. By pursuing the same path of feeling, Electra has persuaded her brother that this is friendly ground; now by following in his steps she makes him reappear. As they meet she cries aloud in anguish, and her word for anguish is the word for labor too: "The pain, like pangs of labor—this is madness!" Indeed Orestes' birth will lead to his mother's death and his own madness, as Anne Lebeck observes, but it will end in the renewal of himself and his society. His torment, like his sister's, is constructive.

The Libation Bearers runs on act upon act of recognition. So it must; it is a play about the continuous readjustment of character and destiny, one's perceptions and one's place. When Electra tries to resist Orestes, he insists upon their kinship, their mutual re-creation of each other. He seizes on a piece of her weaving that he wears, her own creation that she gave him at his birth, perhaps, as a *gnôrisma*, a token of identity and swaddling band in one. She yields, she is euphoric, praises him as a living family in one, and rejoices in the help of Saving

Zeus. But Orestes modulates her joy. Zeus may be the patron of their father, but Agamemnon is dead and his children must be cautious, they must ask the gods for help.

Orestes' help comes from Apollo, his patron *and* tormentor. Apollo has commanded him to avenge his father or suffer pains of guilt as political as exile, as physical as plague, and as psychological as madness and the Furies. Guilt is a strong god, and when he takes the name Apollo, a brutal one as well. Even his agent labors under a death sentence—Orestes has punishments, no incentives. And perhaps Apollo is not even to be trusted, he muses, so he improvises motives of his own: his grief for his father, his patrimony, and his compatriots. He will do Apollo's work, no doubt of that, but his own motives are based on loss, and they are strictly masculine; he seems unaware the work involves his mother. He is still "determined" by Apollo; like Cassandra, another victim of the god, he is denied the power of self-determination. He must find a relationship between his feelings and his fate, the vengeance he must perform and the justice he desires. He must recognize, in fact, that his revenge is just, but that justice takes the form of matricide, the greatest form of guilt. Apollo has brought the gods and the Furies to a new, more lethal deadlock in Orestes. But with the women and his sister he will bring these powers to a new, more fruitful union.

That is what happens in the great chant at the grave that now unfolds before us. Now to turn tender recognition into conspiracy and rough desire. The women pray that the Fates and Zeus conspire in terms of the old law, "stroke for bloody stroke," and as the children join them, the structure of the chant embodies their growing unity and momentum. There are three movements. The first (312–412), by far the longest, has two complementary sections (322–68, 377–412). Orestes leads off with a slow, despairing dirge for Agamemnon, intensified by Electra's prayer that he had never died at all, that his murderers had died instead. Their grief is giving rise to vengefulness and more, as the women evoke the true retributive force of the dirge and of the king himself. To avenge him would be just, and they turn the children's dreams of glory into valid anger in the second, harsher section. Catching fire, the children call for the retribution massed behind their father's ghost; and Electra, in control, cries out for the one power that can drive her brother into action—"Mother dear, you bred our wolves' raw fury"—charging the justice of the gods with the matriarchal energy it requires.

But the gods and Furies clash at the center of the chant (413–42), surrounding Orestes with excruciating pressure. More than just, more than empowered by his mother, his vengeance is provoked by her own act of vengeance now revealed for the first time—she mutilated Agamemnon's body. That horror spurs a further recognition within Orestes. He must kill his *mother*—it is as if Apollo never told him! Justice is matricide. Orestes' peak of personal commitment is a peak of guilt as well: "Oh she'll pay, / she'll pay, by the gods and these bare hands— / just let me take her life and *die!*" At the core of the chant he is torn apart. But in the final movement (443–52), as all three voices merge in a *stretto* swift and tense, Orestes begins to consolidate himself. He is both the avenger and the son, justice and the curse. He exults in both roles, calling out for blood and for his loved ones—"Now force will clash with force, right with right!" Unlike Apollo, he will acknowledge his mother's claims and pit them against his own. He is murderous and moral, predestined and aware, and so he can emerge as the leader, the Aeschylean hero. Electra follows, but the women recoil from what they have unleashed, the "cure" that comes from the children's "bloody strife." Their fury may be homeopathic, as we see in the coda that concludes the chant.

They adopt their mother's fury and train it on their father, taunting him, recriminating him with the ignominy of his death, until they have lashed his spirit back to life not only as a memory but as a force within themselves. Orestes reincarnates Agamemnon. Both must choose between doing something and doing nothing—both are damned if they do and damned if they don't. If Agamemnon fails his mission he incurs the wrath of Zeus; to perform it he must kill his daughter and incur the Furies later. It is a murderous choice, and Agamemnon makes it more so; he personifies vengeance as a law unto itself. But Orestes' choice is worse: to avenge his father he must kill his mother. If he fails his mission he incites the Furies—if he performs it he incites the Furies. They are on both sides of the conflict now, struggling deep within him, asserting both his father's just demand for vengeance and his mother's just revenge in turn. He has no choice at all. Yet as his self-awareness grows he creates a choice between the Furies as administered by Apollo—the mortifying powers of conscience—and the Furies of his mother that may mortify him and electrify him too. This will be the crucial choice of his career, in fact, for even here, as he adopts his mother's fury to revive his father, he radically reforms his father's spirit. Orestes turns revenge into a force that can *preserve* his line from Pelops to posterity. At last Electra knows what to say as she pours her cup, and her brother has the answer to his question, "Dear father, father of dread, / what can I do or say to reach you now?" The words are love-in-hate, the work is murder in behalf of life itself. The range, the promise of the chant is exhilarating. The warlord's lust for glory resounds within his son, the new, moral hero, tortured now but soon triumphant. The witches' Sabbath yields to prophecy, the old law to the new law—to the first real hope for the justice of the gods, yet that justice must be powered by the Furies.

Now for action, say the women, encouraged by the coda. But first Orestes must know more about the libations—why did his mother send them? Only now, thanks to his recognitions in the chant, can he fully respond to his mother's dream. It has portrayed the dead as calling for revenge, yet its first effect is positive; the queen's ritual of riddance has actually enlivened the dead and their avengers. Here we learn the dream itself is a
- blend of life and death: Clytaemnestra has given birth

to a serpent that destroys her. It is a nightmare, but as Orestes absorbs its meaning it becomes a waking vision: "I turn serpent, / I kill her." The serpent is a symbol of the underworld, and Orestes represents the dead—he will play dead, the dead who come to life. For the serpent is also a symbol of the Furies and their dual powers of vengeance and regeneration. Clytaemnestra bears Orestes' fury—she suffers it and nurses it at once. If his first resolve to kill his mother ended in a death wish, this resolve may fulfill himself as well. "No empty dream. The vision of a man." Like the serpent, jaws embracing the breast that it must cut, he is forever in the act of killing what he loves, yet somehow nourished by it.

That is a vision Apollo has never seen, and Orestes (like Cassandra) is inspired by the Furies. As he plots his course of action, however, he tries to bring his two divinities together. To suit the compulsions of Apollo he will disguise his speech with Parnassian dialect, the native eloquence of Delphi, and take Apollo's delegate, Pylades, as his comrade-in-arms. At the same time the Furies within him cry for blood, the "third libation" poured to Saving Zeus, as if insisting on a union between Orestes' compulsion and his impulse, the Olympians and themselves. But between Orestes' rehearsal and his performance lies a difference. Here as he writes his script he omits the Furies from the action. Full of the bravado of the young unseasoned actor, he can relish the killing of Aegisthus with a stroke, but not a word of matricide—he cringes at the thought.

A violent birth is coming. What tells us so is the central chorus that celebrates the "terrible marvels" of creation. Like the voice of the whirlwind in the Book of Job, the voice of "terrible majesty" that brings fair weather from the north, the women trace the Furies from their negative to their positive extreme. The only marvel equal to creation is the fury of women. They multiply crime on crime against creation, and as the chorus turns from women who murdered sons and fathers to those who murdered husbands and destroyed their line, it also moves from the deft, poetic justice of the gods that intercepted Scylla to their revenge that blotted out the Lemnian women. They sing of mounting crimes that are met by mounting retribution from on high, but as they turn to Clytaemnestra, "the wedded love-in-hate . . . the curse of the halls," something startling happens. The closer they come to her, the closer they come to her son who will "wipe clean / the inveterate stain of blood shed long ago." Not only is this constructive retribution; it is human, and what's more, it may even be summoned by the Queen herself, at least by the force they have in common: "Fury brings him home at last, / the brooding mother Fury." Orestes is the minister of the gods, but his mother must impel him. A terrible marvel: only she can generate his justice, only he can embody that justice, destroy her and the curse.

The central chorus is the fulcrum of the play. *The Libation Bearers* has two acts. At the house of the dead an old outrage is remembered and its vengeance is rehearsed. At the house of the living that vengeance is performed, its repercussions felt. We turn from vision to enactment, from a version of Homer's underworld to his final battleground, the hearth. Here the dangers are more familiar and more deadly, and they catch Orestes off his guard. He comes on like a tiger at the gates, bristling for combat with Aegisthus, but the epic day of encounter is over. The hero gropes in a twilight zone—these walls, these echoes, he knows them all as from a childhood dream. Even the gateman's formulaic question, "Where do you come from, stranger? Who are you?" leads toward a fateful recognition. Orestes calls for his enemy—his mother enters. As if recalled from legend Clytaemnestra seems unchanged; her gracious welcome only brings the nightmare rushing back: "We have warm baths and beds to charm away your pains / and the eyes of Justice look on all we do." But the terms of her welcome also reassert her guilt. The eyes of justice belong to the curse, the curse has come to Argos, and Orestes has defenses.

The rites of hospitality ask the guest to identify himself, and Orestes launches out on a cock-and-bull story, like many in the *Odyssey*, that reveals his life and tests his host in turn. He had not planned to meet his mother first, and the Fury in her makes him improvise and begin to sense the impact of his mission:

> I'd just set out,
> *packing my own burden bound for Argos*
> *(here I'd put my burden down and rest),*
> *when I met a perfect stranger, out of the blue,*
> *who asks about my way and tells me his. . . .*
> *"Well, my friend," he says, "out for Argos*
> *in any case? Remember to tell the parents*
> *he is dead, Orestes . . ."*

As an emissary of Apollo, Orestes is a merchant of destruction; he brings his mother death. Yet his story only makes her harder to contend with, especially since he ends by challenging her feelings as a parent. She responds with a typical outburst of grief; it shouts aloud her falseness—her excess may reveal her relief, even her triumph in Orestes' demise—while it stirs with love-in-hate and the hope that he might just survive the worst. The mother in the Fury mourns her son. Strange, he had not thought to find a trace of affection left for him, and perhaps a gift for recognition even more surprising. As Clytaemnestra turns from him—"your words, you storm us, raze us to the roots"—to address the curse itself, "you curse of the house so hard to wrestle down," her subject never changes. She is probably distraught, unless she sees the stranger is the curse or, though this is conjecture, that the curse is Orestes quite alive before her, calling her to die and calling for assistance. In *Agamemnon* she extended sympathy to her victim, here perhaps she extends compassion to her son who must be baptized in her blood. A thing to terrify a mother and to rend her heart.

It also reaches Orestes' heart, introducing him to the basic truth of his disguise. He plays on the custom that the one who brings bad news is punished; he is sorry to announce Orestes' death and distress his hostess, and his ironies dissolve. He *is* sorry the young Orestes is gone and the mature Orestes has to face the destiny that, for the first time, may glimmer in his mother's eyes. "The tie between / the host and stranger," he wonders, "what is kinder?" He might even desert his mission, were he not "bound by honor, bound by the rights / of hospitality." Bound to whom? To his *philoi*, as he says, though the word may mean his friends or his kin, or both. He is bound to his patron Apollo and his friendly hosts in Argos—bound too to avenge his father and perform a dreadful service for his mother, for whom he holds a lingering affection. And she answers him in kind: "For all that you receive what you deserve, / as welcome in these halls as one of us [*philos*]." This is a threat, of course; she knows the stranger is no friend, she will welcome him as if he were that *philos*, Agamemnon home from war. Or is he the *philos* Orestes, her own offspring? Might she even breathe a kind of reassurance? "Whatever the cost, my son," she may almost seem to say, "our destiny lies before us, and it must be fulfilled." Over the years Clytaemnestra's ironies have matured. They still assert her mastery—"we never lack for loved ones [*philoi*]," she warns, meaning Aegisthus while speaking to Orestes; but now her ironies expose her vulnerability as well. Here she is diabolic and deeply human too, the murderess and the mother. Here in the growing dark she may invite her son to suffer into truth—a mutual ordeal.

As they go through the doors, the women reassemble. Orestes needs their help—and here is his old nurse, already on her way to Aegisthus with word of Orestes' death. But she hates her master and will take the women's word as well: Tell him to come without his bodyguard and be an easy kill. Cilissa gives Orestes equal odds, and her long harangue about his infancy, part humor and part heartbreak, gives him something more. The infant she nursed is gone, but as she mourns for him we glimpse a new tie between the innocent and the mature young man. Like her he comes from the shadows of the house, nursed by the bowl of pain that she has sipped, and nursed with her milk of kindness too, that lends a seasoned innocence, a decency to his later years. Cilissa is his second mother, perhaps as legitimate as Clytaemnestra, because the nurse enlarges the issue of their combat. Her monologue rambles from the time she took Orestes from his mother to the time she took him from his father, as the true successor born to liberate their people, the humanity Cilissa represents.

"The sweetest, dearest plague of all our lives" will offer further hardships first, but the captive women want their liberation now. They invoke the gods in all benevolence, they rehearse a song of joy to sing when their hopes have reached their destination, and they speed Aegisthus toward his execution. Here he comes again, unchanged, the mask of a man who pretends concern for the house but revels in its pain, the swaggering activist who, like a crude version of Agamemnon, takes a cue from the women and blunders to his death behind the doors—a death as insignificant as his role in Agamemnon's murder.

There is nothing, in other words, that can compete with the act of matricide that is approaching. Clytaemnestra emerges of her own free will, majestic in anger, and when a servant warns, "The dead are cutting down the quick," she reads the riddle staunchly:

By cunning we die, precisely as we killed.
Hand me the man-ax, someone, hurry!
Now we will see. Win all or lose all,
we have come to this—the crisis of our lives.

Her suspicions are confirmed. "The dead" are the generations of the curse embodied in her living son, her murderer, yet somehow the making of her too, for not until she has engaged with him can she fulfill herself. The main doors open. Over her lover's body stands Orestes. At first he is torn between extremes of hate and love, between a killer and a son who tears at his mother's robes, bares her breast, and cannot take her life. As William Arrowsmith has made so clear, Orestes' hesitation is the most momentous act in the *Oresteia*; it will originate the justice of the gods, exacting and humane. But for the present the gods reject that hesitation —as if they were not ready for the mercies of mankind, or so Apollo's spokesman, Pylades, would suggest. He has not said a word till now, and as he breaks his silence, it seems the god himself is urging on Orestes:

> What of the future? What of the Prophet God Apollo,
> the Delphic voice, the faith and oaths we swear?
> Make all mankind your enemy, not the gods.

Apollo's commandment is a mortal threat as well, and what it evokes within Orestes, as he hurls Clytaemnestra against the body of Aegisthus, is less a sense of principle than sexual envy of his mother and her lover.

Orestes' hesitation is a saving grace that issues from his mother. Not only from the sight of her breast but what we noticed earlier, her grief for the dead Orestes, or was it for her living son and his ordeal? What may have been their recognition at the gates was vital. The mother breeds compassion in her child, and she alone can teach him how to use it. She is the impresario the young unseasoned actor needs. Between Pylades' threats and Orestes' act of murder she conducts another great temptation scene—again she is *Peitho*, but here she persuades her son to take her life, unintentionally at first and then more firmly. She begins, in fact, by pleading for her life, to save herself and save Orestes from the curse that waits for matricides. And when he places her on trial, she meets his charges softly, placing her maternal care against his pains of exile, her adultery against his father's adultery throughout the war, until the trial comes to a standoff. Too raw to combat her self-defense— a blend of regret and justification—he repeats himself, his meaning blurs (906–08), weakened by his adolescent love-in-hate. Self-pity on one hand, histrionics on the other, it saps his will to act.

But Clytaemnestra wants a crisis. Suddenly she "prosecutes" the action—"I see murder in your eyes, my child—

mother's murder!"—a horrified accusation *and* a challenge, and they break into a passionate interchange. It is not matricide, Orestes insists; her guilt will make it suicide. But her curse will hunt him down—no gentle warning now—but unless he murders her his father's curse will do the same:

CLYTAEMNESTRA
  I must be spilling live tears on a tomb of stone.

ORESTES
  Yes, my father's destiny—it decrees your death.

CLYTAEMNESTRA
  Ai—you are the snake I bore—I gave you life!

ORESTES
                                                   Yes!
  That was the great seer, that terror in your dreams.
  You killed and it was outrage—suffer outrage now.

She creates her fate and she accepts it, and she rises to her tragic greatness. Her agony passes into affirmation—the mother's death-cry is a birth-cry too, for she brings forth the destiny of her son; she turns his innocence into power. It is not purity of heart that impels Orestes; it is his mother's heart. Apollo can reduce him to an instrument of vengeance. Only she can generate his action as a man. These are the poles of the tragic quandary: the yoke of necessity and the drive of human will, and Orestes must incorporate them both. He is his father's and his mother's son, but he and Clytaemnestra are better than Agamemnon and his gods. More than enact a brutal destiny blindly, they would counteract it with creative sorrow—with their painful, mutual awareness that outrage must be met by greater outrage.

As Orestes takes his mother through the doors, the women celebrate the gods and sing of justice, oblivious to all that lies ahead. The light of freedom is breaking through the dark, as they maintain, but when the doors swing open and the torches blaze, we behold a "dawn of the darkness" once again, a stunning *déjà vu*. Sword in hand, Orestes rises over the bodies of Clytaemnestra and her lover, as she had risen over his father and Cassandra. Like his mother, he claims to end the curse, to play the role of justice. But history repeats itself, as Joyce advises, with a difference. Orestes is frenzied by the memory of his victim—then, summoned by his own incriminations, the fury of his mother maddens him with deeper and deeper states of moral insight. Her medium is her masterpiece, the robes that entangled Agamemnon's body and now entangle hers. In fact the robes produce a family reunion; they unite the murdered parents with their son, the avenger and the matricide—the robes present the love knot of his mission and his guilt. For Orestes exhibits them, as Clytaemnestra did, to exonerate himself, but he finds the stains not only of his father's blood, his rightful cue to passion, but of his mother's too. He embraces the robes as if they were the king, fulfilling his debt of mourning; embracing them as if they were the queen, he cries aloud his crime. He cannot assume his parents' powers unless he accepts their dark pathologies as well. The public trial that concluded *Agamemnon* has narrowed into the young man's troubled psyche, rendering him the judge and convict both. Standing in his mother's steps, he is the latest victim of the curse.

Yet Orestes is also the consummation of the curse. His father embodied its negative aspect, its murderousness. Orestes adds the fierce humanity of his mother, and in their relationship the curse may begin to find its cure. For he, unlike his father, gives his mother what she always needed, worthy opposition. He is endowed with all her gifts, from verbal agility to moral stature—the mother and the son complete each other. Orestes has an Oedipus complex, with a difference. "Indeed he does," some will object, "he loves his father and murders his mother!" But what we mean is that he rivals his father and replaces him because his authority is more valid, more humane. Perhaps because he hungers for his mother, and that hunger is channeled into the psychic richness and responsibility that flourishes between them. Even though he kills her, yes, for together they will project their bond into the most creative reaches of the *Oresteia*. They not only prefigure the union of Fury and justice that concludes the trilogy. They make that justice worth the suffering in the first place, stringent and compassionate in one.

For the present, however, Orestes must suffer for "the race of man," and as his mission grows his trials grow as well. He appeals to Apollo, who commanded him to avenge his father and promised to purge him in return. At last a god can be held accountable for a murder in the house, and Apollo will participate in Orestes' exoneration. But here, as he is invested with Apollo's insignia and turns toward Delphi, he may have his doubts. "Go through with [your revenge]," Apollo urged, "and you go free of guilt." Perhaps, but Orestes no sooner murders his mother—lops her serpent head, as the women say—than the serpents of her Furies flash and tangle in his eyes. And they are stronger than the bloodguilt which Apollo's arts can purge. They are the forces of conscience and would go their wild way, were it not for the nature of their source—his mother's blood, his own lifeblood that he has shed. Matricide is a kind of suicide for Orestes; at the same time matricide may expand him. The matriarchal Furies are both his punishment and in a sense his power. They are, above all, a terrifying reversal of the mourning women Orestes saw at first. Dressed in black, a "new wound to the house," they drive him mad—they drive him into a new, more desperate flight—yet the Furies also galvanize his perceptions and, as we shall see, they force him on to Delphi, then to Athens where he is restored. As Orestes goes to meet his more climactic trials, he is equipped with all that he inherits from his mother: tragic heroism, the power to suffer into truth, and more. In the midst of terror an act of symbiosis has begun between the mother and the son. Cursed and murderous as they are, they have begun to regenerate the curse.

In *Agamemnon* everyone is in the grip of larger forces. The gates close; the ramparts loom. It is not a play of action. The poetry is the action, but the long casts back to Troy and forward to Argos only tighten the patterns of reprisal like a vise. Violence breeds violence; all that can counteract it is an attitude, the will to suffer more. *The Libation Bearers* breaks the deadlock. Here is a new generation, a new attempt to penetrate the massive walls, a new accommodation with the gods. The tone of the play is deeply inward. The Furies, once an expedition sent to Troy, are assaults within the brain. Aeschylus probes his sources. Scenes that stir with an Odyssean quiet may even tell us more; here at the grave, the dead father hears what he never heard in Homer, the voices of his children. And within the atmosphere of the hearth, the baths, the old nurse and the traveler's ingratiating talk, lies a re-creation of the *Odyssey* at least as psychological and expansive. The hostess welcomes a stranger— the son who returns for vengeance but must kill his mother together with her suitor. Homer's story of revenge turns tragic, yet the family expands with humanity as well. Clytaemnestra rivals her suitor in treachery and Penelope in maternal strength. Orestes rivals Odysseus in savagery, Telemachus in maturity. In terms of Homer he is both the father and the son. He is his own father, one might say: more self-determined than predetermined, his character may improve upon his destiny. That is the purpose of Orestes' play-within-a-play: to create his own identity so fully that, when he enacts his ruthless, destined part, he can recast it with dignity and insight. Orestes is a prophet, as the chorus sees him, because he has a vision of himself.

If people are demonized in *Agamemnon*, here they personalize their gods. The gods remain in Delphi or Olympus, but "the rough work of the world is still to do," and men who go about it find divinity in themselves. The magnificence of the opening play is muted, less because the king is gone and the work at hand is ugly than because a fresh new spirit is required. The gorgeous arias yield to conversations. There is an intimacy breathing in the shadows, warm, confiding, alive. Something can be done. *The Libation Bearers* is a play of action.

The plays are as different as their choruses. The old men of Argos reach back to the heroic past; like Homer they invoke the muse and find that she is Fury. Still they strain to praise the gods, they seize on Olympian doctrines to shield them from the truth. But once it crashes through, they learn what they had never known before—how it feels to suffer—and they convert to the Furies in the end. The captive women have known the Furies all along but fail to use their powers to the full. Victims of the wars abroad and the strife in Argos, they yearn to support Orestes and the mission of Apollo. When they reach to the past, they show how the present exceeds all past example. They live to provide momentum here and now; cajoling, goading, bloody-minded, they are the midwives to the action. They cry to the gods for help, too rushed for doctrine. Their style is stripped, their morality is at last simplistic—too vindictive or too optimistic, they leap to the future when justice will prevail, and flee the arena where Orestes struggles on. They are finally extruded from the action. They leave a vacuum which the Furies fill.

The Furies will unify language and action, and Orestes leads the way. Even when his syntax and his conscience go insane, his shattering holds a kind of promise. His language at the outset, like his conscience, strains for commitment—now too sure, now insecure, too pious or despondent, feverish, overwrought. But after his painful recognitions he can articulate the conflicts of maturity itself. He is torn between his maddening insights and his desire for the rights; his cries clash out against his closing prayers. Orestes' fury and his gods are clashing, but the language of the play predicts their union, especially in that symbol of complicity from *Agamemnon*, the nets of capture and the ceremonious robes. Here they reticulate in subtle ways. First in the strands of hair Orestes places on the grave, one for death and one for life. As Electra animates the strands, she brings her brother forth; and as the children recall the lethal net, they lash their father back to life and invigorate themselves. "Corks to the net, they rescue the linen meshes / from the depths.

This line will never drown!" Their very existence is a weave of life and death, like Electra's web that binds the wild beasts in its design, and unites her with her brother in vengefulness and love.

We see the weave most clearly in another symbol, perhaps the living, coiling extension of the nets, that dominates this play. At first the serpent is the queen who kills the warlord in her coils, but she also presses her children to conspire against her, and the serpent in her nightmare lends Orestes will to act. The meaning of his action springs from a new bond between the serpent and the nets. The bloody robes that trammeled the bodies of Agamemnon and Clytaemnestra, that embody Orestes' mission and his guilt, stimulate the snaky-headed Furies in his mind. And in effect he is doubly invested at the end, with the Furies' swarming cloaks as well as with the trappings of Apollo, a Nessus shirt and a habit of perfection. For Orestes may prefigure a union of the warring moral orders in the *Oresteia*— he may become the fury of the justice of the gods. As he rushes out, his language and his action work together. All that he envisions leads him on.

In *The Libation Bearers* vision enlivens action, for better and for worse. The brother and the sister embrace, yet they only foreshadow the embrace between the mother and the son. The characteristic act of *Agamemnon* is a trampling; here it is an embrace of opposites that may empower each other. Separate images from the first play grow more human and promise to combine. Blended in with the serpent and the net is the image of the eagle, the ominous bird of Zeus. Here the eagle-king has been strangled by the she-snake, but his nestlings will avenge him. This conflict between the eagles and the serpent may suggest a final triumph of the Olympians over the forces of the Earth, but Aeschylus is actually moving toward their union, and Orestes is identified with both. A stranger to the trilogy might have thought Orestes would simply avenge his father by murdering his mother—masculine will suppressing feminine energy.

Not at all. Orestes must embody his mother's energy, and it will drive him from Argos and insanity to the light. In this central play the conflict between male and female has become a dialectic struggle moving toward a resolution. That is why Aeschylus makes the murder of Aegisthus insignificant but lifts the act of matricide to paramount importance. Mother and son are agonizing out their evolution, and the mutual labor of the generations is unique to Aeschylus' *Oresteia*.

In later treatments of the legend it recedes, Orestes' resoluteness slowly crumbles, and a lethal rivalry between Clytaemnestra and Electra takes the stage. As we move from Sophocles to Euripides, from a daughter who reincarnates her mother's proud, tragic vengefulness to one who lashes her mother's failing powers to a maddened pitch within herself, we watch the house of Atreus degenerate. The more Clytaemnestra's maternal energies fail in the later plays, the more the act of matricide is drained of vital impact, and her Furies finally abandon their creative struggle with the gods. What Aeschylus dramatizes as the necessary roots of justice, Sophocles views with the cruel indifference of Olympus, and Euripides condemns. The legend is demythologized in a harsh, more modern light that some find realistic, others cynical and black. "The crisis of our lives" becomes a private nightmare. Evolution turns to incest. The leap across the centuries to O'Neill and Hofmannsthal and Strauss seems brief, as the ancestral house contracts into the prison of one's pathology and one's past. In the opera *Elektra* the suicidal energies of the daughter, mounting into the ecstatic murder of her mother, burn out in her maenadic dance of death. In *Mourning Becomes Electra* the daughter reverts to her mother's phantom spirit and cohabits with the dead—it is the most defeatist, deterministic version of the *Oresteia* that we have. The tale of the tribe becomes a story of the tribe's disintegration.

But in Aeschylus the act of matricide gathers a positive momentum. *The Libation Bearers* has a headlong forward thrust. Its movement is a metaphor for Orestes' surging will; his lust for vengeance is building into justice. Dionysos is dying into life, and here his rite of spring, ultimately unlike the Anthesteria, celebrates his dying into later, ever larger forms of life. This is the traumatic springtime of our culture. The play explodes our perspective once for all. We are breaking free of the walled, claustrophobic citadel—like Mycenae, as Henry Miller saw it, "one of the navels of the human spirit, the place of attachment to the past and of complete severance too." A greater rite of passage has begun; it begins in agony, but it will end on the level, lucid heights of Athens. Only after death can Clytaemnestra pass from mother to the Furies to the Eumenides. Like the serpents in the Gorgon's hair, their serpents imply reprisal and revival, the healing power of the gods. For the serpent was also a prototype of Zeus and it soon will lend the Furies true redemptive strength. And Orestes has a final passage too. Through the onslaught of the Furies he becomes a purgatorial hero, the scapegoat who absorbs his people's guilt and grows into their prince, the living promise of his father's kingdom. Orestes must suffer into Everyman, our last, best hope. The gods and the Furies may exist without him, but it is within his conscience that they live and battle; then, like actors in a drama, they will speak and make their peace.

The crux of the *Oresteia* is the fierce embrace between the mother and the son. Only they can humanize the gods; then the gods can humanize our world. He and she cannot foresee the magnificent unions still to come—they can only create their possibility. Yet the captive women cannot even see the Furies. They see Orestes' triumph and his torment, a baffling repetition of the curse. He seemed a savior in the third generation, like Third Saving Zeus, or was he Death? He is both; he is the prince and outlaw, humanity in ruins and perfection. But this is a vision for the chorus just emerging. The Furies will embrace him still more fiercely and, with Athena as their leader, generate the justice of the gods.

THE EUMENIDES

The Eumenides turns the darkness into light. Dionysos dies and lives again. It is the harvest of the god, the season "barbarous and beautiful," when the waning year is bursting with its fruits, and loss and regeneration seem the same. The *Oresteia* ends with rites of autumn. Aeschylus may recall the Thesmophoria, when the women reap and sow, singing their spells that ban and bless, that purify the present crop and reinforce the next. The final play, as some have said, is so expansive it may even recall the Mysteries of Eleusis. These enlarged the Thesmophoria into rites so guarded, so close to the soul it was heresy to reveal their secrets, yet so democratic—open to free men and slaves alike—that they became the national religion of Greece.

The Mysteries began as a harvest rite that celebrated the gift of agriculture as the fruits of the ordeal of Demeter and her daughter. Kore or Persephone was abducted to the underworld by Hades and cost her mother "all that pain / To seek her through the world." In her fury Demeter loosed a blight on the earth until Zeus interceded, won the release of Kore, and reunited her with her mother. Every year, however, Kore must descend again as the bride of Death; yet as if her potency depended on her dying, she rises in the spring and bears the grain, her grateful mother's gift. And Demeter is admitted to Olympus, the gods of the Earth and Sky unite, rejoicing in a *Theogony* that ends in harmony rather than suppression. It may be our most moving, human story of the gods, for Demeter also gave us the Mysteries that ally us with the gods in suffering and success. The Mysteries transformed the violation of Kore, the trials of Demeter and their reunion into a threefold ritual of purgation, passion play, and pageant. The celebrant might see the purging and the passion as his tribulations in this life, and the final pageant, the return of Kore, as a sacred birth, and the union of the gods as a sacred marriage that renewed him and prepared him for his death.

"Blest is he who goes beneath the earth having seen these things," said Pindar. "He knows the end of life, he knows its god-given beginning too." Those who decline the rites remain among the uninitiate, "the unpurified mob," as Plutarch saw them, "who trample each other underfoot, herded together in thick mire and gloom." Not the initiate—"met by a marvelous light, or welcomed into open country and meadows, with singing and dancing and solemn raptures of holy music and sacred revelations; there, made perfect at last, walking at large, free and absolved, the initiate worships with crowned head, arm-in-arm with the pure and undefiled." He is the pure beholder, purged, transfixed. The Mysteries would become the apocalypse of antiquity, an intimation of immortality, but at the time of Aeschylus they celebrated the things of this world. And the experience was a trauma of terror and reverence, of darkness broken by a blaze of torches, of ritual mounting to drama, drama resolving into vision, gods and mortals wedded here and now. As the Mysteries were absorbed by Athens, they became the force, as an ancient decree described them, that led mankind from savagery to civilization. More than agriculture, human culture was the harvest gift of Athens. Through the Mysteries she bestowed it on the world.

The *Oresteia* and the Mysteries might rival each other, not only as spectacles but as ordeals, initiations into our culture—rites of aggregation. Yet the *Oresteia* finally admits us to society, not a visionary company. Aeschylus is civic, active, dramatic. He transforms the passion of Dionysos into the tragedy and restoration of our lives, the medium through which a culture ridden by its guilt achieves its greatness. The tragic hero, Orestes, becomes a revolutionary hero of his time. Aeschylus departs from Homer's prince, who simply kills his father's assassins and reclaims his native city, to enlarge the later Orestes of lyric poetry, the guilty matricide who must overcome the Furies with the arrows of Apollo. And Aeschylus departs from that physical combat to create an ethical, religious combat that surrounds Orestes and his crime.

The fruits of this struggle may be what no poet, perhaps no legend either, had ever brought to light—a remarkable vision of wedding and rebirth. But first, as at the outset of the Mysteries, the young initiate must suffer "wanderings, exhausting rushing to and fro, and anxious, interminable journeys through the darkness; then, just before the consummation itself, all the terrors, shuddering, trembling, sweat and wonder."

Driven on by the Furies, Orestes has fled to Delphi for the purges of Apollo. Everything seems purged at Delphi, especially this strife between the forces of the Earth and the Olympians. In the priestess' morning prayer she celebrates a peaceful evolution of the oracle and its possessors, from Mother Earth to the Titans to Apollo, who can speak for Father Zeus. Her subject is "cultural evolution," we might say, as it is reflected in this happy union of the gods, their march that civilized our wildness and allows us to foresee our fate. And evolution is the subject of the drama to come, but its spirit will be harsh not peaceful, and so was the history of the Delphic shrine itself. Apollo took the Mother's oracle by force; he butchered her sacred serpent, the Python, and this atrocity brought the Olympian to power. His priestess would rather suppress that violent history, though it seems to surface when she summons the attendant spirits of the shrine: Pallas, the warrior goddess; and Dionysos, whose maenads dismembered Pentheus; and Poseidon in his turbulence; and Zeus *Teleios*, who saw to Agamemnon's execution. Behind the serene façade of Apollo's temple, in other words, a pantheon of violent gods may wait to shape the coming action.

The priestess no sooner enters the sanctuary to receive her prophecy than she rushes back at once, terrified, like a child by a nightmare. And all that unfolds before us now is like a strenuous dream where ghosts may walk, our guilt and our gods may loom and struggle as if at our creation. For this is a vision of the childhood of the race and of our future—"greater than all [the Pythia's] embarkations past," and far beyond her powers of expression. At the Navel of the Earth she finds Orestes and the

Furies, motionless as a still life, mysterious. Orestes holds a suppliant's branch in one hand, wreathed with a shining, pious tuft of wool, but in the other hand a bloody sword—bloody from his mother's wounds or from Apollo's purges, or both, since purging contaminates the purger and Apollo's shrine is polluted either way. The Furies are still more ambiguous. Neither Gorgons nor Harpies, they are terrifying precisely because they are not supernatural; they are women of a sort, and so their transformation into Eumenides will be both more miraculous and more natural at the last. Even now they surround Orestes like a *lochos*, an ambush pressing for revenge, but a *lochos* is a bed of childbirth too, and there may be other ties between them. Some legends say that the Navelstone is the tomb of the Python, and if so the blood on Orestes' sword may serve to revive the bloodguilt of Apollo. The first possessors of Delphi may have risen from the dead to seek revenge. Another watch has seen another sign, another interchange of men and women, but now the gods of the Sky and forces of the Earth have joined the action. There is a light in the darkness of Apollo's temple. Is it the dawn of civilization or the advent of a new barbarism? Gods and men together will determine its significance.

The doors open. Over Orestes and the Furies stands Apollo, the god of prophecy, purgation, and the law. According to popular belief his powers are "external" in a strong sense: his prophecies are fiats, his purges are ritualistic, and his laws enforce our peaceful coexistence with the gods, essentially through our skills of self-effacement and restraint. "Nothing in excess" is Apollo's creed, and he had become its hero, lucid, formal, intellectual, civilized, through his victory over all that was dark, amorphous, irrational, primitive—the Earth. But Aeschylus has spared Apollo that struggle, and Apollo's powers, never tempered from within, may be eroded. Clearly his purges have begun to dissolve Orestes' bloodguilt and insanity, but his purges seem superficial. He knows, or thinks he knows, these Furies for what they are—emissaries of "the world of death"—so he stupefies them for a moment, only to make them livelier as Orestes' pangs of conscience. Clearly the purges of Delphi formed a bridge from the blood vendetta to social justice (they "detoxified" the murderer, preparing him for common courts of law), but because they were simply ritualistic, some believe they impeded the advance of ethics, and Aeschylus increases this impression. Apollo orders Orestes on to Athens less for a probing, moral restoration than for a kind of magic absolution of his crime. Apollo the Healer has a power of referral, the Justicer knows "the rules of justice," but as Orestes may imply—in a surprising imperative—the god must learn compassion.

Apollo is prophetic, it is true. Orestes will be absolved and the Olympians will prevail, but in a way Apollo could not foresee, and dependent on the Furies for success. That is another vision, and as Orestes leaves, his mother's ghost appears, a spume that rises from the Navelstone and speaks the Mother's true prophetic voice. Clytaemnestra, unlike Apollo, is the voice of conscience. She is guilty of murder, yet she was murdered in return, and still her Furies sleep. She awakes them from their origins, the silent dead, to rouse their powers of revenge. They begin defeated. Apollo has inspired the matricide and snatched him from their grasp. Now it is their turn to suffer incriminations—all the nightmares, spurs, and chills they dealt their guilty victims—but they quickly turn their suffering against the guilty god. The Navelstone is hemorrhaging again, and they know what that means: another Olympian violation of the Mother and the Fates. Now by taking revenge on the matricide, Orestes, the Furies will repay the matricidal gods. They would wage the *Theogony* again, not on the Olympians' grounds of Might Makes Right but on their own grounds, the Furies' older, more moral law of retaliation.

A subtle distinction perhaps, yet it may govern their encounter with Apollo, striding forth in arms to drive them out. Here is the opening skirmish between the Titans and the gods, in effect, and in this battle of opposites each side has its claims, though each is so extreme a reconciliation seems impossible, and Apollo may be even less cooperative than the Furies. His values—Law and Order—are undermined by his methods of enforcement: he would slaughter the Furies to preserve his sense of justice, he is murderously self-righteous. And the Furies calmly, rationally expose him in debate. First he justifies matricide in terms of vengeance, then he pardons it with absolution. But if murder calls for murder in return, should it be forgiven with a prayer? Perhaps in behalf of the marriage bond, which Apollo defends as sanctified by Zeus and Hera, more binding than the bonds of blood and Fate defended by the Furies. But Apollo, the champion of marriage, has murdered one of its partners and mortified its children. Faced with his contradictions, the Furies are consistent but clearly limited: they punish matricides, other murderers go free. Yet at least they are reactive, defensive of their order, while the Olympians promote their order with a brutal will. By facing Apollo with his wilfulness, moreover, the Furies force the action on to Athens, not for a blanket pardon but a trial, a weighing of the rights and wrongs. While Apollo would absolve Orestes in the name of *force majeure*, they pursue him in behalf of rudimentary justice.

As we move from Delphi to Athens, from an oracle to an altar of communion, it is like moving from the purges of the Mysteries to the passion play itself. The purges of Apollo have their limits. Orestes has had to suffer a further purgatorial journey, and even now, as he grasps Athena's idol, he is "curst and an outcast." He was a skeptic at Delphi; here he strains for belief, for the Furies press him toward a more intense ordeal. In full cry, they would hale Orestes down to the underworld for judgment. There the three commandments of Greek religion—honor your gods, your parents, and your guests—are enforced by Hades, the recording angel of antiquity. Orestes invokes Athena in despair, in a voice like Everyman's appealing for salvation. Greek Hell and Heaven are contending for his soul, and the Furies' binding-song that follows binds him to the implications of his crime, expanding it from matricide to the ruin of his house, the curse that every act of *hubris* breeds. The Furies also bind Orestes to themselves, expanding from primitive magic forces to the forces of revenge, the *lex talionis*, the binding law that regulates mankind. For the bond between them is as complex as that between Orestes and his mother. They are bound not only as victim and avenger but as equal victims of the gods, equally frenzied, reviled, destined to the darkness. Yet the Furies turn their deprivations into achievements; that is the weave of their binding-song—they shuttle, they suffer into higher states of awareness. Advancing from pathology to principle, in fact, in their closing lines they become majestic moral powers. Not until the Furies enter Athens can they realize their potential. Here their bond with Orestes may even be symbiotic—the making of them both—though first they make his life a living hell.

The new *Theogony* begins. Athena takes the stage, the warrioress and a force of peace as well. She is the *Parthenos*, the virgin, the Olympian *par excellence*, who sprang from the brow of Zeus in battle gear—"terrible, rouser of war-cries, marshal of armies," in Hesiod's description, but she often lays aside her helmet to rejoice the heart of Zeus. Here she enters like Agamemnon, flushed with victory over Troy, but she bequeaths that victory to Theseus and his peaceful federation of Athens. Athena *Parthenos* inclines toward Athena *Polias*, the goddess of the city. Together they guard and guide all forms of human victory, as Vincent Scully observes, for Athena is both Olympian and of the Earth, the Father's daughter and the Mother's too. Behind the goddess stands a matriarchal spirit of the hearth whose symbol was the serpent, the symbol of the Furies, and her provinces were fertility and the loom. Athena becomes the force of public discipline, the instigator of our actions and their judge, for in a case of homicide she can detect the involuntary murderer and release him.

Where Apollo simply purges, Athena probes to matters of the heart. Like him she sees the Furies and Orestes at her shrine, but she will not prejudge her guests, she asks them to introduce themselves. In response the Furies expand their targets from matricides to murderers in general, though their punishments, as Athena sees them, are extreme. So was the crime, they answer, despite her sense that a higher power forced Orestes on. "What spur could force a man to kill his mother?" they ask, pressing for a verdict, since Orestes will not take the traditional oath of innocence. Incriminating evidence, yet Athena uses it to demonstrate the Furies' dogmatism—more moral but no less ritualistic than Apollo's—and their binding-song has just committed them to *acts* of retribution rather than pompous declarations. Athena makes the Furies' terms recoil, in other words, in a way that does them honor. And so they volunteer for what they had refused: adjudication of this issue by a god. "We respect you. You show us respect." A startling conversion, but understandable and prophetic. The warrioress is turning conflict into peace, her battleground into the depths of conscience.

These are depths which she must learn herself. When she probes Orestes, he reveals a guilt that purges cannot touch. Once more he is torn between his father and his mother, his mission and his guilt. Was his action just or not? he asks, and probes Athena's conscience; for his father was her partisan at Troy, her brother Apollo drove Orestes on. Conscience alone might lead Athena to acquit him, but she perceives that the Furies "have their destiny too, hard to dismiss," and once defeated, they will destroy her land. The choice is too grave for men to make, too emotional for a god. It is the tragic choice, and now it is Athena's turn to feel it. "A crisis either way. / Embrace the one? expel the other? It defeats me." Like the tragic heroes before her, *she* is damned if she does and damned if she doesn't. If she plays an Olympian role and frees Orestes, she incites the Furies. If she consigns Orestes to them, she incites the Olympians instead. Athena's choice intensifies Orestes'—now the gods and the Furies are on both sides of the conflict; if she embraces one, she must expel the other. Yet her approach to the choice intensifies Orestes' too. Like him she hesitates, but Athena's hesitation is even more constructive, for she is turning her ordeal into a trial, a legal judgment, and creating the procedures to control it. Her examination of the Furies and Orestes is like an *anakrisis*, the magistrate's initial hearing of the contenders, preliminary to selecting proper judges. These will be men and gods together—the best Athenians, with Athena as their leader. As she brings on this great debate between conscience and command—dual sides of her own inner nature—she reveals a deep desire for balance.

The Furies want to help her. At the core of *The Eumenides*, as in the first two plays, stands a chorus that relates the Furies to the justice of the gods. Here that relationship involves the tragic choice itself, and the Furies are embroiled with Athena. If she lets the matricide go free, an age of lawlessness will follow, leaving the Furies with no choice but to hasten on a "blood-dimmed tide" that sweeps society. That is a course which they deplore. Think what men might gain, they argue, if Athena *lets* the Furies choose for good instead of evil. Why together they might turn the tragic choice into a victory, nothing less than the birth of law itself, the Furies' evolution from their origins to the ministers of justice. That, in fact, is the subject of their chorus. Rising up in the face of lawlessness—the tides, the rampant plagues, collapsing houses—the Furies return to their firm, original foundation: the terror that can reinforce our reverence for the rights. For now the Furies suffer into justice rather than revenge. That has been their promise all along, and that is why they (of all creatures in the world) can erect the ruling law of Greece. At the center of this chorus the Furies erect a shrine to the doctrine of the Mean—Apollo's doctrine, ironically enough. It is the Mean as they conceive it however; not the golden mediocrity of Delphi which avoids extremes, but the interplay of one against another, a dialectic, a moral tension. The very weave of their stanzas binds our powers of restraint to our potential, for this is a binding-song far larger than the first. Here the Furies bind us to the three

Greek commandments not for punishment but for health; and here they strengthen earlier strands from the *Oresteia*. The altar of the rights that Paris trampled is resurrected as a standard of behavior. The law of Zeus may at last become the way to justice.

But before the Furies can bind themselves to the gods, they must discover what their bond with Orestes represents. At the end of their chorus they can prophesy the coming age of conscience, but they cannot see that Orestes is its herald. They see him as a perversion of the Mean more drastic than his storm-tossed father; he must "ram on the reef of law and drown unwept, unseen." And so the Furies have raised the tragic choice to a higher power. Now civilization hangs on Orestes' execution, unless Athena can release him and empower the Furies too, fulfilling their hopes for justice while conserving human life. She herself must seize upon the Mean.

That is the purpose of her trial, and it has a hopeful start. As the Furies carry morality toward a higher goal, so the scene has moved to the Areopagus where Athena will establish her tribunal. She and her judges enter, her battle-trumpet sounds for peace, she begins to state her law. But a towering figure breaks the peace—Apollo, her enemy at Troy, the crucial witness who has purged Orestes. Athena improvises, turns to the Furies; the prosecution must begin, and we shift to a new, more urgent version of Athenian legal procedure. The Furies waive the prosecutor's customary speech; they cross-examine Orestes, leading him from heroic claims to his most contradictory disclaimer: "Does mother's blood run in my veins?" Yes, he said so himself at the end of *The Libation Bearers*. In despair he turns to Apollo, almost challenging him to justify their crime. And now one wonders if Apollo even knows "the rules of justice." He can only swell Orestes' defenses with his own windy threats; he relies on Father Zeus, not only because Zeus's might makes right an act of matricide but because it relieves Apollo of responsibility. The Furies cross-examine him tersely. Could the Father avenge a father by abusing a mother so? On the defensive, Apollo expands

Clytaemnestra's guilt, but the more he exonerates her victim Agamemnon, the more he is exposed for lashing the jury with his rhetoric. Moreover, as the Furies insist, Clytaemnestra's treatment of Agamemnon was no worse than Zeus's treatment of his father. Apollo sputters with contempt: Zeus merely shackled Kronos, he did not murder him, and not even Zeus can bring the dead to life. Precisely the point, the Furies object. Orestes killed his mother; what can pardon that? Only Apollo's disclaimer of motherhood itself:

> The woman you call the mother of the child
> is not the parent, just a nurse to the seed,
> the new-sown seed that grows and swells inside her.
> The man is the source of life—the one who mounts.

Hardly an endearing argument to feminists, though it was of biological, even sociological interest to the Athenians, since it offered propaganda for the patrilineal democratic state. But in its context here it may be called into question. It not only undermines Apollo's earlier endorsements of marriage, especially his praise for the equality of the partners. Now, to prove "the father can father forth without a mother" he exhibits Athena who leapt fullblown from the brow of Zeus, and here the myth may have a certain power of recoil. Zeus overpowered Mêtis, a Titaness; she conceived a daughter, and Mother Earth prophesied that if Mêtis conceived again she would bear a son who would dethrone his father. So Zeus swallowed her whole and then was seized with a raging headache, Hephaistos split his skull, and Athena sprang to light. The myth may demonstrate the fatherhood of Zeus but it hardly excludes the motherhood of Mêtis, even her irrepressible vitality in the face of the Father's typical violence. As Apollo uses the story here, it becomes, in Jane Harrison's words, "a desperate theological expedient to rid [Athena] of her matriarchal conditions." Worst of all, in the context of her trial it is a kind of blackmail—You are an Olympian, Apollo thunders, you will vote for us.

Athena cuts him short before he makes a mockery of the proceedings. Some have actually found the trial comic; and like all great comedy it threatens us with disorder so that we may cherish order all the more. The trial is a constructive parody, a re-creation of court procedure which reminds us of its flaws and flexibility; it can be poked but it regains its powers of control. Apollo's intrusion, in fact, only serves to make the trial more momentous. He "Olympianizes" the issues, forcing Athena to assume a new Olympian role. Her tragic choice expands into cosmic terms—now she must mediate between the Titans and the gods. And as she resumes the declaration of her law, it resolves the conflicts of this new *Theogony* in a lasting human institution, Athena's high tribunal on the Areopagus. According to one legend, it was on "the Crag of Ares" that the god of war was acquitted for manslaughter by a jury of his fellow gods. But in Athena's eyes it must remain the scene of human struggle, hence her derivation of the name. It was from the Areopagus that Theseus repelled the Amazons, the invaders who sacrificed to Ares, and here his heirs will defend their law, as Heracleitos urged, as if it were the city wall. That law is strong, moreover, because Athena incorporates the new invaders, the Furies and their powers. Terror and reverence become her people's kindred powers, and seizing on the Furies' most creative hopes, Athena commands her people not only to repel injustice but to preserve the rights of men. Through her court, in other words, the Furies' doctrine of the Mean becomes the actual, working basis of communal justice.

Principle must turn to practice, Orestes must be judged. And as the judges rise to cast their ballots, Apollo and the Furies rise to such vituperation that this *Theogony* may erupt into a clash between Zeus and the Fates themselves if Athena does not cast her ballot as she does:

> *My work is here, to render the final judgment.*
> *Orestes, I will cast my lot for you.*
> *No mother gave me birth.*

I honor the male, in all things but marriage.
Yes, with all my heart I am my Father's child.
I cannot set more store by the woman's death—
she killed her husband, guardian of their house.
Even if the vote is equal, Orestes wins.

The one who has just endorsed the Mean could scarcely strike a more one-sided, more Olympian stance. "We cannot love a goddess who on principle forgets the Earth from which she sprang," Jane Harrison laments, "always from the lips of the Lost Leader we hear the shameful denial." Yet we may hear some other things as well, though the issues are complex, and certainty is probably out of reach. Athena may be defending Zeus, at any rate, less than she is admitting her undeniable kinship with the Father and the masculine gods. Nor is she fully espousing Apollo's male biology with its social, political extensions. She may say, in effect, the murder of a husband by a wife is worse than the murder of a mother by a son, and so she may lend support to the ties of marriage, a civic institution, rather than the ties of blood. But according to her statement, it is precisely in marriage that her loyalties are not exclusively with the male. And rather than totally justify Orestes for his crime, she simply cannot favor Clytaemnestra for hers—a statement of negative preference.

Then why does Athena cast her ballot for Orestes? Her critics will argue that she yields to religious pressures and sexual politics, and her judgment is not only biased but predetermined. "Even if the vote is equal, Orestes wins." Yet her ability to sense an equality in this case, plus her firm independence of her fellow-jurors, may also point to her judiciousness and rigor. She may have decided on Orestes less from bias, we suggest, than to exemplify— with great precision—the origin of the Athenian practice that acquitted all defendants who received an equally divided vote. Whereas a later age would ascribe Athena's action to mercy pure and simple, however, Aeschylus would have her act according to the mercy of her means, her strict sense of equity. For the blanket pardon that

Apollo orders would contravene the facts, painstakingly gathered throughout the trial, and the facts are what compel Athena's decision now. Not only the fact of her kinship with the gods, but the more important fact that they drove Orestes, however willing to avenge his father, to commit his terrible act of matricide. Understandably torn between the rights and wrongs of the case, the jury appears to be deadlocked (or so it appears to us, as we explain in the note on line 767). And Athena will uphold Orestes' crime as justifiable homicide, but not innocence outright. Even in her statement of acquittal—"The man goes free, / cleared of the charge of blood. The lots are equal"—her words reveal that, despite Orestes' innocence, Orestes' guilt remains.

That is a contradiction as arbitrary as the will of Zeus himself, and perhaps the very point Athena wants to make. By maintaining the moral ambiguity of Orestes' action, she maintains the gods' continuing involvement in its consequences. "With all my heart I am my Father's child"—Athena is obedient to, and responsible for, her father. Not for Apollo, who leaves unceremoniously, certain perhaps of victory, though this is moot and the Furies will receive a settlement he would despise. No, Athena is responsible for her father, especially for improving his sense of right and wrong, and this is a burden she has just begun to feel. As Kitto says of the trial, "as a debate it is poor; as conflict it is magnificent." It is so dramatic. Its issue cannot be resolved, it can only be experienced. The law is only medial; its contradictions call for the harmony, the social justice that is its goal. If Athena's position here is too one-sided, too Olympian, she must right the balance. She is "all for the male, in all things but marriage." And now marriage—unions of every sort—becomes Athena's labor, and through these unions she will justify her father.

Her model is Orestes. Adopted by her city, the outlaw is reborn. He returns to Argos, his patrimony, where he redeems his murderous fathers as a just, lawful prince. Thanks to the gods, especially Third Saving Zeus who unites the Olympians and the forces of the Earth. For

Orestes is his mother's son as well, and as he swears an alliance between Argos and Athens, he regenerates his bond with Clytaemnestra. He will curse the men who break his oath, even if he must rise up from the grave, and bless the ones who keep it. He returns to his mother's powers of love and hate, transforming them into a fondness that empowers, a curb that regulates society. He resolves his parents' strife. He is a successful version of Oedipus; neither the banished king of Sophocles nor the wounded private citizen of Freud, by suffering his filial traumas Orestes has regained his throne. He is the pathology of his people, yet he grows into the victor of the *polis*, his people's great good health. He is a martyr in the first sense of the word, a living witness, and a far cry from later martyrs who will leave the living centers of their world. Far from Sartre's Orestes in *The Flies*— the scapegoat who carries off our guilt to an isolated life of fierce, self-gratifying freedom. Far from the Orestes in *The Family Reunion*—the passionate pilgrim who takes "the only way out," in Eliot's words, "purgation and holiness," and an even sharper abdication from his people. In the *Oresteia* the ordeals of Orestes are an *aristeia*, a heroic proof of human victory, individual and social. The tragic hero becomes an epic hero, and his exploits never end; legends of further trials still cling to his future, and further triumphs too. Through Orestes we may glimpse a union of the Titans and the gods. Cursing and blessing both, he promises to be *eumenês*—he may prepare us for the Eumenides, the Kindly Ones, the fury of the justice of the gods. His passion play is the crux of the Mysteries before us, casting us toward the larger birth, the larger sacred marriage still to come.

But first the larger agony. As Athena frees Orestes she inflames the Furies. Like him and his mother, she declares a victory for justice that only provokes the forces of the curse. Now Athena must be tried, and again the prosecution will begin. The Furies cry in pain and turn their pain into the lawless bloody tide they dreaded most. They are like Demeter in her fury, forced to destroy the world, unless Athena can assuage them. She reminds them that the vote was tied, the verdict merely acknowledged Zeus's power. But that is what they deplore, and even when Athena offers them thrones beneath the earth, they repeat their cries against the younger gods. So she threatens them with the lightning-bolt she trained against the Titans—a threat of power politics, yet a reluctant one as well, no sooner made than modulated with her offer of the land's first fruits. And the Furies' rage, in turn, now that it can only hurt themselves, modulates to anguish. Both are dispensing with their rage, in short; their consciences are making them creative. Lest Athena abuse the older gods, she offers them still more, a conscious social role—"do great things, feel greatness, greatly honored." She pleads that they remain and prosper, for if she fails, both sides will lose. Now the tragic choice is not a choice of evils but the effort to secure a total victory. And under this pressure Athena discovers herself, her godly power. It is Persuasion, *Peitho*, not the compulsion of Helen or the temptation of Clytaemnestra, but compassion, the power Cassandra first expressed and now Athena turns to action.

For the third time in the trilogy *Peitho* rises to conduct a swift exchange, but in this persuasion scene the prize is mutual. Through compassion Athena sees that her opponents' strength and weakness are her own. She resembles Prospero in *The Tempest* less than some have thought—she might find him condescending when he turns to Caliban and says, "This thing of darkness I acknowledge mine," and self-righteous when he pardons the rebels in his kingdom:

> Though with their high wrongs I am struck to th' quick,
> Yet with my nobler reason 'gainst my fury
> Do I take part. The rarer action is
> In virtue than in vengeance.

Athena reasons with their mutual fury; she helps them find the virtue in their vengeance, its vital energy. She makes *life* their mutual province, and she wins the Furies over. For she returns them to what they always wanted, what they always were, and in the process she reclaims her own maternal roots—Athena, the spirit of the hearth, savage in defense of all she fosters, not unlike a Fury. They have shared their terms, their values, even their tragic burdens, and now they share the resolution of their trial. It is very moving, like a dialogue of mother and daughter, power and potential, Demeter and Kore reunited. The Furies will generate life; Athena will lead that life to social victory. Together they express a "blessed rage for order."

Together they sing a final binding-song of blessings, founding a new *sunoikia*, a federation that expands the first federation of Theseus into a new cosmology. We begin with prophecy and the gods. The Furies foresee a new union between the Earth and Sky, while Athena, mediating between them and her citizens, will bring the Furies' vision to fruition. Yet as they shower down their blessings, she reasserts their regulatory powers, their severity, for this is like a Thesmophoria of the Furies. They are like the women singing spells that ban and bless at harvest, dispensing joy for some and blinding pain for others. That is our fate, the enduring possibility of tragedy in our lives, but the Furies' second round of blessings shows us how to counteract its harshness. As spirits of fertility they invigorate the rite of marriage—the Olympian rite Apollo unsuccessfully defended—and as they ally themselves with Zeus and Hera they unite with the Fates as guardians of our laws. It is a grand alliance, thanks to *Peitho*, as Athena tells us; thanks above all, the Furies tell us, to ourselves. By rejecting civil strife and promoting brotherhood we can turn their love-in-hate into a national code of conduct:

> Give joy in return for joy,
> one common will for love,
> and hate with one strong heart:
> such union heals a thousand ills of man.

The crux of this binding-song is man. What begins as prophecy ends in a public exhortation of us all. In the third, final round of blessings the Furies urge us to rejoice in the gods' gifts, but only as we use our native gifts and "achieve humanity at last."

The play ends as it began, with the evolution of a culture. But in Delphi we simply foresee our fate, in Athens we create it. These are the Mysteries of Athens, and the sacred marriage here is a wedding of opposites overwhelming in their joy. Vengeance yields to regeneration, the Furies yield to Athena and embrace. Together they complete their rites of passage. Athena becomes what she would become in Plato: the Kore always among us, the virgin brilliant in armor and exulting in our dances—in Wallace Stevens' phrase, she is "war's miracle begetting that of peace." She is the Kore in her fruitfulness, what's more, and as her children imitate her ways, she becomes an image of their psychic wholeness too. Aeschylus has warmed Athena's civic discipline, her imposing statuesque authority, with love. She is magnificently human, the spirit of Athens incarnate in the unions that consummate the *Oresteia*.

A great procession forms, not unlike the Panathenaic Procession that moved throughout the city at every harvest to celebrate Athena's birth and consecrate her gift of human culture. As if that gift derived from other roots as well, the Metics, the resident aliens, were yearly clad in crimson robes and included in the torchlit march. Like Metics imported for their strengths, the Furies are also clad in crimson, but they are invested as permanent citizens and then renamed Eumenides, the Kindly Ones, who never cease to be the Furies too. The parts of their nature wed, and as they join the torchlit march that conducts them to their shrine beneath the Areopagus, they also become the Semnai Theai, the Awesome Goddesses who sanctify the law. Only in Athens can the Furies be the Semnai and Eumenides in one. That is the measure of the city's breadth—passionate and lawful and magnanimous. Athena's citizens are wedded to these spirits, and their common issue is justice, a union of rigor and resilience. Their issue is "neither anarchy nor tyranny" but *isonomia*, social balance. It is the Mean, democracy.

THE ORESTEIA

The *Oresteia* ends in a great mutual victory. At last, as Athena urged, there is no "brutal conquest" of light over darkness, patriarchy over matriarchy, Olympians over Titans and the Earth. In this *Theogony* all enjoy the triumph they desired—"All-seeing Zeus and Fate embrace." The old antagonists, Will and Necessity, have been married by Persuasion, and according to Aeschylus (and Pythagoras and Plato) they produce the world. The *Oresteia* is like a story of creation, yet as the cosmic forces grow creative they become more human and humane. It is in our progress from savagery to democracy, it would seem, that the gods may find the balance which they lacked, and earn a better warrant for authority. In the words of Aeschylus' most expansive couplet, "Zeus is the air, Zeus is the earth, Zeus is the heaven, / Zeus is all in all, and all that lies beyond" —but not until he turns from the use of power politics to the rights of humankind. In the old *Theogony* he acquired power; in the new *Theogony* he refines it. And if Zeus is not a character in the *Oresteia*, capable of improvement, his spokesmen clearly do improve, from Apollo, rationality belligerent, to Athena, the force of reason victorious. She had always been Zeus's ultimate weapon; her birth in armor protected him against his fathers' sorry fates. Now she legitimates her father, and she does so in profoundly human terms. As if Orestes were her model, she enacts her father's will with the energies of her mother, Mêtis, Wisdom. And so the *Oresteia* culminates in a union of male and female strengths, a healthy unisexuality of the spirit. It seems the opposite of Clytaemnestra at the start—the terrifying hermaphrodite—yet the final unions may remind us of her maternal powers too. If the finale recalls the Panathenaia, a harvest festival, Athena's birth may issue, in effect, equally from the brow of the Father and the depths of Mother Earth.

The *Oresteia* may also have a clear maternal bias. Athena is the virgin goddess yet she bears a mortal offspring, Athens. The trilogy consecrates her city, and "the city is a maternal symbol," as Jung describes it, "a woman who harbors the inhabitants in herself like children." More than an official Olympian statement, exclusively masculine as many have asserted, the *Oresteia* makes a boldly innovative, feminine appeal. And this appeal may well be crucial to Athens *because* of the supremacy of the male, the inferiority of the female in the democratic state. Far from an apologist for the status quo, Aeschylus defends the faith by reminding his Athenians of the tribal, matriarchal roots from which they came. While Athena's trial, as we have said, may lend support to the ties of marriage, a civic institution, against the ties of blood, the *polis* against the family, Athena's even-handed verdict on Orestes— justifiable homicide, not innocence outright—enables her to redress the balance, to redeem the claims of the family in a sequel even more conclusive. She awards the Furies a handsome restitution, embracing them into Athens as citizens with equal rights, incorporated, even institutionalized, yet also greatly strengthened and enlarged. In fact the *Oresteia* grows into its final unions mainly by reestablishing the feminine and its powers. Necessarily so; for throughout these plays, men without women appear myopic and destructive. Women dominate the trilogy, especially its resounding climax; not, as some suggest, because they are castrating females, unsexed at last by a threatened, mannish Athens, but because the Mother is the source of life itself. There Athena finds the one necessity that can humanize her Father. And Aeschylus finds the counterweight essential to the democratic balance. It is woman.

The Furies are the force that empowers *The Eumenides*. At last a chorus sings and acts in equal measure. The old men of Argos could only sing; the captive women could only urge the action on until it grew too fierce. The Furies *are* the action, "the heart of the past" that drives the future, and the Furies are its music. Never has a chorus had such range, from silence to complete articulation, joyous, warm and clear. Through the Furies the language of Aeschylus suffers into truth, *pathos* into *mathos* more genuine for every mark it bears. Their song is a *mimesis*, a re-creation of pain that redeems the pain with meaning. The Furies are the artists of pain. They are the pangs of conscience that give rise to self-fulfillment. Without them Orestes would never strive for restoration, and Athena could never justify her father or bring Athens and human consciousness to birth. More than child-avengers, *teknopoinos*, the Furies are *teknopoios*, child-breeding too. They are the Process, like the Great Mother as Nietzsche saw her, "eternally creating, eternally driving into life, in this rushing, whirling flux eternally seizing satisfaction." They send us through a rush of recognitions, dramatic shocks that frighten us and further us at once, and the movement of their drama is unique.

The *Agamemnon* coils, tightens; the light in the dark is strangled off at last. *The Libation Bearers* plunges out of darkness toward the light—the disaster that plunges us into darkness once again. *The Eumenides* sweeps us through a phantasmagoria of light and dark, of darkness breeding light, until the night brings forth the torches of our triumph, like the torches of that Fury Clytaemnestra, "glorious from the womb of Mother Night." Night and day are mother and daughter, suffering and the illumination it can bring. For the energy of the Furies is as great with order as the energy of Dionysos. They are his wild maenads gathering moral force. They are the Mean Dynamic.

So they will become if we embrace them. Surely the gods of Aeschylus are superhuman powers, yet the *Oresteia* is such a humanistic statement one may often wonder if the gods could exist without us. They endure our tragic choices, and they build upon our strengths. The Will of Zeus becomes the will to human justice. Necessity becomes the force of life. Character is destiny after all, not in the ruinous spirit of Agamemnon at the start, but in the spirit of Athena who creates our destination—democracy, a human institution. The *Oresteia* is a theodicy, but as Nietzsche observed, "the gods justified human life by living it themselves—the only satisfactory theodicy!" The gods become our powers, our energies and our ideals, and they are wedded by Athena, our compassion that alone can breed our culture.

More than a story of creation, the *Oresteia* is a story of our re-creation as we struggle from the past to meet the future. The struggle and the union are inseparable, or so the double vision of *The Eumenides* suggests. We are in Athens of the heroic age which embodies Athens in her fifth-century prime; the original battle to found our institutions becomes our constant battle to preserve them. This is the oracular style that Calchas first employed, the historical present that reveals what is to come, and these are the poetics of the play. Everything from the first two plays is painfully recollected and renewed, yet all comes right at last. The imaginary trial that convicted Troy and Agamemnon comes to life, the judges are poised, the sense of crisis mounts, yet the verdict leads to acquittal and restitution. Images had come to life before, but never with so much fear that turns to so much hope. The blighted earth blooms; the storms of ruin become an auspicious, running wind; the sea that heaved with corpses is a rising tide of joy. We not only hear the Furies in full cry and feel them breathing down our necks—at the first performances women miscarried, others fainted, according to an ancient Life of Aeschylus—but we see them turn their hunt into a dance and then a march that leads to rightful ends, the Athenians' pursuance of their culture. In fact every act of trampling in these plays becomes the progress of a civilization. All the blood weddings become the *proteleia*, the sacrifices preliminary to the marriage of the Eumenides and Athens. And Athena comprises all the embattled heroines before her—Athena, the wonderful revision of their suffering into all mankind's success. Here is great clarity rising from great complexity, terror giving rise to reverence for life.

Nowhere is such regeneration felt more clearly than in the dominant symbol of the *Oresteia*, the nets of capture and the robes of ceremony. The robes materialize in the white robes of the gods and the aegis of Athena, the battle cape she lays aside. The nets materialize in the black cloaks of the Furies and the hunting-nets through which Orestes slips and which they lay aside. Both robes and nets will yield to a freely weaving play of image and enactment. The Furies' nets extend into their binding-songs that bind them to their victim, but Orestes is "twined" in Athena's idol too. His guilt and his innocence can never be disentangled, and neither can the Furies and the gods, the threads of the Fates and the grand design of Zeus. Their final binding-song connects us all, mortals and immortals, in a vast moral network, not of retaliation as in the *Agamemnon*, or of recrimination as in *The Libation Bearers*, but of mutual responsibility. The chains of revenge are not so much broken as they are welded into the bonds of justice. We never lose our complicity with the curse, but now our cruelties may be referred to a magisterial court of law, as the closing symbol would imply. As the Furies don the Metics' crimson robes, the color of blood becomes the color of authority, royal crimson worn by gods and kings. The nets of capture finally reinforce the robes of ceremony.

And if the closing procession recalls the Panathenaia, a greater piece of weaving rises before us—if only in imagination—the *peplos* of Athena, the magnificent robe her citizens wove for her at every harvest. It was the bridal color, saffron, like the robes of Iphigeneia, but it renewed Athena's life, her perennial, golden ripeness. In the weave were scenes of her triumph over the Giants, and the Gorgon's snaky head. For her robe incorporated her winged aegis, her Olympian prowess, and her ties to Mother Earth. "Now is the strong prayer folded in thine arms," in Hart Crane's lines, "the serpent with the eagle in the boughs." Athena is both the Victor and the spirit of the loom; and as her citizens raised her robe to the wind, like a sail to buoy forth their ship of state, it may have symbolized the fabric of Athenian society, resilient and controlled, which they bestowed upon posterity.

The *Oresteia* is the triumph of the Mean. The only trilogy that remains to us from Greece embodies "the offence, the counter-offence, and the reconciliation," as George Thomson says, "the resolution of discord into harmony, the triumph of democracy." While *The Eumenides* may seem distinctly optimistic, however— an epilogue where "good wins out in glory in the end"— its ties with the first two tragedies are strong and binding. The final play has three suggestive settings: the house of Apollo expands the house of Atreus haunted by the Furies; Athena's shrine on the Acropolis expands the tragic choice at the hearth; the Areopagus resolves the tragic burden. And so the entire trilogy may seem to consist of three libations. After the libations poured to the gods, then poured to the dead, we have the third libation poured to Saving Zeus, and the third depends on the harshness of the first and second for its savor. *The Eumenides* not only reconciles the *Agamemnon* and *The Libation Bearers*; it preserves their special torments. The trilogy is like Eliot's "ragged rock in the restless waters,"

> *On a halcyon day it is merely a monument,*
> *In navigable weather it is always a seamark*
> *To lay a course by: but in the sombre season*
> *Or the sudden fury, is what it always was.*

It is all a matter of perspective. The craggy grandeur of *Agamemnon* may always dominate our vision—massive and immobile. Or when we consider the seasonal, ritualistic rhythm of the trilogy, *The Libation Bearers* may dominate the center all the more—the rite of spring that follows a costly harvest of the past and impels the great good harvest still to come. In some sense it is always spring in the *Oresteia*, Orestes' agony is so crucial.

But for many *The Eumenides* may predominate; it is the final vision, for better and for worse. For better, since it answers to a human need for respite after so much suffering, perhaps for a wedding of Hegelian opposites to crown the advance of history, idealized and perfected. But for others any optimistic vision may seem unreal, or worse, a delusion. And this particular vision may contain, despite itself, the seeds of historical ruin soon to come. *The Eumenides* celebrates the founding of the Argos League that would, in reality, rouse the Spartan columns and bring Athens to her knees. She would turn, as her new ally had turned, from an international victory to a fatal civil war. And her demise could only be hastened, especially in the eyes of later ages, by those urgings of Athena toward the end of *The Eumenides* which seem to launch an expansionist, imperialistic Athens on her way. But either reaction to the final play is probably a distortion. Far from Utopian and self-complete, its vision appeals for lasting endurance and endeavor. Its optimism has its price; "a contradiction is reconciled," as David Lenson says, "and we count the dead." And its chauvinism has its limits. In the continuous present of her play, in fact, Athena sounds a warning and a promise—a challenge to safeguard her civilization from the barbarism that surrounds it and infects it from within.

The *Oresteia* is Hegelian in its challenge. Not only do its three plays form a thesis, antithesis and synthesis, but its final synthesis is a spur to further struggle. Compare the trilogy to other visions of disobedience, woe, and restoration—Milton's grand three-part design for our salvation—and the more distinct it grows. Through the crimes in the house of Atreus the *Oresteia* may recall an original fall from paradise, the golden age of ease when men and gods were equal, before Tantalus prepared the first disastrous feast. But Aeschylus translates our fallen state from heredity to the conscience where the Furies urge us onward. Our fall is fortunate, not because the Furies are *agents provocateurs*, forces of evil manipulated by a god who acts in our behalf. Nor are they Sartre's flies, the morbid forces of our guilt that enslave us to a fascist tyrant; or Eliot's "bright angels" who warn that worldly affection is a sin, and society a trap. The

Furies are our positive allies, "the fortunes of our lives" because they make us love our lives, they root our lives within a vigorous social order.

Perhaps the *Oresteia* is the *Divine Comedy* of the antique world (a suggestion made by others that needs a study in reply), the *Agamemnon* an *Inferno*, *The Libation Bearers* a *Purgatorio*, *The Eumenides* a *Paradiso*. "In both tripartite works," as C. J. Herington has pointed out so clearly, "there is a similar movement, a gradual climb from torment, through testing, into the light." Yet as we journey from the dark to the light in Aeschylus, we cannot leave the dark behind—the darkness breeds the light. Here the *Inferno* is not only a great tide of destruction; it is also a source of human energy waiting to be channeled. And so this *Purgatorio* is less a sublimation of our mortality, a preparation for a realm beyond the human, than it is a deeper immersion in mortality itself. And it prepares us for a *Paradiso* very Greek indeed, an earthly paradise that is eternally demanding. We regain the golden age; men and gods join hands again, not in their ease but in their labor to create a brave new world.

The end of the trilogy may recall the final phase of Shakespeare's work. After the tragic straits we reach a harbor like that of the late romances. But what makes the kingdom of *The Tempest* peaceable may be its distance, its atmosphere of dream and sea-change and miraculous reunion. In Aeschylus' *Eumenides* we have a dream that turns to drama, a passionate encounter with reality. His salvation is neither in the imagination, "a paradise within thee, happier far," nor in the city of god. It is in the city of man, where paradise must be earned with every passing day, and it exists in our very struggle to achieve it. Struggle is salvation, as Nietzsche would say. Or in the words of a modern revolutionary, "To climb Mount Everest is a premature aspiration, until you learn the way—the learning, that is the action." If Aeschylus celebrates progress, it is not as a limp myth of perfectibility but as a march, a never-ending effort.

Homer might agree, but Aeschylus' vision of our destiny is larger. In *The Eumenides* he has worked loose from his master, to engage more freely with him and surpass him at the last. In this final *Odyssey*, after the bloody returns of Agamemnon and Orestes, it is a goddess who journeys home and brings her people to a point where vendettas may yield to justice once for all. As we move away from an *Iliad*, from a city razed by men and gods to a city they restore—a league of cities formerly hostile—the *Oresteia* presents a sweeping homeward turning, a universal harvest home. It is tragedy becoming epic in its affirmation and its scope. The ultimate *pathos* breeds the ultimate *mathos*, never losing sight of the labor and the danger still to come, not even in conclusion.

Originally the trilogy ended with a satyr-play called *Proteus*, also based on the *Odyssey*. Although it has not survived, it probably re-enacted the adventures of Agamemnon's brother, Menelaus, who had been driven to Egypt by the storm that struck the fleets. It would have explained his absence at the time of the assassination and showed another son of Atreus—in a clearly lighter vein—coming to grips with destiny and its powers. Proteus was the Old Man of the Sea, the prophet of Poseidon (invoked at the outset of *The Eumenides*); and by wrestling with his shifting, slippery flux—now lion, now serpent, boar, tree, the sea itself—Menelaus wrings a prophecy of his future "with golden Rhadamanthos at the world's end," as Fitzgerald translates Homer, "where all existence is a dream of ease." But in Aeschylus the theme of hard-won transformation, the harnessing of elemental forces, may have bound the satyr-play and trilogy together. For all its optimism, the *Proteus* may have reminded the Athenians that their lives were based on conflict, indeed that Athena had prevailed over Poseidon for possession of their city. So in the trilogy we reach an accommodation with the earth, but the sea, like Poseidon in the *Odyssey*, may remain to be placated. Almost all that remains of the buoyant *Proteus*, in fact, is one of Aeschylus' more violent images—"a wretched struggling dove on the wing for food, / crushed by the winnowing fans, its breast split open"—and a grim reminder of "a masterwork, irresistible, hard to strip away."

Conflict remains the medium of our destiny in the *Oresteia*. Here it is always anxious spring, yet always harvest too. Sown in tears and reaped in joy, Dionysos is continuously dismembered and reborn. How could the trilogy embody so much grief and so much joy at once? Perhaps it arose at a time, never again recovered, when tragedy was so inspired by Dionysos it could reenact his death and resurrection in one dramatic span. Perhaps the suffering of the Greeks seemed totally constructive—out of the Persian wars emerged a truly stronger nation. Art and history might conspire, the birth of tragedy and the birth of democracy might be one.

Aeschylus is the creator of tragedy and, as Thomson describes him, "a democrat who fought as well as wrote." His epitaph may tell us so:

Beneath this stone lies Aeschylus of Athens, Euphorion's son
who died in the fields of Gela rich in wheat.
His strength, his glory the grove of Marathon can praise
and the longhaired Persian too—he learned it well.

He fought with his tragedies, his compatriot George Seferis has said, as if they were weapons that might keep his country free. And his soldiery of song, like that of the old men of Argos, grew as he grew older. We may surmise from what remains—seven out of perhaps ninety plays—that he turned from dread to hope, as Herington suggests, and that he probed, ever more deeply, the bond between the two. It was a triumph of concentration, perfected after he had reached the age of fifty. In *The Persians* the invaders are destroyed and Athens gathers strength. The Suppliant Maidens are coerced into a union with society, reflecting a fruitful union of the Heavens and the Earth. And this bond between destruction and creation, this symbiosis, lies at the heart of Aeschylus' last work, the *Prometheia* and the *Oresteia*. The latter, created two years before his death and awarded first prize by his city, represents the maturity of Aeschylus and Athens. It is a kind of national biography, and he rehearsed it in public as a playwright who directed and actually performed his work. Aeschylus the actor emulated Aeschylus the poet; he galvanized his words upon the stage. We may imagine him striving together with Orestes, torn by the forces that contended for his world, the archaic against the modern, and eager to unite them. For Aeschylus was born in Eleusis, close to the Mysteries, yet Athens was his city. One of the ancient nobility, he was also a democrat—a fine amphibian, adapted to the present and the past. He epitomized Ortega's man of antiquity: "before he did anything, [he] took a step backward, like the bullfighter who leaps back to deliver his mortal thrust." As Aeschylus portrays the founding of the Areopagus, he may endorse the latest, radical reforms that curbed its jurisdiction to cases of homicide, but he also recalls its older senatorial powers that had been stripped, he urges against all innovations in the court, and lends it a broad humanitarian cast that should govern life to come. A conservative democrat, he conserves his origins by competing with them, evincing their potential for the future.

Aeschylus is the great religious visionary. He makes old myths new with all the arrogance of the Chosen. He may well have been the first to present the Furies on the stage, then identify them as the Furies, Semnai and Eumenides in one. Imagine him as the leader of his chorus—an old man, rising up from the elders of the city, he rejuvenated his native spirits at the last, his "children always young." They were impulsive, aggressive, at times irrational, yet he redeemed their fierce vitality through his art; he trained them into song and social value. For he had a mission too: to make the crisis between the Furies and the gods the origin not only of the Areopagus but of Athens in her prime. Ultimately like Athena, he reclaimed the energies of his mothers for the greatness of his fathers. It was as if he had returned to his birthplace, where he prayed, as Aristophanes had him pray, "O Demeter, you who nursed my heart, /

make me worthy of your mystic rites." Never an initiate himself, it seems, he proved his worth as a kind of initiating priest who led those rites in his own inimitable ways—in the savage parody of *Agamemnon*, the tragic parody of *The Libation Bearers*, finally the sacred parody of *The Eumenides*, where the closing pageant is a civic marriage of men and gods, the civic birth of Athens. The Mysteries of Eleusis leave us rapt as saints. The Mysteries of Aeschylus, breaking out of ritual into drama, lead us toward a living waking vision, a state of consciousness where we must act as citizens. Aeschylus recasts the secrets of the Mysteries in spectacular public form. This was heresy, and legend tells that he was brought to trial, perhaps for this offense, but he won his freedom by appealing to his performance at Marathon or seeking refuge at the altar of Dionysos. Or both, we may say, since his exploits for democracy and the religious power of his art were intertwined. His *authadeia* had merged with his *megaloprepeia*; his arrogance became magnificence in the service of his maker. At the end of the *Oresteia*, when the joy of the people blends with the Escorts' song of praise to the gods, Aeschylus might say with the Psalmist, "Not unto us, O Lord, not unto us, but unto thy name give glory."

Aeschylus had achieved pure unity of being, the Mean in art and life. Athens granted him a kind of immortality. A public decree insured the reproduction of his work, and after he died his work won many victories—in effect his tragedies became enshrined. Yet in life the man was restless, striving to the end. One of the old breed, politically disenchanted perhaps, probably no longer at home in an Athens captious, brilliant, somewhat overripe, he died in Sicily, "the America of the day," as Lattimore describes it, "the new Greek world, rich, generous and young." He was approaching seventy. Some say he had gone to produce his *Oresteia*. "Old men ought to be explorers," as Eliot advises,

Here and there does not matter
We must be still and still moving

Into another intensity
For a further union, a deeper communion
Through the dark cold and the empty desolation,
The wave cry, the wind cry, the vast waters
Of the petrel and the porpoise. In my end is my beginning.

Aeschylus' rite of passage is our own. The final act of *mimesis* is our re-creation of his world. We may see the house of Atreus become the house of Athens and the city of mankind. We see as Cassandra sees. Civilization rises from barbarity and it is perishable, its progress is the fruit of human struggle, a new barbarity may engulf the future. Yet seeing is believing too. An act of commemoration is asking for commitment from us all, a spirit of desire far from Aristotle's blend of pity and fear that purges us of both emotions, "calm of mind, all passion spent." In the *Oresteia* we are not purged, we are overmastered by the spirit of Dionysos—"Heaven blazing into the head." It is not pity and fear but reverence and terror, tragic joy, the only spirit that could lead a people to *become* a myth by charging myth with all the fullness of their hearts. Here tragedy stands between the ecstasy from which it may have risen and the spectacle it would become. Here tragedy sounds a call to action. The torches blaze. The drums begin. The riders of Athens mount. Ahead are "girls and mothers, / trains of aged women grave in movement." And following them the audience and ourselves. Athena leads us toward a creation always new. The end of the *Oresteia* is simply our beginning. Performance is all. "Cry, cry in triumph, carry on the dancing on and on."

Robert Fagles
W. B. Stanford

AESCHYLUS: THE Oresteia

AGAMEMNON

FOR
MY MOTHER AND FATHER

*Be like me!—amid the incessant flux
of appearances, eternally creating,
eternally driving into life, in this
rushing, whirling flux eternally seizing
satisfaction—I am the Great Mother!*

—NIETZSCHE, *The Birth of Tragedy*

CHARACTERS

WATCHMAN

CLYTAEMNESTRA

HERALD

AGAMEMNON

CASSANDRA

AEGISTHUS

CHORUS, THE OLD MEN OF ARGOS
AND THEIR LEADER

Attendants of Clytaemnestra
and of Agamemnon,
bodyguard of Aegisthus

TIME AND SCENE: *A night in the tenth and final autumn of the Trojan war. The house of Atreus in Argos. Before it, an altar stands unlit; a watchman on the high roofs fights to stay awake.*

WATCHMAN

Dear gods, set me free from all the pain,
the long watch I keep, one whole year awake . . .
propped on my arms, crouched on the roofs of Atreus
like a dog.

       I know the stars by heart,
the armies of the night, and there in the lead   5
the ones that bring us snow or the crops of summer,
bring us all we have—
our great blazing kings of the sky,
I know them, when they rise and when they fall . . .
and now I watch for the light, the signal-fire   10
breaking out of Troy, shouting Troy is taken.
So she commands, full of her high hopes.
That woman—she maneuvers like a man.

And when I keep to my bed, soaked in dew,
and the thoughts go groping through the night   15
and the good dreams that used to guard my sleep . . .
not here, it's the old comrade, terror at my neck.
I mustn't sleep, no—

               [Shaking himself awake.]

       Look alive, sentry.

And I try to pick out tunes, I hum a little,
a good cure for sleep, and the tears start,   20
I cry for the hard times come to the house,
no longer run like the great place of old.

Oh for a blessed end to all our pain,
some godsend burning through the dark—

> [Light appears slowly in the east; he
> struggles to his feet and scans it.]

                        I salute you!
You dawn of the darkness, you turn night to day—   25
I see the light at last.
They'll be dancing in the streets of Argos
thanks to you, thanks to this new stroke of—
                             Aieeeeee!
There's your signal clear and true, my queen!
Rise up from bed—hurry, lift a cry of triumph   30
through the house, praise the gods for the beacon,
if they've taken Troy . . .
                  But there it burns,
fire all the way. I'm for the morning dances.
Master's luck is mine. A throw of the torch
has brought us triple-sixes—we have won!   35
My move now—

> [Beginning to dance, then breaking
> off, lost in thought.]

                Just bring him home. My king,
I'll take your loving hand in mine and then . . .
the rest is silence. The ox is on my tongue.
Aye, but the house and these old stones,
give them a voice and what a tale they'd tell.   40
And so would I, gladly . . .
I speak to those who know; to those who don't
my mind's a blank. I never say a word.

CHORUS

Ten years gone, ten to the day
our great avenger went for Priam—   45
    Menelaus and lord Agamemnon,
two kings with the power of Zeus,
the twin throne, twin scepter,
Atreus' sturdy yoke of sons
launched Greece in a thousand ships,   50
armadas cutting loose from the land,
armies massed for the cause, the rescue—

[From within the palace Clytaemnestra raises a cry of triumph.]

the heart within them screamed for all-out war!
Like vultures robbed of their young,
    the agony sends them frenzied,   55
soaring high from the nest, round and
round they wheel, they row their wings,
stroke upon churning thrashing stroke,
but all the labor, the bed of pain,
    the young are lost forever.   60
Yet someone hears on high—Apollo,
Pan or Zeus—the piercing wail
these guests of heaven raise,
and drives at the outlaws, late
but true to revenge, a stabbing Fury!   65

[Clytaemnestra appears at the doors and pauses with her entourage.]

So towering Zeus the god of guests
drives Atreus' sons at Paris,
all for a woman manned by many
the generations wrestle, knees
grinding the dust, the manhood drains,   70
the spear snaps in the first blood rites
    that marry Greece and Troy.
And now it goes as it goes
and where it ends is Fate.
And neither by singeing flesh   75
nor tipping cups of wine
nor shedding burning tears can you
enchant away the rigid Fury.

                        [Clytaemnestra lights the altar-fires.]

We are the old, dishonored ones,
the broken husks of men.   80
Even then they cast us off,
the rescue mission left us here
to prop a child's strength upon a stick.
What if the new sap rises in his chest?
He has no soldiery in him,   85
    no more than we,
and we are aged past aging,
gloss of the leaf shriveled,
three legs at a time we falter on.
Old men are children once again,   90
    a dream that sways and wavers
into the hard light of day.

                        But you,
daughter of Leda, queen Clytaemnestra,
what now, what news, what message
drives you through the citadel   95
    burning victims? Look,
the city gods, the gods of Olympus,
gods of the earth and public markets—
all the altars blazing with your gifts!
    Argos blazes! Torches   100
race the sunrise up her skies—
drugged by the lulling holy oils,
    unadulterated,
run from the dark vaults of kings.
    Tell us the news!   105
What you can, what is right—
Heal us, soothe our fears!
Now the darkness comes to the fore,
now the hope glows through your victims,
beating back this raw, relentless anguish   110
    gnawing at the heart.

> [Clytaemnestra ignores them and pur-
> sues her rituals; they assemble for the
> opening chorus.]

O but I still have power to sound the gods' command at the roads
that launched the kings. The gods breathe power through my song,
   my fighting strength, Persuasion grows with the years—
I sing how the flight of fury hurled the twin command,   115
                one will that hurled young Greece
and winged the spear of vengeance straight for Troy!
The kings of birds to kings of the beaking prows, one black,
        one with a blaze of silver
                skimmed the palace spearhand right   120
                    and swooping lower, all could see,
                        plunged their claws in a hare, a mother
        bursting with unborn young—the babies spilling,
quick spurts of blood—cut off the race just dashing into life!
Cry, cry for death, but good win out in glory in the end.   125

But the loyal seer of the armies studied Atreus' sons,
two sons with warring hearts—he saw two eagle-kings
   devour the hare and spoke the things to come,
"Years pass, and the long hunt nets the city of Priam,
                the flocks beyond the walls,   130
a kingdom's life and soul—Fate stamps them out.
Just let no curse of the gods lour on us first,
        shatter our giant armor
           forged to strangle Troy. I see
                pure Artemis bristle in pity—   135
                    yes, the flying hounds of the Father
        slaughter for armies . . . their own victim . . . a woman
trembling young, all born to die—She loathes the eagles' feast!"
Cry, cry for death, but good win out in glory in the end.

"Artemis, lovely Artemis, so kind   140
to the ravening lion's tender, helpless cubs,
the suckling young of beasts that stalk the wilds—
     bring this sign for all its fortune,
      all its brutal torment home to birth!
I beg you, Healing Apollo, soothe her before   145
her crosswinds hold us down and moor the ships too long,
pressing us on to another victim . . .
     nothing sacred, no
       no feast to be eaten
         the architect of vengeance   150

[Turning to the palace.]

     growing strong in the house
    with no fear of the husband
here she waits
the terror raging back and back in the future
     the stealth, the law of the hearth, the mother—   155
       Memory womb of Fury child-avenging Fury!"
  So as the eagles wheeled at the crossroads,
Calchas clashed out the great good blessings mixed with doom
  for the halls of kings, and singing with our fate
we cry, cry for death, but good win out in glory in the end.   160

Zeus, great nameless all in all,
if that name will gain his favor,
I will call him Zeus.
I have no words to do him justice,
weighing all in the balance,
all I have is Zeus, Zeus—
Lift this weight, this torment from my spirit,
cast it once for all.

165

He who was so mighty once,
storming for the wars of heaven,
he has had his day.
And then his son who came to power
met his match in the third fall
and he is gone. Zeus, Zeus—
raise your cries and sing him Zeus the Victor!
You will reach the truth:

170

175

Zeus has led us on to know,
the Helmsman lays it down as law
that we must suffer, suffer into truth.
We cannot sleep, and drop by drop at the heart
the pain of pain remembered comes again,
and we resist, but ripeness comes as well.
From the gods enthroned on the awesome rowing-bench
there comes a violent love.

180

So it was that day the king,
the steersman at the helm of Greece,
would never blame a word the prophet said—
swept away by the wrenching winds of fortune
he conspired! Weatherbound we could not sail,
our stores exhausted, fighting strength hard-pressed,
and the squadrons rode in the shallows off Chalkis
where the riptide crashes, drags,

185

190

and winds from the north pinned down our hulls at Aulis,
port of anguish . . . head winds starving,
sheets and the cables snapped   195
   and the men's minds strayed,
   the pride, the bloom of Greece
   was raked as time ground on,
ground down, and then the cure for the storm
and it was harsher—Calchas cried,   200
"My captains, Artemis must have blood!"—
   as harsh the sons of Atreus
    dashed their scepters on the rocks,
   could not hold back the tears,

and I still can hear the older warlord saying,   205
"Obey, obey, or a heavy doom will crush me—
Oh but doom *will* crush me
   once I rend my child,
    the glory of my house—
   a father's hands are stained,   210
blood of a young girl streaks the altar.
Pain both ways and what is worse?
Desert the fleets, fail the alliance?
   No, but stop the winds with a virgin's blood,
    feed their lust, their fury?—feed their fury!—   215
   Law is law!—
        Let all go well."

And once he slipped his neck in the strap of Fate,
his spirit veering black, impure, unholy,
once he turned he stopped at nothing,
    seized with the frenzy   220
          blinding driving to outrage—
wretched frenzy, cause of all our grief!
Yes, he had the heart
    to sacrifice his daughter!—
  to bless the war that avenged a woman's loss,   225
        a bridal rite that sped the men-of-war.

"My father, father!"—she might pray to the winds;
no innocence moves her judges mad for war.
Her father called his henchmen on,
    on with a prayer,   230
        "Hoist her over the altar
like a yearling, give it all your strength!
She's fainting—lift her,
    sweep her robes around her,
  but slip this strap in her gentle curving lips . . .   235
        here, gag her hard, a sound will curse the house"—

and the bridle chokes her voice . . . her saffron robes
pouring over the sand

                     her glance like arrows showering
wounding every murderer through with pity
        clear as a picture, live,   240
she strains to call their names . . .
I remember often the days with father's guests
when over the feast her voice unbroken,
   pure as the hymn her loving father
bearing third libations, sang to Saving Zeus—   245
transfixed with joy, Atreus' offspring
    throbbing out their love.

What comes next? I cannot see it, cannot say.
The strong techniques of Calchas do their work.
But Justice turns the balance scales,   250
   sees that we suffer
and we suffer and we learn.
And we will know the future when it comes.
Greet it too early, weep too soon.
   It all comes clear in the light of day.   255
Let all go well today, well as she could want,

[Turning to Clytaemnestra.]

our midnight watch, our lone defender,
   single-minded queen.

LEADER

We've come,
Clytaemnestra. We respect your power.
Right it is to honor the warlord's woman   260
once he leaves the throne.

But why these fires?
Good news, or more good hopes? We're loyal,
we want to hear, but never blame your silence.

CLYTAEMNESTRA

Let the new day shine, as the proverb says,
glorious from the womb of Mother Night.   265

*[Lost in prayer, then turning to the
chorus.]*

You will hear a joy beyond your hopes.
Priam's citadel—the Greeks have taken Troy!

LEADER

No, what do you mean? I can't believe it.

CLYTAEMNESTRA

Troy is ours. Is that clear enough?

LEADER

The joy of it,
stealing over me, calling up my tears—   270

CLYTAEMNESTRA

Yes, your eyes expose your loyal hearts.

LEADER
And you have proof?

CLYTAEMNESTRA
                    I do,
I must. Unless the god is lying.

LEADER
                         That,
or a phantom spirit sends you into raptures.

CLYTAEMNESTRA
No one takes me in with visions—senseless dreams.   275

LEADER
Or giddy rumor, you haven't indulged yourself—

CLYTAEMNESTRA
You treat me like a child, you mock me?

LEADER
Then when did they storm the city?

CLYTAEMNESTRA
Last night, I say, the mother of this morning.

LEADER
And who on earth could run the news so fast?   280

CLYTAEMNESTRA

The god of fire—rushing fire from Ida!
And beacon to beacon rushed it on to me,
my couriers riding home the torch.

                           From Troy
to the bare rock of Lemnos, Hermes' Spur,
and the Escort winged the great light west   285
to the Saving Father's face, Mount Athos hurled it
third in the chain and leaping Ocean's back
the blaze went dancing on to ecstasy—pitch-pine
streaming gold like a newborn sun—and brought
the word in flame to Mount Makistos' brow.   290
No time to waste, straining, fighting sleep,
that lookout heaved a torch glowing over
the murderous straits of Euripos to reach
Messapion's watchmen craning for the signal.
Fire for word of fire! tense with the heather   295
withered gray, they stack it, set it ablaze—
the hot force of the beacon never flags,
it springs the Plain of Asôpos, rears
like a harvest moon to hit Kithairon's crest
and drives new men to drive the fire on.   300
That relay pants for the farflung torch,
they swell its strength outstripping my commands
and the light inflames the marsh, the Gorgon's Eye,
it strikes the peak where the wild goats range—
my law, my fire whips that camp!   305
They spare nothing, eager to build its heat,
and a huge beard of flame overcomes the headland
beetling down the Saronic Gulf, and flaring south
it brings the dawn to the Black Widow's face—
the watch that looms above your heads—and now   310
the true son of the burning flanks of Ida
crashes on the roofs of Atreus' sons!

And I ordained it all.
Torch to torch, running for their lives,
one long succession racing home my fire.   315

One,

first in the laps and last, wins out in triumph.
There you have my proof, *my* burning sign, I tell you—
the power my lord passed on from Troy to me.

LEADER

We'll thank the gods, my lady—first this story,
let me lose myself in the wonder of it all!   320
Tell it start to finish, tell us all.

CLYTAEMNESTRA

The city's ours—in our hands this very day!
I can hear the cries in crossfire rock the walls.
Pour oil and wine in the same bowl,
what have you, friendship? A struggle to the end.   325
So with the victors and the victims—outcries,
you can hear them clashing like their fates.

They are kneeling by the bodies of the dead,
embracing men and brothers, infants over
the aged loins that gave them life, and sobbing,   330
as the yoke constricts their last free breath,
for every dear one lost.
               And the others,
there, plunging breakneck through the night—
the labor of battle sets them down, ravenous,
to breakfast on the last remains of Troy.   335
Not by rank but the lots of chance they draw,
they lodge in the houses captured by the spear,
settling in so soon, released from the open sky,
the frost and dew. Lucky men, off guard at last,
they sleep away their first good night in years.   340

If only they are revering the city's gods,
the shrines of the gods who love the conquered land,
no plunderer will be plundered in return.

Just let no lust, no mad desire seize the armies
to ravish what they must not touch—
overwhelmed by all they've won!   345
                                    The run for home
and safety waits, the swerve at the post,
the final lap of the grueling two-lap race.
And even if the men come back with no offense
to the gods, the avenging dead may never rest—   350
Oh let no new disaster strike! And here
you have it, what a woman has to say.
Let the best win out, clear to see.
A small desire but all that I could want.

LEADER

Spoken like a man, my lady, loyal,   355
full of self-command. I've heard your sign
and now your vision.

> [*Reaching toward her as she turns
> and re-enters the palace.*]

                    Now to praise the gods.
The joy is worth the labor.

CHORUS

O Zeus my king and Night, dear Night,
queen of the house who covers us with glories,   360
you slung your net on the towers of Troy,
neither young nor strong could leap
the giant dredge net of slavery,
   all-embracing ruin.
I adore you, iron Zeus of the guests   365
and your revenge—you drew your longbow
year by year to a taut full draw
till one bolt, not falling short
or arching over the stars,
   could split the mark of Paris!   370

The sky stroke of god!—it is all Troy's to tell,
but even I can trace it to its cause:
god does as god decrees.
   And still some say
that heaven would never stoop to punish men   375
who trample the lovely grace of things
untouchable. How wrong they are!
   A curse burns bright on crime—
     full-blown, the father's crimes will blossom,
       burst into the son's.   380
Let there be less suffering . . .
give us the sense to live on what we need.

         Bastions of wealth
         are no defense for the man
         who treads the grand altar of Justice   385
            down and out of sight.

Persuasion, maddening child of Ruin
overpowers him—Ruin plans it all.
And the wound will smolder on,
   there is no cure,   390
a terrible brilliance kindles on the night.
He is bad bronze scraped on a touchstone:
put to the test, the man goes black.
   Like the boy who chases
     a bird on the wing, brands his city,   395
       brings it down and prays,
but the gods are deaf
to the one who turns to crime, they tear him down.

         So Paris learned:
         he came to Atreus' house   400
         and shamed the tables spread for guests,
            he stole away the queen.

And she left her land *chaos*, clanging shields,
companions tramping, bronze prows, men in bronze,
    and she came to Troy with a dowry, death,   405
strode through the gates
        defiant in every stride,
as prophets of the house looked on and wept,
"Oh the halls and the lords of war,
    the bed and the fresh prints of love.   410
I *see* him, unavenging, unavenged,
the stun of his desolation is so clear—
    he longs for the one who lies across the sea
until her phantom seems to sway the house.

        Her curving images,   415
        her beauty hurts her lord,
        the eyes starve and the touch
        of love is gone,

"and radiant dreams are passing in the night,
the memories throb with sorrow, joy with pain . . .   420
    it is pain to dream and see desires
slip through the arms,
        a vision lost forever
winging down the moving drifts of sleep."
So he grieves at the royal hearth   425
    yet others' grief is worse, far worse.
All through Greece for those who flocked to war
they are holding back the anguish now,
    you can feel it rising now in every house;
I tell you there is much to tear the heart.   430

        They knew the men they sent,
        but now in place of men
        ashes and urns come back
        to every hearth.

War, War, the great gold-broker of corpses   435
holds the balance of the battle on his spear!
Home from the pyres he sends them,
    home from Troy to the loved ones,
weighted with tears, the urns brimmed full,
    the heroes return in gold-dust,   440
dear, light ash for men; and they weep,
they praise them, "He had skill in the swordplay,"
    "He went down so tall in the onslaught,"
"All for another's woman." So they mutter
in secret and the rancor steals   445
toward our staunch defenders, Atreus' sons.

            And there they ring the walls, the young,
            the lithe, the handsome hold the graves
            they won in Troy; the enemy earth
                    rides over those who conquered.   450

The people's voice is heavy with hatred,
now the curses of the people must be paid,
and now I wait, I listen . . .
    there—there is something breathing
under the night's shroud. God takes aim   455
    at the ones who murder many;
the swarthy Furies stalk the man
gone rich beyond all rights—with a twist
    of fortune grind him down, dissolve him
into the blurring dead—there is no help.   460
The reach for power can recoil,
the bolt of god can strike you at a glance.

            Make me rich with no man's envy,
            neither a raider of cities, no,
            nor slave come face to face with life   465
                    overpowered by another.

—Fire comes and the news is good,
 it races through the streets
but is it true? Who knows?
Or just another lie from heaven?   470

—Show us the man so childish, wonderstruck,
 he's fired up with the first torch,
then when the message shifts
he's sick at heart.

      —Just like a woman
to fill with thanks before the truth is clear.   475

—So gullible. Their stories spread like wildfire,
 they fly fast and die faster;
rumors voiced by women come to nothing.

LEADER
Soon we'll know her fires for what they are,
her relay race of torches hand-to-hand—   480
know if they're real or just a dream,
the hope of a morning here to take our senses.
I see a herald running from the beach
and a victor's spray of olive shades his eyes
and the dust he kicks, twin to the mud of Troy,   485
shows he has a voice—no kindling timber
on the cliffs, no signal-fires for him.
He can shout the news and give us joy,
or else . . . please, not that.
       Bring it on,
good fuel to build the first good fires.   490
And if anyone calls down the worst on Argos
let him reap the rotten harvest of his mind.

       [The herald rushes in and kneels on
       the ground.]

HERALD

Good Greek earth, the soil of my fathers!
Ten years out, and a morning brings me back.
All hopes snapped but one—I'm home at last. 495
Never dreamed I'd die in Greece, assigned
the narrow plot I love the best.
                                        And now
I salute the land, the light of the sun,
our high lord Zeus and the king of Pytho—
no more arrows, master, raining on our heads! 500
At Scamander's banks we took our share,
your longbow brought us down like plague.
Now come, deliver us, heal us—lord Apollo!
Gods of the market, here, take my salute.
And you, my Hermes, Escort, 505
loving Herald, the heralds' shield and prayer!—
And the shining dead of the land who launched the armies,
warm us home . . . we're all the spear has left.

You halls of the kings, you roofs I cherish,
sacred seats—you gods that catch the sun, 510
if your glances ever shone on him in the old days,
greet him well—so many years are lost.
He comes, he brings us light in the darkness,
free for every comrade, Agamemnon lord of men.

Give him the royal welcome he deserves! 515
He hoisted the pickax of Zeus who brings revenge,
he dug Troy down, he worked her soil down,
the shrines of her gods and the high altars, gone!—
and the seed of her wide earth he ground to bits.
That's the yoke he claps on Troy. The king, 520
the son of Atreus comes. The man is blest,
the one man alive to merit such rewards.

Neither Paris nor Troy, partners to the end,
can say their work outweighs their wages now.
Convicted of rapine, stripped of all his spoils, 525
and his father's house and the land that gave it life—
he's scythed them to the roots. The sons of Priam
pay the price twice over.

LEADER

                        Welcome home
from the wars, herald, long live your joy.

HERALD

                              Our joy—
now I could die gladly. Say the word, dear gods. 530

LEADER

Longing for your country left you raw?

HERALD

The tears fill my eyes, for joy.

LEADER

                        You too,
down the sweet disease that kills a man
with kindness . . .

HERALD

                  Go on, I don't see what you—

LEADER

                                           Love

for the ones who love you—that's what took you.

HERALD

                               You mean   535

the land and the armies hungered for each other?

LEADER

There were times I thought I'd faint with longing.

HERALD

So anxious for the armies, why?

LEADER

                          For years now,

only my silence kept me free from harm.

HERALD

                                    What,

with the kings gone did someone threaten you?

LEADER

                              So much ...   540

now as you say, it would be good to die.

HERALD

True, we *have* done well.
Think back in the years and what have you?
A few runs of luck, a lot that's bad.
Who but a god can go through life unmarked?   545

A long, hard pull we had, if I would tell it all.
The iron rations, penned in the gangways
hock by jowl like sheep. Whatever miseries
break a man, our quota, every sunstarved day.

Then on the beaches it was worse. Dug in   550
under the enemy ramparts—deadly going.
Out of the sky, out of the marshy flats
the dews soaked us, turned the ruts we fought from
into gullies, made our gear, our scalps
crawl with lice.

           And talk of the cold,   555
the sleet to freeze the gulls, and the big snows
come avalanching down from Ida. Oh but the heat,
the sea and the windless noons, the swells asleep,
dropped to a dead calm . . .

But why weep now?   560
It's over for us, over for them.
The dead can rest and never rise again;
no need to call their muster. We're alive,
do we have to go on raking up old wounds?
Good-by to all that. Glad I am to say it.   565

For us, the remains of the Greek contingents,
the good wins out, no pain can tip the scales,
not now. So shout this boast to the bright sun—
fitting it is—wing it over the seas and rolling earth:

"Once when an Argive expedition captured Troy   570
they hauled these spoils back to the gods of Greece,
they bolted them high across the temple doors,
the glory of the past!"
                        And hearing that,
men will applaud our city and our chiefs,
and Zeus will have the hero's share of fame—   575
he did the work.
                    That's all I have to say.

LEADER
I'm convinced, glad that I was wrong.
Never too old to learn; it keeps me young.

                          *[Clytaemnestra   enters   with   her
                          women.]*

First the house and the queen, it's their affair,
but I can taste the riches.

CLYTAEMNESTRA
                        I cried out long ago!—   580
for joy, when the first herald came burning
through the night and told the city's fall.
And there were some who smiled and said,
"A few fires persuade you Troy's in ashes.
Women, women, elated over nothing."   585

You made me seem deranged.
For all that I sacrificed—a woman's way,
you'll say—station to station on the walls
we lifted cries of triumph that resounded
in the temples of the gods. We lulled and blessed   590
the fires with myrrh and they consumed our victims.

                    [Turning to the herald.]

But enough. Why prolong the story?
From the king himself I'll gather all I need.
Now for the best way to welcome home
my lord, my good lord . . .
                              No time to lose!   595
What dawn can feast a woman's eyes like this?
I can see the light, the husband plucked from war
by the Saving God and open wide the gates.

Tell him that, and have him come with speed,
the people's darling—how they long for him.   600
And for his wife,
may he return and find her true at hall,
just as the day he left her, faithful to the last.
A watchdog gentle to him alone,

[Glancing toward the palace.]

                              savage
to those who cross his path. I have not changed.   605
The strains of time can never break our seal.
In love with a new lord, in ill repute I am
as practiced as I am in dyeing bronze.

That is my boast, teeming with the truth.
I am proud, a woman of my nobility—   610
I'd hurl it from the roofs!

[She turns sharply, enters the palace.]

LEADER
She speaks well, but it takes no seer to know
she only says what's right.

*[The herald attempts to leave; the
leader takes him by the arm.]*

                              Wait, one thing.
Menelaus, is he home too, safe with the men?
The power of the land—dear king.   615

HERALD
I doubt that lies will help my friends,
in the lean months to come.

LEADER
Help us somehow, tell the truth as well.
But when the two conflict it's hard to hide—
out with it.

HERALD
        He's lost, gone from the fleets!   620
He and his ship, it's true.

LEADER
          After you watched him
pull away from Troy? Or did some storm
attack you all and tear him off the line?

HERALD
              There,
like a marksman, the whole disaster cut to a word.

LEADER
How do the escorts give him out—dead or alive?   625

HERALD
No clear report. No one knows . . .
only the wheeling sun that heats the earth to life.

LEADER
But then the storm—how did it reach the ships?
How did it end? Were the angry gods on hand?

HERALD
This blessed day, ruin it with *them*?   630
Better to keep their trophies far apart.

When a runner comes, his face in tears,
saddled with what his city dreaded most,
the armies routed; two wounds in one,
one to the city, one to hearth and home . . .   635
our best men, droves of them, victims
herded from every house by the two-barb whip
that Ares likes to crack,
                              that charioteer
who packs destruction shaft by shaft,
careening on with his brace of bloody mares—   640
When he comes in, I tell you, dragging that much pain,
wail your battle-hymn to the Furies, and high time!

But when he brings salvation home to a city
singing out her heart—
how can I mix the good with so much bad   645
and blurt out this?—
                              "Storms swept the Greeks,
and not without the anger of the gods!"

Those enemies for ages, fire and water,
sealed a pact and showed it to the world—
they crushed our wretched squadrons.
                              Night looming,   650
breakers lunging in for the kill
and the black gales come brawling out of the north—
ships ramming, prow into hooking prow, gored

by the rush-and-buck of hurricane pounding rain
by the cloudburst—
                      ships stampeding into the darkness,   655
lashed and spun by the savage shepherd's hand!

But when the sun comes up to light the skies
I see the Aegean heaving into a great bloom
of corpses . . . Greeks, the pick of a generation
scattered through the wrecks and broken spars.   660

But not us, not our ship, our hull untouched.
Someone stole us away or begged us off.
No mortal—a god, death grip on the tiller,
or lady luck herself, perched on the helm,
she pulled us through, she saved us. Aye,   665
we'll never battle the heavy surf at anchor,
never shipwreck up some rocky coast.

But once we cleared that sea-hell, not even
trusting luck in the cold light of day,
we battened on our troubles, they were fresh—   670
the armada punished, bludgeoned into nothing.

And now if one of them still has the breath
he's saying *we* are lost. Why not?
We say the same of him. Well,
here's to the best.
              And Menelaus?   675
Look to it, he's come back, and yet . . .
if a shaft of the sun can track him down,
alive, and his eyes full of the old fire—
thanks to the strategies of Zeus, Zeus
would never tear the house out by the roots—   680
then there's hope our man will make it home.

You've heard it all. Now you have the truth.

[Rushing out.]

CHORUS
Who—what power named the name that drove your fate?—
what hidden brain could divine your future,
steer that word to the mark, 685
to the bride of spears,
   the whirlpool churning armies,
               Oh for all the world a Helen!
Hell at the prows, hell at the gates
hell on the men-of-war, 690
from her lair's sheer veils she drifted
    launched by the giant western wind,
      and the long tall waves of men in armor,
huntsmen trailing the oarblades' dying spoor
slipped into her moorings, 695
   Simois' mouth that chokes with foliage,
             bayed for bloody strife,

for Troy's Blood Wedding Day—she drives her word,
her burning will to the birth, the Fury
late but true to the cause, 700
to the tables shamed
   and Zeus who guards the hearth—
           the Fury makes the Trojans pay!
Shouting their hymns, hymns for the bride
hymns for the kinsmen doomed 705
to the wedding march of Fate,
    Troy changed her tune in her late age,
      and I think I hear the dirges mourning
"Paris, born and groomed for the bed of Fate!"
They mourn with their life breath, 710
   they sing their last, the sons of Priam
          born for bloody slaughter.

So a man once reared
a lion cub at hall, snatched
from the breast, still craving milk   715
    in the first flush of life.
A captivating pet for the young,
and the old men-adored it, pampered it
    in their arms, day in, day out,
like an infant just born.   720
Its eyes on fire, little beggar,
fawning for its belly, slave to food.

    But it came of age
and the parent strain broke out
and it paid its breeders back.   725
    Grateful it was, it went
through the flock to prepare a feast,
an illicit orgy—the house swam with blood,
    none could resist that agony—
                    massacre vast and raw!   730
From god there came a priest of ruin,
adopted by the house to lend it warmth.

And the first sensation Helen brought to Troy . . .
call it a spirit
    shimmer of winds dying   735
        glory light as gold
    shaft of the eyes dissolving, open bloom
  that wounds the heart with love.
But veering wild in mid-flight
she whirled her wedding on to a stabbing end,   740
slashed at the sons of Priam—hearthmate, friend to the death,
    sped by Zeus who speeds the guest,
a bide of tears, a Fury.

There's an ancient saying, old as man himself:
men's prosperity   745
    never will die childless,
        once full-grown it breeds.
    Sprung from the great good fortune in the race
  comes bloom on bloom of pain—
insatiable wealth. But not I,   750
I alone say this. Only the reckless act
can breed impiety, multiplying crime on crime,
    while the house kept straight and just
is blessed with radiant children.

        But ancient Violence longs to breed,   755
           new Violence comes
    when its fatal hour comes, the demon comes
    to take her toll—no war, no force, no prayer
      can hinder the midnight Fury stamped
    with parent Fury moving through the house.   760

      But Justice shines in sooty hovels,
        loves the decent life.
  From proud halls crusted with gilt by filthy hands
    she turns her eyes to find the pure in spirit—
spurning the wealth stamped counterfeit with praise,   765
  she steers all things toward their destined end.

[Agamemnon enters in his chariot, his plunder borne before him by his entourage; behind him, half hidden, stands Cassandra. The old men press toward him.]

Come, my king, the scourge of Troy,
   the true son of Atreus—
How to salute you, how to praise you
neither too high nor low, but hit   770
the note of praise that suits the hour?
So many prize some brave display,
they prefer some flaunt of honor
   once they break the bounds.
When a man fails they share his grief,   775
but the pain can never cut them to the quick.
When a man succeeds they share his glory,
torturing their faces into smiles.
But the good shepherd knows his flock.
When the eyes seem to brim with love   780
   and it is only unction,
he will know, better than we can know.
That day you marshaled the armies
all for Helen—no hiding it now—
I drew you in my mind in black;   785
you seemed a menace at the helm,
   sending men to the grave
to bring her home, that hell on earth.
But now from the depths of trust and love
I say Well fought, well won—   790
   the end is worth the labor!
Search, my king, and learn at last
who stayed at home and kept their faith
   and who betrayed the city.

AGAMEMNON

First,
with justice I salute my Argos and my gods,   795
my accomplices who brought me home and won
my rights from Priam's Troy—the just gods.
No need to hear our pleas. Once for all
they consigned their lots to the urn of blood,
they pitched on death for men, annihilation   800
for the city. Hope's hand, hovering
over the urn of mercy, left it empty.
Look for the smoke—it is the city's seamark,
building even now.

The storms of ruin live!
Her last dying breath, rising up from the ashes   805
sends us gales of incense rich in gold.

For that we must thank the gods with a sacrifice
our sons will long remember. For their mad outrage
of a queen we raped their city—we were right.
The beast of Argos, foals of the wild mare,   810
thousands massed in armor rose on the night
the Pleiades went down, and crashing through
their walls our bloody lion lapped its fill,
gorging on the blood of kings.

Our thanks to the gods,
long drawn out, but it is just the prelude.   815

*[Clytaemnestra approaches with her
women; they are carrying dark red
tapestries. Agamemnon turns to the
leader.]*

And your concern, old man, is on my mind.
I hear you and agree, I will support you.
How rare, men with the character to praise
a friend's success without a trace of envy,
poison to the heart—it deals a double blow.   820
Your own losses weigh you down but then,

look at your neighbor's fortune and you weep.
Well I know. I understand society,
the fawning mirror of the proud.

                    My comrades . . .
they're shadows, I tell you, ghosts of men   825
who swore they'd die for me. Only Odysseus:
I dragged that man to the wars but once in harness
he was a trace-horse, he gave his all for me.
Dead or alive, no matter, I can praise him.

And now this cause involving men and gods.   830
We must summon the city for a trial,
found a national tribunal. Whatever's healthy,
shore it up with law and help it flourish.
Wherever something calls for drastic cures
we make our noblest effort: amputate or wield   835
the healing iron, burn the cancer at the roots.

Now I go to my father's house—
I give the gods my right hand, my first salute.
The ones who sent me forth have brought me home.

> [He starts down from the chariot,
> looks at Clytaemnestra, stops, and
> offers up a prayer.]

Victory, you have sped my way before,   840
now speed me to the last.

> [Clytaemnestra turns from the king
> to the chorus.]

CLYTAEMNESTRA
                    Old nobility of Argos
gathered here, I am not ashamed to tell you
how I love the man. I am older,
and the fear dies away . . . I am human.
Nothing I say was learned from others.   845
This is my life, my ordeal, long as the siege
he laid at Troy and more demanding.

                                First,
when a woman sits at home and the man is gone,
the loneliness is terrible,
unconscionable . . .   850
and the rumors spread and fester,
a runner comes with something dreadful,
close on his heels the next and his news worse,
and they shout it out and the whole house can hear;
and wounds—if he took one wound for each report   855
to penetrate these walls, he's gashed like a dragnet,
more, if he had only died . . .
for each death that swelled his record, he could boast
like a triple-bodied Geryon risen from the grave,
"Three shrouds I dug from the earth, one for every body   860
that went down!"
                    The rumors broke like fever,
broke and then rose higher. There were times
they cut me down and eased my throat from the noose.
I wavered between the living and the dead.

                          [Turning to Agamemnon.]

                          And so
our child is gone, not standing by our side,   865
the bond of our dearest pledges, mine and yours;
by all rights our child should be here . . .
Orestes. You seem startled.
You needn't be. Our loyal brother-in-arms
will take good care of him, Strophios the Phocian.   870
He warned from the start we court two griefs in one.
You risk all on the wars—and what if the people
rise up howling for the king, and anarchy
should dash our plans?
                    Men, it is their nature,
trampling on the fighter once he's down.   875
Our child is gone. That is my self-defense
and it is true.

> For me, the tears that welled
> like springs are dry. I have no tears to spare.
> I'd watch till late at night, my eyes still burn,
> I sobbed by the torch I lit for you alone. 880

[Glancing toward the palace.]

> I never let it die . . . but in my dreams
> the high thin wail of a gnat would rouse me,
> piercing like a trumpet—I could see you
> suffer more than all
> the hours that slept with me could ever bear. 885

> I endured it all. And now, free of grief,
> I would salute that man the watchdog of the fold,
> the mainroyal, saving stay of the vessel,
> rooted oak that thrusts the roof sky-high,
> the father's one true heir. 890
> Land at dawn to the shipwrecked past all hope,
> light of the morning burning off the night of storm,
> the cold clear spring to the parched horseman—
> ☉ the ecstasy, to flee the yoke of Fate!

> It is right to use the titles he deserves. 895
> Let envy keep her distance. We have suffered
> long enough.

[Reaching toward Agamemnon.]

> Come to me now, my dearest,
> down from the car of war, but never set the foot
> that stamped out Troy on earth again, my great one.

> Women, why delay? You have your orders. 900
> Pave his way with tapestries.

[They begin to spread the crimson tap-
estries between the king and the palace
doors.]

                    Quickly.
Let the red stream flow and bear him home
to the home he never hoped to see—Justice,
lead him in!
                    Leave all the rest to me.
The spirit within me never yields to sleep.   905
We will set things right, with the gods' help.
We will do whatever Fate requires.

AGAMEMNON
                                    There
is Leda's daughter, the keeper of my house.
And the speech to suit my absence, much too long.
But the praise that does us justice,   910
let it come from others, then we prize it.
                                    This—
You treat me like a woman, groveling, gaping up at me!
What am I, some barbarian peacocking out of Asia?
Never cross my path with robes and draw the lightning.
Never—only the gods deserve the pomps of honor   915
and the stiff brocades of fame. To walk on them . . .
I am human, and it makes my pulses stir
with dread.
                    Give me the tributes of a man
and not a god, a little earth to walk on,
not this gorgeous work.   920
There is no need to sound my reputation.
I have a sense of right and wrong, what's more—
heaven's proudest gift. Call no man blest
until he ends his life in peace, fulfilled.
If I can live by what I say, I have no fear.   925

CLYTAEMNESTRA
One thing more. Be true to your ideals and tell me—

AGAMEMNON
True to my ideals? Once I violate them I am lost.

CLYTAEMNESTRA
Would you have sworn this act to god in a time of terror?

AGAMEMNON
Yes, if a prophet called for a last, drastic rite.

CLYTAEMNESTRA
But Priam—can you see him if he had your success?   930

AGAMEMNON
Striding on the tapestries of god, I see him now.

CLYTAEMNESTRA
And *you* fear the reproach of common men?

AGAMEMNON
The voice of the people—aye, they have enormous power.

CLYTAEMNESTRA
Perhaps, but where's the glory without a little gall?

AGAMEMNON
And where's the woman in all this lust for glory?   935

CLYTAEMNESTRA

But the great victor—it becomes him to give away.

AGAMEMNON

Victory in this . . . war of ours, it means so much to you?

CLYTAEMNESTRA

O give way! The power is yours if you surrender
all of your own free will to me.

AGAMEMNON

               Enough.

If you are so determined—   940

*[Turning to the women, pointing to
his boots.]*

Let someone help me off with these at least.
Old slaves, they've stood me well.

               Hurry,
and while I tread his splendors dyed red in the sea,
may no god watch and strike me down with envy
from on high. I feel such shame—   945
to tread the life of the house, a kingdom's worth
of silver in the weaving.

*[He steps down from the chariot to
the tapestries and reveals Cassandra,
dressed in the sacred regalia, the fil-
lets, robes, and scepter of Apollo.]*

               Done is done.
Escort this stranger in, be gentle.
Conquer with compassion. Then the gods
shine down upon you, gently. No one chooses   950
the yoke of slavery, not of one's free will—
and she least of all. The gift of the armies,
flower and pride of all the wealth we won,
she follows me from Troy.

And now,
since you have brought me down with your insistence,   955
just this once I enter my father's house,
trampling royal crimson as I go.

[He takes his first steps and pauses.]

CLYTAEMNESTRA
                              There is the sea
and who will drain it dry? Precious as silver,
inexhaustible, ever-new, it breeds the more we reap it—
tides on tides of crimson dye our robes blood-red.   960
Our lives are based on wealth, my king,
the gods have seen to that.
Destitution, our house has never heard the word.
I would have sworn to tread on legacies of robes,
at one command from an oracle, deplete the house—   965
suffer the worst to bring that dear life back!

[Encouraged, Agamemnon strides to the entrance.]

When the root lives on, the new leaves come back,
spreading a dense shroud of shade across the house
to thwart the Dog Star's fury. So you return
to the father's hearth, you bring us warmth in winter   970
like the sun—
                 And you are Zeus when Zeus
tramples the bitter virgin grape for new wine
and the welcome chill steals through the halls, at last
the master moves among the shadows of his house, fulfilled.

[Agamemnon goes over the threshold; the women gather up the tapestries while Clytaemnestra prays.]

Zeus, Zeus, master of all fulfillment, now fulfill our prayers—   975
speed our rites to their fulfillment once for all!

[She enters the palace, the doors close, the old men huddle in terror.]

CHORUS
Why, why does it rock me, never stops,
this terror beating down my heart,
         this seer that sees it all—
it beats its wings, uncalled unpaid   980
thrust on the lungs
the mercenary song beats on and on
singing a prophet's strain—
        and I can't throw it off
like dreams that make no sense,   985
and the strength drains
that filled the mind with trust,
and the years drift by and the driven sand
        has buried the mooring lines
that churned when the armored squadrons cut for Troy . . .   990
and now I believe it, I can prove he's home,
        my own clear eyes for witness—

                                 Agamemnon!
Still it's chanting, beating deep so deep in the heart
this dirge of the Furies, oh dear god,
not fit for the lyre, its own master   995
    it kills our spirit
kills our hopes
and it's real, true, no fantasy—
        stark terror whirls the brain
            and the end is coming   1000
                Justice comes to birth—
I pray my fears prove false and fall
and die and never come to birth!

Even exultant health, well we know,
    exceeds its limits, comes so near disease   1005
it can breach the wall between them.

Even a man's fate, held true on course,
    in a blinding flash rams some hidden reef;
but if caution only casts the pick of the cargo—
one well-balanced cast—   1010
the house will not go down, not outright;
laboring under its wealth of grief
the ship of state rides on.

Yes, and the great green bounty of god,
sown in the furrows year by year and reaped each fall   1015
can end the plague of famine.

But a man's lifeblood
    is dark and mortal.
Once it wets the earth
what song can sing it back?   1020
Not even the master-healer
    who brought the dead to life—
Zeus stopped the man before he did more harm.

Oh, if only the gods had never forged
the chain that curbs our excess,   1025
    one man's fate curbing the next man's fate,
my heart would outrace my song, I'd pour out all I feel—
                but no, I choke with anguish,
        mutter through the nights.
Never to ravel out a hope in time   1030
and the brain is swarming, burning—

*[Clytaemnestra emerges from the pal-
ace and goes to Cassandra, impassive
in the chariot.]*

CLYTAEMNESTRA
Won't you come inside? I mean you, Cassandra.
Zeus in all his mercy wants you to share
some victory libations with the house.
The slaves are flocking. Come, lead them   1035
up to the altar of the god who guards
our dearest treasures.

             Down from the chariot,
no time for pride. Why even Heracles,
they say, was sold into bondage long ago,
he had to endure the bitter bread of slaves.   1040
But if the yoke descends on you, be grateful
for a master born and reared in ancient wealth.
Those who reap a harvest past their hopes
are merciless to their slaves.

                    From us
you will receive what custom says is right.   1045

[Cassandra remains impassive.]

LEADER
It's *you* she is speaking to, it's all too clear.
You're caught in the nets of doom—obey
if you can obey, unless you cannot bear to.

CLYTAEMNESTRA
Unless she's like a swallow, possessed
of her own barbaric song, strange, dark.   1050
I speak directly as I can—she must obey.

LEADER
Go with her. Make the best of it, she's right.
Step down from the seat, obey her.

CLYTAEMNESTRA

Do it *now*—
I have no time to spend outside. Already
the victims crowd the hearth, the Navelstone,   1055
to bless this day of joy I never hoped to see!—
our victims waiting for the fire and the knife,
and you,
if you want to taste our mystic rites, come now.
If my words can't reach you—

[Turning to the leader.]

Give her a sign,   1060
one of her exotic handsigns.

LEADER

I think
the stranger needs an interpreter, someone clear.
She's like a wild creature, fresh caught.

CLYTAEMNESTRA

She's mad,
her evil genius murmuring in her ears.
She comes from a *city* fresh caught.   1065
She must learn to take the cutting bridle
before she foams her spirit off in blood—
and that's the last I waste on her contempt!

*[Wheeling, re-entering the palace.
The leader turns to Cassandra, who
remains transfixed.]*

LEADER

Not I, I pity her. I will be gentle.
Come, poor thing. Leave the empty chariot—   1070
Of your own free will try on the yoke of Fate.

CASSANDRA

Aieeeeeel Earth—Mother—
                        Curse of the Earth—Apollo Apollo!

LEADER

Why cry to Apollo?
He's not the god to call with sounds of mourning.

CASSANDRA

Aieeeeeel Earth—Mother—   1075
                        Rape of the Earth—Apollo Apollo!

LEADER

Again, it's a bad omen.
She cries for the god who wants no part of grief.

> *[Cassandra steps from the chariot,
> looks slowly toward the rooftops of
> the palace.]*

CASSANDRA
God of the long road,

Apollo *Apollo* my destroyer—
you destroy me once, destroy me twice— 1080

LEADER
She's about to sense her own ordeal, I think.
Slave that she is, the god lives on inside her.

CASSANDRA
God of the iron marches,

Apollo *Apollo* my destroyer—
where, where have you led me now? what house— 1085

LEADER
The house of Atreus and his sons. Really—
don't you know? It's true, see for yourself.

CASSANDRA
No . . . the house that hates god,
   an echoing womb of guilt, kinsmen
      torturing kinsmen, severed heads,   1090
slaughterhouse of heroes, soil streaming blood—

LEADER
A keen hound, this stranger.
Trailing murder, and murder she will find.

CASSANDRA
See, my witnesses—
   I trust to them, to the babies   1095
      wailing, skewered on the sword,
their flesh charred, the father gorging on their parts—

LEADER
We'd heard your fame as a seer,
but no one looks for seers in Argos.

CASSANDRA

   Oh no, what horror, what new plot,   1100
new agony this?—
it's growing, massing, deep in the house,
             a plot, a monstrous—*thing*
                    to crush the loved ones, no,
   there is no cure, and rescue's far away and—   1105

LEADER

I can't read these signs; I knew the first,
the city rings with them.

CASSANDRA

   You, you godforsaken—you'd do *this*?
The lord of your bed,
you bathe him . . . his body glistens, then—   1110
              how to tell the climax?—
                  comes so quickly, see,
   hand over hand shoots out, hauling ropes—
                      then lunge!

LEADER

Still lost. Her riddles, her dark words of god—
I'm groping, helpless.

CASSANDRA

                No no, look *there!*— 1115
what's that? some net flung out of hell—
    No, *she* is the snare,
the bedmate, deathmate, murder's strong right arm!
            Let the insatiate discord in the race
rear up and shriek "Avenge the victim—stone them dead!" 1120

LEADER

What Fury is this? Why rouse it, lift its wailing
through the house? I hear you and lose hope.

CHORUS

Drop by drop at the heart, the gold of life ebbs out.
    We are the old soldiers . . . wounds will come
with the crushing sunset of our lives. 1125
Death is close, and quick.

CASSANDRA

            Look out! *look out!*—
Ai, drag the great bull from the mate!—
    a thrash of robes, she traps him—
writhing—
        black horn glints, twists—
                she gores him through!
          And now he buckles, look, the bath swirls red— 1130
There's stealth and murder in that caldron, do you hear?

LEADER

I'm no judge, I've little skill with the oracles,
but even I know danger when I hear it.

CHORUS
What good are the oracles to men? Words, more words,
    and the hurt comes on us, endless words   1135
and a seer's techniques have brought us
terror and the truth.

CASSANDRA
The agony—O I am breaking!—Fate's so hard,
    and the pain that floods my voice is mine alone.
Why have you brought me here, tormented as I am?   1140
Why, unless to die with him, why else?

LEADER and CHORUS
Mad with the rapture—god speeds you on
    to the song, the deathsong,
like the nightingale that broods on sorrow,
    mourns her son, her son,   1145
her life inspired with grief for him,
she lilts and shrills, dark bird that lives for night.

CASSANDRA
The nightingale—O for a song, a fate like hers!
    The gods gave her a life of ease, swathed her in wings,
no tears, no wailing. The knife waits for me.   1150
They'll splay me on the iron's double edge.

LEADER and CHORUS
Why?—what god hurls you on, stroke on stroke
    to the long dying fall?
Why the horror clashing through your music,
    terror struck to song?—   1155
why the anguish, the wild dance?
Where do your words of god and grief begin?

CASSANDRA

Ai, the wedding, wedding of Paris,
death to the loved ones. Oh Scamander,
you nursed my father . . . once at your banks   1160
   I nursed and grew, and now at the banks
of Acheron, the stream that carries sorrow,
it seems I'll chant my prophecies too soon.

LEADER and CHORUS

  What are you saying? Wait, it's clear,
a child could see the truth, it wounds within,   1165
             like a bloody fang it tears—
   I hear your destiny—breaking sobs,
         cries that stab the ears.

CASSANDRA

Oh the grief, the grief of the city
ripped to oblivion. Oh the victims,   1170
the flocks my father burned at the wall,
   rich herds in flames . . . no cure for the doom
that took the city after all, and I,
her last ember, I go down with her.

LEADER and CHORUS

  You cannot stop, your song goes on—   1175
some spirit drops from the heights and treads you down
            and the brutal strain grows—
    your death-throes come and come and
        I cannot see the end!

CASSANDRA

Then off with the veils that hid the fresh young bride—   1180
we will see the truth.
Flare up once more, my oracle! Clear and sharp
as the wind that blows toward the rising sun,
I can feel a deeper swell now, gathering head
to break at last and bring the dawn of grief.   1185

No more riddles. I will teach you.
Come, bear witness, run and hunt with me.
We trail the old barbaric works of slaughter.

These roofs—look up—there is a dancing troupe
that never leaves. And they have their harmony   1190
but it is harsh, their words are harsh, they drink
beyond the limit. Flushed on the blood of men
their spirit grows and none can turn away
their revel breeding in the veins—the Furies!
They cling to the house for life. They sing,   1195
sing of the frenzy that began it all,
strain rising on strain, showering curses
on the man who tramples on his brother's bed.

There. Have I hit the mark or not? Am I a fraud,
a fortune-teller babbling lies from door to door?   1200
Swear how well I know the ancient crimes
that live within this house.

LEADER

                    And if I did?
Would an oath bind the wounds and heal us?
But you amaze me. Bred across the sea,
your language strange and still you sense the truth   1205
as if you had been here.

CASSANDRA
                    Apollo the Prophet
introduced me to his gift.

LEADER
A *god*—and moved with love?

CASSANDRA
I was ashamed to tell this once,
but now . . .

LEADER
                    We spoil ourselves with scruples,   1210
long as things go well.

CASSANDRA
                    He came like a wrestler,
magnificent, took me down and breathed his fire
through me and—

LEADER
                    You bore him a child?

CASSANDRA
                              I yielded,
then at the climax I recoiled—I deceived Apollo!

LEADER
But the god's skills—they seized you even then?   1215

CASSANDRA

Even then I told my people all the grief to come.

LEADER

And Apollo's anger never touched you?—is it possible?

CASSANDRA

Once I betrayed him I could never be believed.

LEADER

We believe you. Your visions seem so true.

CASSANDRA

Aieeee!—
the pain, the terror! the birth-pang of the seer   1220
who tells the truth—

it whirls me, oh,
the storm comes again, the crashing chords!

Look, you see them nestling at the threshold?
Young, young in the darkness like a dream,
like children really, yes, and their loved ones   1225
brought them down . . .

their hands, they fill their hands
with their own flesh, they are serving it like food,
holding out their entrails . . . now it's clear,
I can see the armfuls of compassion, see the father
reach to taste and—

For so much suffering,   1230
I tell you, someone plots revenge.
A lion who lacks a lion's heart,
he sprawled at home in the royal lair
and set a trap for the lord on his return.
My lord . . . I must wear his yoke, I am his slave.   1235
The lord of the men-of-war, he obliterated Troy—
he is so blind, so lost to that detestable hellhound
who pricks her ears and fawns and her tongue draws out
her glittering words of welcome—

No, he cannot see
the stroke that Fury's hiding, stealth, murder.   1240
What outrage—the woman kills the man!

What to call
that . . . monster of Greece, and bring my quarry down?
Viper coiling back and forth?

Some sea-witch?—
Scylla crouched in her rocky nest—nightmare of sailors?
Raging mother of death, storming deathless war against   1245
the ones she loves!

                    And how she howled in triumph,
boundless outrage. Just as the tide of battle
broke her way, she seems to rejoice that he
is safe at home from war, saved for her.

Believe me if you will. What will it matter   1250
if you won't? It comes when it comes,
and soon you'll see it face to face
and say the seer was all too true.
You will be moved with pity.

LEADER
                              Thyestes' feast,
the children's flesh—that I know,   1255
and the fear shudders through me. It's true,
real, no dark signs about it. I hear the rest
but it throws me off the scent.

CASSANDRA
                         Agamemnon.
You will see him dead.

LEADER
                         Peace, poor girl!
Put those words to sleep.

CASSANDRA
                    No use,   1260
the Healer has no hand in this affair.

LEADER
Not if it's true—but god forbid it is!

CASSANDRA
You pray, and they close in to kill!

LEADER
What man prepares this, this dreadful—

CASSANDRA

Man?
You *are* lost, to every word I've said.

LEADER

Yes—   1265
I don't see who can bring the evil off.

CASSANDRA
And yet I know my Greek, too well.

LEADER
So does the Delphic oracle,
but he's hard to understand.

CASSANDRA

His *fire*!—
sears me, sweeps me again—the torture!   1270
Apollo Lord of the Light, you burn,
you blind me—

Agony!

She is the lioness,
she rears on her hind legs, she beds with the wolf
when her lion king goes ranging—

she will kill me—

Ai, the torture!

        She is mixing her drugs,   1275
adding a measure more of hate for me.
She gloats as she whets the sword for him.
He brought me home and we will pay in carnage.

Why mock yourself with these—trappings, the rod,
the god's wreath, his yoke around my throat?   1280
Before I die I'll tread you—

          *[Ripping off her regalia, stamping it
          into the ground.]*

        Down, out,
die die die!
Now you're down. I've paid you back.
Look for another victim—I am free at last—
make her rich in all your curse and doom.

          *[Staggering backward as if wrestling
          with a spirit tearing at her robes.]*

        See,   1285
Apollo himself, his fiery hands—I feel him again,
he's stripping off my robes, the Seer's robes!
And after he looked down and saw me mocked,
even in these, his glories, mortified by friends
I loved, and they hated me, they were so blind   1290
to their own demise—

          I went from door to door,
I was wild with the god, I heard them call me
"Beggar! Wretch! Starve for bread in hell!"

And I endured it all, and now he will
extort me as his due. A seer for the Seer.   1295
He brings me here to die like this,
not to serve at my father's altar. No,
the block is waiting. The cleaver steams
with my life blood, the first blood drawn
for the king's last rites.

[Regaining her composure and moving to the altar.]

We will die, 1300
but not without some honor from the gods.
There will come another to avenge us,
born to kill his mother, born
his father's champion. A wanderer, a fugitive
driven off his native land, he will come home 1305
to cope the stones of hate that menace all he loves.
The gods have sworn a monumental oath: as his father lies
upon the ground he draws him home with power like a prayer.

Then why so pitiful, why so many tears?
I have seen my city faring as she fared, 1310
and those who took her, judged by the gods,
faring as they fare. I must be brave.
It is my turn to die.

[Approaching the doors.]

I address you as the Gates of Death.
I pray it comes with one clean stroke, 1315
no convulsions, the pulses ebbing out
in gentle death. I'll close my eyes and sleep.

LEADER
So much pain, poor girl, and so much truth,
you've told so much. But if you *see* it coming,
clearly—how can you go to your own death, 1320
like a beast to the altar driven on by god,
and hold your head so high?

CASSANDRA
No escape, my friends,
not now.

LEADER

        But the last hour should be savored.

CASSANDRA

My time has come. Little to gain from flight.

LEADER

You're brave, believe me, full of gallant heart.   1325

CASSANDRA

Only the wretched go with praise like that.

LEADER

But to go nobly lends a man some grace.

CASSANDRA

My noble father—you and your noble children.

                    [She nears the threshold and recoils,
                    groaning in revulsion.]

LEADER

What now? what terror flings you back?
Why? Unless some horror in the brain—

CASSANDRA

                    Murder.   1330
The house breathes with murder—bloody shambles!

LEADER

No, no, only the victims at the hearth.

CASSANDRA

I know that odor. I smell the open grave.

LEADER

But the Syrian myrrh, it fills the halls with splendor,
can't you sense it?

CASSANDRA

        Well, I must go in now,   1335
mourning Agamemnon's death and mine.
Enough of life!

> *[Approaching the doors again and crying out.]*

        Friends—I cried out,
not from fear like a bird fresh caught,
but that you will testify to *how* I died.
When the queen, woman for woman, dies for me,   1340
and a man falls for the man who married grief.
That's all I ask, my friends. A stranger's gift
for one about to die.

LEADER

        Poor creature, you
and the end you see so clearly. I pity you.

CASSANDRA

I'd like a few words more, a kind of dirge,   1345
it is my own. I pray to the sun,
the last light I'll see,
that when the avengers cut the assassins down
they will avenge me too, a slave who died,
an easy conquest.
                Oh men, your destiny.   1350
When all is well a shadow can overturn it.
When trouble comes a stroke of the wet sponge,
and the picture's blotted out. And that,
I think that breaks the heart.

[She goes through the doors.]

CHORUS

But the lust for power never dies—   1355
   men cannot have enough.
No one will lift a hand to send it
from his door, to give it warning,
"Power, never come again!"
Take this man: the gods in glory   1360
gave him Priam's city to plunder,
brought him home in splendor like a god.
But now if he must pay for the blood
his fathers shed, and die for the deaths
he brought to pass, and bring more death   1365
to avenge his dying, show us one
   who boasts himself born free
of the raging angel, once he hears—

[Cries break out within the palace.]

AGAMEMNON

Aagh!

Struck deep—the death-blow, deep—

LEADER

Quiet. Cries,

but who? Someone's stabbed—

AGAMEMNON

Aaagh, again . . .   1370

second blow—struck home.

LEADER

The work is done,

you can feel it. The king, and the great cries—

Close ranks now, find the right way out.

[But the old men scatter, each speaks singly.]

CHORUS

—I say send out heralds, muster the guard,
   they'll save the house.

                            —And I say rush in now,   1375
   catch them red-handed—butchery running on their blades.

—Right with you, do something—now or never!

—Look at them, beating the drum for insurrection.

                                        —Yes,
   we're wasting time. They rape the name of caution,
   their hands will never sleep.

                            —Not a plan in sight.   1380
   Let men of action do the planning too.

—I'm helpless. Who can raise the dead with words?

—What, drag out our lives? bow down to the tyrants,
   the ruin of the house?

                        —Never, better to die
   on your feet than live on your knees.

                                —Wait,   1385
   do we take the cries for signs, prophesy like seers
   and give him up for dead?

                            —No more suspicions,
   not another word till we have proof.

                            —Confusion
   on all sides—one thing to do. See how it stands
   with Agamemnon, once and for all we'll see—   1390

[He rushes at the doors. They open and reveal a silver caldron that holds the body of Agamemnon shrouded in bloody robes, with the body of Cassandra to his left and Clytaemnestra standing to his right, sword in hand. She strides toward the chorus.]

CLYTAEMNESTRA

Words, endless words I've said to serve the moment!
Now it makes me proud to tell the truth.
How else to prepare a death for deadly men
who seem to love you? How to rig the nets
of pain so high no man can overleap them?   1395

I brooded on this trial, this ancient blood feud
year by year. At last my hour came.
Here I stand and here I struck
and here my work is done.
I did it all. I don't deny it, no.   1400
He had no way to flee or fight his destiny—

[Unwinding the robes from Agamemnon's body, spreading them before the altar where the old men cluster around them, unified as a chorus once again.]

our never-ending, all-embracing net, I cast it
wide for the royal haul, I coil him round and round
in the wealth, the robes of doom, and then I strike him
once, twice, and at each stroke he cries in agony—   1405
he buckles at the knees and crashes here!
And when he's down I add the third, last blow,
to the Zeus who saves the dead beneath the ground
I send that third blow home in homage like a prayer.

So he goes down, and the life is bursting out of him—   1410
great sprays of blood, and the murderous shower
wounds me, dyes me black and I, I revel
like the Earth when the spring rains come down,
the blessed gifts of god, and the new green spear
splits the sheath and rips to birth in glory!   1415

So it stands, elders of Argos gathered here.
Rejoice if you can rejoice—I glory.
And if I'd pour upon his body the libation
it deserves, what wine could match my words?
It is right and more than right. He flooded   1420
the vessel of our proud house with misery,
with the vintage of the curse and now
he drains the dregs. My lord is home at last.

LEADER

You appall me, you, your brazen words—
exulting over your fallen king.

CLYTAEMNESTRA

                  And you,   1425
you try me like some desperate woman.
My heart is steel, well you know. Praise me,
blame me as you choose. It's all one.
Here is Agamemnon, my husband made a corpse
by this right hand—a masterpiece of Justice.   1430
Done is done.

CHORUS
                    Woman!—what poison cropped from the soil
or strained from the heaving sea, what nursed you,
drove you insane? You brave the curse of Greece.
    You have cut away and flung away and now
the people cast you off to exile,   1435
broken with our hate.

CLYTAEMNESTRA
                    And now you sentence me?—
you banish *me* from the city, curses breathing
down my neck? But *he*—
name one charge you brought against him then.
He thought no more of it than killing a beast,   1440
and his flocks were rich, teeming in their fleece,
but he sacrificed his own child, our daughter,
the agony I labored into love
to charm away the savage winds of Thrace.

Didn't the law demand you banish him?—   1445
hunt him from the land for all his guilt?
But now you witness what I've done
and you are ruthless judges.
                    Threaten away!
I'll meet you blow for blow. And if I fall
the throne is yours. If god decrees the reverse,   1450
late as it is, old men, you'll learn your place.

CHORUS

Mad with ambition,
shrilling pride!—some Fury
crazed with the carnage rages through your brain—
I can see the flecks of blood inflame your eyes! 1455
But vengeance comes—you'll lose your loved ones,
stroke for painful stroke.

CLYTAEMNESTRA

Then learn this too, the power of my oaths.
By the child's Rights I brought to birth,
by Ruin, by Fury—the three gods to whom 1460
I sacrificed this man—I swear my hopes
will never walk the halls of fear so long
as Aegisthus lights the fire on my hearth.
Loyal to me as always, no small shield
to buttress my defiance.
Here he lies. 1465
He brutalized me. The darling of all
the golden girls who spread the gates of Troy.
And here his spearprize . . . what wonders she beheld!—
the seer of Apollo shared my husband's bed,
his faithful mate who knelt at the rowing-benches, 1470
worked by every hand.
They have their rewards.
He as you know. And she, the swan of the gods
who lived to sing her latest, dying song—
his lover lies beside him.
She brings a fresh, voluptuous relish to my bed! 1475

CHORUS

Oh quickly, let me die—
no bed of labor, no, no wasting illness . . .
bear me off in the sleep that never ends,
        now that he has fallen,
now that our dearest shield lies battered—   1480
   Woman made him suffer,
               woman struck him down.

Helen the wild, maddening Helen,
one for the many, the thousand lives
you murdered under Troy. Now you are crowned   1485
with this consummate wreath, the blood
that lives in memory, glistens age to age.
Once in the halls she walked and she was war,
angel of war, angel of agony, lighting men to death.

CLYTAEMNESTRA

Pray no more for death, broken   1490
as you are. And never turn
   your wrath on her, call her
the scourge of men, the one alone
who destroyed a myriad Greek lives—
Helen the grief that never heals.   1495

CHORUS

The *spirit*!—you who tread
the house and the twinborn sons of Tantalus—
you empower the sisters, Fury's twins
                    whose power tears the heart!
Perched on the corpse your carrion raven   1500
        glories in her hymn,
                    her screaming hymn of pride.

CLYTAEMNESTRA

Now you set your judgment straight,
you summon *him*! Three generations
        feed the spirit in the race.   1505
Deep in the veins he feeds our bloodlust—
aye, before the old wound dies
it ripens in another flow of blood.

CHORUS

The great curse of the house, the spirit,
   dead weight wrath—and you can praise it!   1510
Praise the insatiate doom that feeds
relentless on our future and our sons.
Oh all through the will of Zeus,
the cause of all, the one who works it all.
   What comes to birth that is not Zeus?   1515
Our lives are pain, what part not come from god?

   Oh my king, my captain,
   how to salute you, how to mourn you?
   What can I say with all my warmth and love?
   Here in the black widow's web you lie,   1520
   gasping out your life
   in a sacrilegious death, dear god,
   reduced to a slave's bed,
   my king of men, yoked by stealth and Fate,
   by the wife's hand that thrust the two-edged sword.   1525

CLYTAEMNESTRA

   You claim the work is mine, call me
   Agamemnon's wife—you are so wrong.
   Fleshed in the wife of this dead man,
     the spirit lives within me,
   our savage ancient spirit of revenge.   1530
   In return for Atreus' brutal feast
   he kills his perfect son—for every
   murdered child, a crowning sacrifice.

CHORUS

And *you*, innocent of his murder?
  And who could swear to that? and how? . . .   1535
and still an avenger could arise,
bred by the fathers' crimes, and lend a hand.
He wades in the blood of brothers,
stream on mounting stream—black war erupts
  and where he strides revenge will stride,   1540
clots will mass for the young who were devoured.

Oh my king, my captain,
  how to salute you, how to mourn you?
  What can I say with all my warmth and love?
Here in the black widow's web you lie,   1545
gasping out your life
in a sacrilegious death, dear god,
reduced to a slave's bed,
my king of men, yoked by stealth and Fate,
by the wife's hand that thrust the two-edged sword.   1550

CLYTAEMNESTRA

No slave's death, I think—
no stealthier than the death he dealt
our house and the offspring of our loins,
    Iphigeneia, girl of tears.
Act for act, wound for wound!   1555
Never exult in Hades, swordsman,
here you are repaid. By the sword
you did your work and by the sword you die.

CHORUS

The mind reels—where to turn?
All plans dashed, all hope! I cannot think ...   1560
the roofs are toppling, I dread the drumbeat thunder
the heavy rains of blood will crush the house
the first light rains are over—
Justice brings new acts of agony, yes,
on new grindstones Fate is grinding sharp the sword of Justice.

Earth, dear Earth,
if only you'd drawn me under
long before I saw him huddled
in the beaten silver bath.
Who will bury him, lift his dirge?   1570

                        [Turning to Clytaemnestra.]

You, can you dare *this*?
To kill your lord with your own hand
then mourn his soul with tributes, terrible tributes—
do his enormous works a great dishonor.
This godlike man, this hero. Who at the grave   1575
will sing his praises, pour the wine of tears?
Who will labor there with truth of heart?

CLYTAEMNESTRA

This is no concern of yours.
The hand that bore and cut him down
will hand him down to Mother Earth.   1580
This house will never mourn for him.
    Only our daughter Iphigeneia,
by all rights, will rush to meet him
first at the churning straits,
the ferry over tears—   1585
she'll fling her arms around her father,
pierce him with her love.

CHORUS

> Each charge meets countercharge.
> None can judge between them. Justice.
> The plunderer plundered, the killer pays the price.   1590
> The truth still holds while Zeus still holds the throne:
>   the one who acts must suffer—
> that is law. Who, who can tear from the veins
> the bad seed, the curse? The race is welded to its ruin.

CLYTAEMNESTRA

At last you see the future and the truth!   1595
But I will swear a pact with the spirit
born within us. I embrace his works,
cruel as they are but done at last,
    if he will leave our house
in the future, bleed another line   1600
with kinsmen murdering kinsmen.
Whatever he may ask. A few things
are all I need, once I have purged
our fury to destroy each other—
    purged it from our halls.

AEGISTHUS

O what a brilliant day   1605
it is for vengeance! Now I can say once more
there are gods in heaven avenging men,
blazing down on all the crimes of earth.
Now at last I see this man brought down
in the Furies' tangling robes. It feasts my eyes—   1610
he pays for the plot his father's hand contrived.

Atreus, this man's father, was king of Argos.
My father, Thyestes—let me make this clear—
Atreus' brother challenged him for the crown,
and Atreus drove him out of house and home   1615
then lured him back, and home Thyestes came,
poor man, a suppliant to his own hearth,
to pray that Fate might save him.
So it did.
There was no dying, no staining our native ground
with *his* blood. Thyestes was the guest,   1620
and this man's godless father—

[Pointing to Agamemnon.]

the zeal of the host outstripping a brother's love,
made my father a feast that seemed a feast for gods,
a love feast of his children's flesh.
He cuts
the extremities, feet and delicate hands   1625
into small pieces, scatters them over the dish
and serves it to Thyestes throned on high.
He picks at the flesh he cannot recognize,
the soul of innocence eating the food of ruin—
look,

[Pointing to the bodies at his feet.]

that feeds upon the house! And then,   1630
when he sees the monstrous thing he's done, he shrieks,
he reels back head first and vomits up that butchery,
tramples the feast—brings down the curse of Justice:
"Crash to ruin, all the race of Pleisthenes, crash down!"

So you see him, down. And I, the weaver of Justice,   1635
plotted out the kill. Atreus drove us into exile,
my struggling father and I, a babe-in-arms,
his last son, but I became a man
and Justice brought me home. I was abroad
but I reached out and seized my man,   1640
link by link I clamped the fatal scheme
together. Now I could die gladly, even I—
now I see this monster in the nets of Justice.

LEADER
Aegisthus, you revel in pain—you sicken me.
You say you killed the king in cold blood,   1645
singlehanded planned his pitiful death?
I say there's no escape. In the hour of judgment,
trust to this, your head will meet the people's
rocks and curses.

AEGISTHUS
                  You say! you slaves at the oars—
while the master on the benches cracks the whip?   1650
You'll learn, in your late age, how much it hurts
to teach old bones their place. We have techniques—
chains and the pangs of hunger,
two effective teachers, excellent healers.
They can even cure old men of pride and gall.   1655
Look—can't you see? The more you kick
against the pricks, the more you suffer.

LEADER
You, pathetic—
the king had just returned from battle.
You waited out the war and fouled his lair,   1660
you planned my great commander's fall.

AEGISTHUS
                                        Talk on—
you'll scream for every word, my little Orpheus.
We'll see if the world comes dancing to your song,
your absurd barking—snarl your breath away!
I'll make you dance, I'll bring you all to heel.   1665

LEADER
You rule Argos? You who schemed his death
but cringed to cut him down with your own hand?

AEGISTHUS
The treachery was the woman's work, clearly.
I was a marked man, his enemy for ages.
But I will use his riches, stop at nothing   1670
to civilize his people. All but the rebel:
him I'll yoke and break—
no cornfed colt, running free in the traces.
Hunger, ruthless mate of the dark torture-chamber,
trains her eyes upon him till he drops!   1675

LEADER
Coward, why not kill the man yourself?
Why did the woman, the corruption of Greece
and the gods of Greece, have to bring him down?
Orestes—
            If he still sees the light of day,
bring him home, good Fates, home to kill   1680
this pair at last. Our champion in slaughter!

AEGISTHUS
Bent on insolence? Well, you'll learn, quickly.
At them, men—you have your work at hand!

[His men draw swords; the old men take up their sticks.]

LEADER
At them, fist at the hilt, to the last man—

AEGISTHUS
Fist at the hilt, I'm not afraid to die.   1685

LEADER
It's death you want and death you'll have—
we'll make that word your last.

[Clytaemnestra moves between them, restraining Aegisthus.]

CLYTAEMNESTRA
                              No more, my dearest,
no more grief. We have too much to reap
right here, our mighty harvest of despair.
Our lives are based on pain. No bloodshed now.   1690

Fathers of Argos, turn for home before you act
and suffer for it. What we did was destiny.
If we could end the suffering, how we would rejoice.
The spirit's brutal hoof has struck our heart.
And that is what a woman has to say.   1695
Can you accept the truth?

[Clytaemnestra turns to leave.]

AEGISTHUS

                But these . . . mouths
that bloom in filth—spitting insults in my teeth.
You tempt your fates, you insubordinate dogs—
to hurl abuse at me, your master!

LEADER

                No Greek
worth his salt would grovel at your feet.   1700

AEGISTHUS

I—I'll stalk you all your days!

LEADER

Not if the spirit brings Orestes home.

AEGISTHUS

Exiles feed on hope—well I know.

LEADER

                More,
gorge yourself to bursting—soil justice, while you can.

AEGISTHUS

I promise you, you'll pay, old fools—in good time too!   1705

LEADER

Strut on your own dunghill, you cock beside your mate.

CLYTAEMNESTRA

Let them howl—they're impotent. You and I have power now.
We will set the house in order once for all.

[*They enter the palace; the great doors close behind them; the old men disband and wander off.*]

AESCHYLUS: THE Oresteia

THE LIBATION BEARERS

FOR MY WIFE

... in my heart there was a kind of fighting
That would not let me sleep. Methought I lay
Worse than the mutines in the bilboes. Rashly—
And prais'd be rashness for it; let us know,
Our indiscretion sometime serves us well
When our deep plots do pall; and that should learn us
There's a divinity that shapes our ends,
Rough-hew them how we will—

—SHAKESPEARE, *Hamlet*

CHARACTERS

ORESTES, *son of Agamemnon and Clytaemnestra*

PYLADES, *his companion*

ELECTRA, *his sister*

CHORUS OF SLAVEWOMEN AND THEIR LEADER

CLYTAEMNESTRA

CILISSA, *Orestes' old nurse*

AEGISTHUS

A servant of Aegisthus

Attendants of Orestes, bodyguard of Aegisthus

*TIME AND SCENE: Several years have
passed since Agamemnon's death. At
Argos, before the tomb of the king and
his fathers, stands an altar; behind it
looms the house of Atreus. Orestes
and Pylades enter, dressed as travelers. Orestes kneels and prays.*

ORESTES
Hermes, lord of the dead, look down and guard
the fathers' power. Be my savior, I beg you,
be my comrade now.
              I have come home
to my own soil, an exile home at last.
Here at the mounded grave I call my father,   5
Hear me—I am crying out to you . . .

*[He cuts two locks of hair and lays
them on the grave.]*

There is a lock for Inachos who nursed me
into manhood, there is one for death.

I was not here to mourn you when you died,
my father, never gave the last salute   10
when they bore your corpse away.

*[Electra and a chorus of slave-women
enter in procession. They are dressed
in black and bear libations, moving
toward Orestes at the grave.]*

            What's this?
Look, a company moving toward us. Women,
robed in black . . . so clear in the early light.

I wonder what they mean, what turn of fate?—
some new wound to the house?   15
Or perhaps they come to honor you, my father,
bearing cups to soothe and still the dead.
That's right, it must be . . .
Electra, I think I see *her* coming, there,
my own sister, worn, radiant in her grief—'   20
Dear god, let me avenge my father's murder—
fight beside me now with all your might!

Out of their way, Pylades. I must know
what they mean, these women turning toward us,
what their prayers call forth.   25

[They withdraw behind the tomb.]

CHORUS
Rushed from the house we come
   escorting cups for the dead,
in step with the hands' hard beat,
          our cheeks glistening,
flushed where the nails have raked new furrows running blood;   30
and life beats on, and through it all
we nurse our lives with tears,
to the sound of ripping linen beat our robes in sorrow,
   close to the breast the beats throb
and laughter's gone and fortune throbs and throbs.   35

Aie!—bristling Terror struck—
   Terror the seer of the house,
the nightmare ringing clear
          breathed its wrath in sleep,
in the midnight watch a cry!—the voice of Terror   40
deep in the house, bursting down
on the women's darkened chambers, yes,
and the old ones, skilled at dreams, swore oaths to god and called,
   "The proud dead stir under earth,
they rage against the ones who took their lives."   45

But the gifts, the empty gifts
        she hopes will ward them off—
good Mother Earth!—that godless woman sends me here . . .
        I dread to say her prayer.
What can redeem the blood that wets the soil?   50
Oh for the hearthfire banked with grief,
    the ramparts down, a fine house down—
dark, dark, and the sun, the life is curst,
    and mist enshrouds the halls
        where the lords of war went down.   55

And the ancient pride no war,
        no storm, no force could tame,
ringing in all men's ears, in all men's hearts is gone.
        They are afraid. Success,
they bow to success, more god than god himself.   60
But Justice waits and turns the scales:
    a sudden blow for some at dawn,
for some in the no man's land of dusk
    her torments grow with time,
        and the lethal night takes others.   65

And the blood that Mother Earth consumes
clots hard, it won't seep through, it breeds revenge
                       and frenzy goes through the guilty,
seething like infection, swarming through the brain.

For the one who treads a virgin's bed   70
there is no cure. All the streams of the world,
    all channels run into one
to cleanse a man's red hands will swell the bloody tide.

And I . . . Fate and the gods brought down their yoke,
they ringed our city, out of our fathers' halls   75
   they led us here as slaves.
And the will breaks, we kneel at their command—
     our masters right or wrong!
  And we beat the tearing hatred down,
 behind our veils we weep for her,   80

[Turning to Electra.]

her senseless fate.
Sorrow turns the secret heart to ice.

ELECTRA
      Dear women,
you keep the house in order, best you can;
and now you've come to the grave to say a prayer
with me, my escorts. I'll need your help with this.   85
What to say when I pour the cup of sorrow?

[Lifting her libation cup.]

What kindness, what prayer can touch my father?
Shall I say I bring him love for love, a woman's
love for husband? My mother, love from her?
I've no taste for that, no words to say   90
as I run the honeyed oil on father's tomb.

Or try the salute we often use at graves?
"A wreath for a wreath. Now bring the givers
gifts to match" . . . no, give them pain for pain.

Or silent, dishonored, just as father died,
empty it out for the soil to drink and then
retrace my steps, like a slave sent out with scourings
left from the purging of the halls, and throw
the cup behind me, looking straight ahead.

Help me decide, my friends. Join me here.   100
We nurse a common hatred in the house.
Don't hide your feelings—no, fear no one.
Destiny waits us all,

[Looking toward the tomb.]

           born free,
or slaves who labor under another's hand.
Speak to me, please. Perhaps you've had   105
a glimpse of something better.

LEADER
                    I revere
your father's death-mound like an altar.
I'll say a word, now that you ask,
that comes from deep within me.

ELECTRA
                Speak on,
with everything you feel for father's grave.   110

LEADER
Say a blessing as you pour, for those who love you.

ELECTRA
And of the loved ones, whom to call my friends?

LEADER
First yourself, then all who hate Aegisthus.

ELECTRA
I and you. I can say a prayer for us
and then for—

LEADER
You know, try to say it.   115

ELECTRA
There is someone else to rally to our side?

LEADER
Remember Orestes, even abroad and gone.

ELECTRA
Well said, the best advice I've had.

LEADER
Now for the murderers. Remember them and—

ELECTRA
                                                    What?
I'm so unseasoned, teach me what to say.   120

LEADER
Let some god or man come down upon them.

ELECTRA
Judge or avenger, which?

LEADER
Just say "the one who murders in return!"

ELECTRA
How can I ask the gods for that
and keep my conscience clear?

LEADER
                              How not,   125
and pay the enemy back in kind?

                    [Electra kneels at the grave in prayer.]

ELECTRA
                              —Herald king
of the world above and the quiet world below,
lord of the dead, my Hermes, help me now.
Tell the spirits underground to hear my prayers,
and the high watch hovering over father's roofs,   130
and have her listen too, the Earth herself
who brings all things to life and makes them strong,
then gathers in the rising tide once more.

And I will tip libations to the dead.
I call out to my father, Pity me,   135
dear Orestes too.
Rekindle the light that saves our house!
We're auctioned off, drift like vagrants now.
Mother has pawned us for a husband, Aegisthus,
her partner in her murdering.
                              I go like a slave,   140
Orestes driven from his estates while they,
they roll in the fruits of all your labors,
magnificent and sleek. O bring Orestes home,

with a happy twist of fate, my father. Hear me,
make me far more self-possessed than mother,   145
make this hand more pure.

These prayers for us. For our enemies I say,
Raise up your avenger, into the light, my father—
kill the killers in return, with justice!
So in the midst of prayers for good I place   150
this curse for them.
                          Bring up your blessings,
up into the air, led by the gods and Earth
and all the rights that bring us triumph.

> [Pouring libations on the tomb and
> turning to the women.]

These are my prayers. Over them I pour libations.
Yours to adorn them with laments, to make them bloom,   155
so custom says—sing out and praise the dead.

CHORUS

Let the tears fall, ring out and die,
          die with the warlord at this bank,
this bulwark of the good, defense against the bad,
the guilt, the curse we ward away   160
with prayer and all we pour. Hear me, majesty, hear me,
    lord of glory, from the darkness of your heart.
                                         Ohhhhhh!—
      Dear god, let him come! Some man
with a strong spear, born to free the house,
    with the torsion bow of Scythia bent for slaughter,   165
splattering shafts like a god of war—sword in fist
      for the slash-and-hack of battle!

> [Electra remains at the grave, staring
> at the ground.]

ELECTRA

                                Father,
you have it now, the earth has drunk your wine.
Wait, friends, here's news. Come share it.

LEADER

                                Speak on,
my heart's a dance of fear.

ELECTRA

                    A lock of hair,   170
here on the grave . . .

LEADER

                    Whose? A man's?
A growing girl's?

ELECTRA

                    And it has the marks,
and anyone would think—

LEADER

                    What?
We're old. You're young, now you teach us.

ELECTRA
No one could have cut this lock but I and—   175

LEADER
Callous they are, the ones who ought to shear
the hair and mourn.

ELECTRA
                        Look at the texture, just like—

LEADER
Whose? I want to know.

ELECTRA
                        Like mine, identical,
can't you see?

LEADER
                    Orestes . . . he brought a gift
in secret?

ELECTRA
            It's *his*—I can see his curls.   180

LEADER
And how could he risk the journey here?

ELECTRA
He sent it, true, a lock to honor father.

LEADER

All the more cause for tears. You mean
we'll never set foot on native ground again.

ELECTRA

                                Yes!
It's sweeping over me too—anguish   185
like a breaker—a sword ripping through my heart!
Tears come like the winter rains that flood the gates—
can't hold them back, when I see this strand of hair.

How could I think another Greek could play
the prince with this?
                        She'd never cut it,   190
the murderess, my mother. She insults the name,
she and her godless spirit preying on her children.

But how, how can I come right out and say it *is*
the glory of the dearest man I know, Orestes?
Stop, I'm fawning on hope.
                            Oh, if only   195
it had a herald's voice, kind and human—
I'm so shaken, torn—and told me clearly
to throw it away, they severed it from a head
that I detest. Or it could sorrow with me
like a brother, aye,   200
this splendor come to honor father's grave.

We call on the gods, and the gods well know
what storms torment us, sailors whirled to nothing.
But if we are to live and reach the haven,
one small seed could grow a mighty tree—   205
Look, tracks.

A new sign to tell us more.
Footmarks . . . pairs of them, like mine.
Two outlines, two prints, his own, and there,
a fellow traveler's.

[Putting her foot into Orestes' print.]

The heel, the curve of the arch
like twins.

*[While Orestes emerges from behind
the grave, she follows cautiously in his
steps until they come together.]*

Step by step, my step in his . . .
we meet—   210
Oh the pain, like pangs of labor—this is madness!

ORESTES
Pray for the future. Tell the gods they've brought
your prayers to birth, and pray that we succeed.

*[Electra draws back, struggling for
composure.]*

ELECTRA
The gods—why now? What have I ever won from them?

ORESTES
The sight you prayed to see for many years.   215

ELECTRA
And you know the one I call?

ORESTES

I know Orestes,
know he moves you deeply.

ELECTRA

Yes,
but now what's come to fill my prayers?

ORESTES

Here I am. Look no further.
No one loves you more than I.

ELECTRA

No,   220
it's a trap, stranger ... a net you tie around me?

ORESTES

Then I tie myself as well.

ELECTRA

But the pain,
you're laughing at all—

ORESTES

Your pain is mine.
If I laugh at yours, I only laugh at mine.

ELECTRA

Orestes— 225
can I call you?—are you really—

ORESTES

I am!
Open your eyes. So slow to learn.
You saw the lock of hair I cut in mourning.
You scanned my tracks, you could see my marks,
your breath leapt, you all but saw me in the flesh— 230
Look—

*[Holding the lock to his temple, then
to Electra's.]*

put it where I cut it.
It's your brother's. Try, it matches yours.

*[Removing a strip of weaving from
his clothing.]*

Work of your own hand, you tamped the loom,
look, there are wild creatures in the weaving.

*[She kneels beside him, weeping; he
lifts her to her feet and they embrace.]*

No, no, control yourself—don't lose yourself in joy! 235
Our loved ones, well I know, would slit our throats.

LEADER

Dearest, the darling of your father's house,
hope of the seed we nursed with tears—you save us.
Trust to your power, win your father's house once more!

ELECTRA

You light to my eyes, four loves in one!   240
I have to call you father, it is fate;
and I turn to you the love I gave my mother—
I despise her, she deserves it, yes,
and the love I gave my sister, sacrificed
on the cruel sword, I turn to you.   245
You were my faith, my brother—
you alone restore my self-respect.

[Praying.]

Power and Justice, Saving Zeus, Third Zeus,
almighty all in all, be with us now.

ORESTES

Zeus, Zeus, watch over all we do,   250
fledglings reft of the noble eagle father.
He died in the coils, the viper's dark embrace.
We are his orphans worn down with hunger,
weak, too young to haul the father's quarry
home to shelter.
               Look down on us!   255
I and Electra too, I tell you, children
robbed of our father, both of us bound
in exile from our house.
               And what a father—
a priest at sacrifice, he showered you
with honors. Put an end to his nestlings now   260
and who will serve you banquets rich as his?
Destroy the eagle's brood, you can never
send a sign that wins all men's belief.
Rot the stock of a proud dynastic tree—
it can never shore your altar steaming   265
with the oxen in the mornings.
               Tend us—
we seem in ruins now, I know. Up from nothing
rear a house to greatness.

LEADER

Softly, children,
white hopes of your father's hearth. Someone
might hear you, children, charmed with his own voice   270
blurt all this out to the masters. Oh, just once
to see them—live bones crackling in the fire
spitting pitch!

ORESTES

Apollo will never fail me, no,
his tremendous power, his oracle charges me
to see this trial through.

I can still hear the god—   275
a high voice ringing with winters of disaster,
piercing the heart within me, warm and strong,
unless I hunt my father's murderers, cut them down
in their own style—they destroyed my birthright.
"Gore them like a bull!" he called, "or pay their debt   280
with your own life, one long career of grief."

He revealed so much about us,
told how the dead take root beneath the soil,
they grow with hate and plague the lives of men.
He told of the leprous boils that ride the flesh,   285
their wild teeth gnawing the mother tissue, aye,
and a white scurf spreads like cancer over these,
and worse, he told how assaults of Furies spring
to life on the father's blood . . .

You can *see* them—
the eyes burning, grim brows working over you in the dark—   290
the dark sword of the dead—your murdered kinsmen
pleading for revenge. And the madness haunts
the midnight watch, the empty terror shakes you,
harries, drives you on—an exile from your city—
a brazen whip will mutilate your back.   295

For such as us, no share in the winebowl,
no libations poured in love. You never see
your father's wrath but it pulls you from the altars.
There is no refuge, none to take you in.
A pariah, reviled, at long last you die,   300
withered in the grip of all this dying.

Such oracles are persuasive,
don't you think? And even if I am not convinced,
the rough work of the world is still to do.
So many yearnings meet and urge me on.   305
The god's commands. Mounting sorrow for father.
Besides, the lack of patrimony presses hard;
and my compatriots, the glory of men
who toppled Troy with nerves of singing steel,
go at the beck and call of a brace of women.   310
Womanhearted he is—if not, we'll soon see.

> [The leader lights the altar fires.
> Orestes, Electra and the chorus gather
> for the invocation at the grave.]

CHORUS
Powers of destiny, mighty queens of Fate!—
by the will of Zeus your will be done,
press on to the end now,
    Justice turns the wheel.   315
"Word for word, curse for curse
be born now," Justice thunders,
    hungry for retribution,
"stroke for bloody stroke be paid.
    The one who acts must suffer."   320
Three generations strong the word resounds.

ORESTES
Dear father, father of dread,
what can I do or say to reach you now?
What breath can reach from here
to the bank where you lie moored at anchor?   325
What light can match your darkness? None,
but there is a kind of grace that comes
    when the tears revive a proud old house
and Atreus' sons, the warlords lost and gone.

LEADER
The ruthless jaws of the fire,   330
    my child, can never tame the dead,
                         his rage inflames his sons.
Men die and the voices rise, they light the guilty, true—
cries raised for the fathers, clear and just,
    will hunt their killers harried to the end.   335

ELECTRA
Then hear me now, my father,
it is my turn, my tears are welling now,
    as child by child we come
to the tomb and raise the dirge, my father.
Your grave receives a girl in prayer   340
and a man in flight, and we are one,
    and the pain is equal, whose is worse?
And who outwrestles death—what third last fall?

CHORUS
But still some god, if he desires,
may work our strains to a song of joy,   345
from the dirges chanted over the grave
    may lift a hymn in the kings' halls
and warm the loving cup you stir this morning.

ORESTES

If only at Troy
a Lycian cut you down, my father—
gone, with an aura left at home behind you,
            children to go their ways
and the eyes look on them bright with awe,
and the tomb you win on headlands seas away
      would buoy up the house . . .   350

                                                              355

LEADER

And loved by the men you loved
      who died in glory, there you'd rule
                        beneath the earth—lord, prince,
stern aide to the giant kings who judge the shadows there.
You were a king of kings when you drew breath;   360
      the mace you held could make men kneel or die.

ELECTRA

No, not under Troy!—
not dead and gone with them, my father,
hordes pierced by the spear Scamander washes down.
      Sooner the killers die   365
as they killed you—at the hands of friends,
and the news of death would come from far away,
      we'd never know this grief.

CHORUS

You are dreaming, children,
dreams dearer than gold, more blest   370
than the Blest beyond the Northwind's raging.
      Dreams are easy, oh,
but the double lash is striking home.
Now our comrades group underground.
Our masters' reeking hands are doomed—   375
      the children take the day!

ORESTES
That thrills his ear,
    that arrow lands!
        Zeus, Zeus, force up from the earth
destruction, late but true to the mark,   380
to the reckless heart, the killing hand—
  for parents of revenge revenge be done.

LEADER
And the ripping cries of triumph mine
to sing when the man is stabbed,
          the woman dies—   385
  why, why hide what's deep inside me,
    black wings beating, storming the spirit's prow—
          hurricane, slashing hatred!

ELECTRA
Both fists at once
    come down, come down—
        Zeus, *crush* their skulls! Kill! Kill!   390
Now give the land some faith, I beg you,
from these ancient wrongs bring forth our rights.
  Hear me, Earth, and all you lords of death.

CHORUS
  It is the law: when the blood of slaughter
  wets the ground it wants more blood.   395
    Slaughter cries for the Fury
  of those long dead to bring destruction
  on destruction churning in its wake!

ORESTES

Sweet Earth, how long?—great lords of death, look on,
   you mighty curses of the dead. Look on   400
the last of Atreus' children, here, the remnant
   helpless, cast from home . . . god, where to turn?

LEADER

And again my pulses race and leap,
I can feel your sobs, and hope
                    becomes despair   405
   and the heart goes dark to hear you—
    then the anguish ebbs, I see you stronger,
              hope and the light come on me.

ELECTRA

What hope?—what force to summon, what can help?
   What but the pain we suffer, bred by her?   410
So let her fawn. She can never soothe her young wolves—
   Mother dear, you bred our wolves' raw fury.

LEADER and CHORUS
I beat and beat the dirge like a Persian mourner,
hands clenched tight and the blows are coming thick and fast,
you can see the hands shoot out,
    now hand over hand and down—the head pulsates,
        blood at the temples pounding to explode! 415

ELECTRA
Reckless, brutal mother—oh dear god!—
    The brutal, cruel cortege,
the warlord stripped of his honor guard
    and stripped of mourning rites— 420
you dared entomb your lord unwept, unsung.

ORESTES
Shamed for all the world, you mean—
dear god, my father degraded so!
Oh she'll pay,
she'll pay, by the gods and these bare hands— 425
    just let me take her life and *die*!

LEADER and CHORUS
Shamed? *Butchered*, I tell you—hands lopped,
strung to shackle his neck and arms!
So she worked,   430
she buried him, made your life a hell.
    Your father mutilated—do you hear?

ELECTRA
    You tell him of father's death, but I was an outcast,
worthless, leashed like a vicious dog in a dark cell.
    I wept—laughter died that day . . .   435
        I wept, pouring out the tears behind my veils.
            Hear *that*, my brother, carve it on your heart!

LEADER and CHORUS
    Let it ring in your ears
        but let your heart stand firm.
    The outrage stands as it stands,   440
        you burn to know the end,
but first be strong, be steel, then down and fight.

ORESTES
I am calling you, my father—be with all you love!

ELECTRA
I am with you, calling through my tears.

LEADER and CHORUS
We band together now, the call resounds—   445
    hear us now, come back into the light.
Be with us, battle all you hate.

ORESTES
Now force *clash* with force, right with right!

ELECTRA
Dear gods, be just—win back our rights.

LEADER and CHORUS
The flesh crawls to hear them pray.   450
    The hour of doom has waited long . . .
pray for it once, and oh my god, it comes.

CHORUS
Oh, the torment bred in the race,
            the grinding scream of death
                  and the stroke that hits the vein,   455
      the hemorrhage none can stanch, the grief,
the curse no man can bear.

But there is a cure in the house
            and not outside it, no,
                  not from others but from *them*,   460
      their bloody strife. We sing to you,
dark gods beneath the earth.

Now hear, you blissful powers underground—
      answer the call, send help.
Bless the children, give them triumph now.   465

                            *[They withdraw, while Electra and
                            Orestes come to the altar.]*

ORESTES
Father, king, no royal death you died—
give me the power now to rule our house.

ELECTRA
I need you too, my father.
Help me kill her lover, then go free.

ORESTES
Then men will extend the sacred feast to you.   470
Or else, when the steam and the rich savor burn
for Mother Earth, you will starve for honor.

ELECTRA
And I will pour my birthright out to you—
the wine of the fathers' house, my bridal wine,
and first of all the shrines revere your tomb.   475

ORESTES
O Earth, bring father up to watch me fight.

ELECTRA
O Persephone, give us power—lovely, gorgeous power!

ORESTES
Remember the bath—they stripped away your life, my father.

ELECTRA
Remember the all-embracing net—they made it first for you.

ORESTES
Chained like a beast—chains of hate, not bronze, my father!   480

ELECTRA
Shamed in the schemes, the hoods they slung around you!

ORESTES
Does our taunting wake you, oh my father?

ELECTRA
Do you lift your beloved head?

ORESTES

Send us justice, fight for all you love,
or help us pin them grip for grip. They threw you—
don't you long to throw them down in turn?   485

ELECTRA

One last cry, father. Look at your nestlings
stationed at your tomb—pity
your son and daughter. We are all you have.

ORESTES

Never blot out the seed of Pelops here.   490
Then in the face of death you cannot die.

[The leader comes forward again.]

LEADER

The voices of children—salvation to the dead!
Corks to the net, they rescue the linen meshes
from the depths. This line will never drown!

ELECTRA

Hear us—the long wail we raise is all for you.   495
Honor our call and you will save yourself.

LEADER

And a fine thing it is to lengthen out the dirge;
you adore a grave and fate they never mourned.
But now for action—now you're set on action,
put your stars to proof.

ORESTES

So we will.   500
One thing first, I think it's on the track.
Why did she send libations? What possessed her,
so late, to salve a wound past healing?
To the unforgiving dead she sends this sop,
this . . . who am I to appreciate her gifts?   505
They fall so short of all her failings. True,
"pour out your all to atone an act of blood,
you work for nothing." So the saying goes.
I'm ready. Tell me what you know.

LEADER

I know, my boy,
I was there. She had bad dreams. Some terror   510
came groping through the night—it shook her,
and she sent these cups, unholy woman.

ORESTES

And you know the dream, you can tell it clearly?

LEADER

She dreamed she bore a snake, said so herself and . . .

ORESTES

Come to the point—where does the story end?   515

LEADER
. . . she swaddled it like a baby, laid it to rest.

ORESTES
And food, what did the little monster want?

LEADER
She gave it her breast to suck—she was dreaming.

ORESTES
And didn't it tear her nipple, the brute inhuman—

LEADER
Blood curdled the milk with each sharp tug . . .   520

ORESTES
No empty dream. The vision of a man.

LEADER
. . . and she woke with a scream, appalled,
and rows of torches, burning out of the blind dark,
flared across the halls to soothe the queen,
and then she sent the libations for the dead,   525
an easy cure she hopes will cut the pain.

ORESTES

No,

I pray to the Earth and father's grave to bring
that dream to life in me. I'll play the seer—
it all fits together, watch!
If the serpent came from the same place as I,   530
and slept in the bands that swaddled me, and its jaws
spread wide for the breast that nursed me into life
and clots stained the milk, mother's milk,
and she cried in fear and agony—so be it.
As she bred this sign, this violent prodigy,   535
so she dies by violence. I turn serpent,
I kill her. So the vision says.

LEADER

You are the seer for me, I like your reading.
Let it come! But now rehearse your friends.
Say do this, or don't do that—   540

ORESTES

The plan is simple. My sister goes inside.
And I'd have her keep the bond with me a secret.
They killed an honored man by cunning, so
they die by cunning, caught in the same noose.
So he commands,   545
Apollo the Seer who's never lied before.

And I like a stranger, equipped for all events,
go to the outer gates with this man here,
Pylades, a friend, the house's friend-in-arms.
And we both will speak Parnassian, both try   550
for the native tones of Delphi.

                    Now, say none
at the doors will give us a royal welcome
(after all the house is ridden by a curse),
well then we wait . . . till a passer-by will stop
and puzzle and make insinuations at the house,   555
"Aegisthus shuts his door on the man who needs him.
Why, I wonder—does he know? Is he home?"

But once through the gates, across the threshold,
once I find that man on *my* father's throne,
or returning late to meet me face to face,   560
and his eyes shift and fall—
                    I promise you,
before he can ask me, "Stranger, who are you?"—
I drop him dead, a thrust of the sword, and twist!
Our Fury never wants for blood. *His* she drinks unmixed,
our third libation poured to Saving Zeus.   ·   565

                [Turning to Electra.]

Keep a close watch inside, dear, be careful.
We must work together step by step.

                [To the chorus.]

                    And you,
better hold your tongues, religiously.
Silence, friends, or speak when it will help.

                *[Looking toward Pylades and the
                death-mound and beyond.]*

For the rest, watch over me, I need you—   570
guide my sword through struggle, guide me home!

                *[As Orestes, Pylades and Electra leave,
                the women reassemble for the chorus.]*

CHORUS

Marvels, the Earth breeds many marvels,
terrible marvels overwhelm us.
The heaving arms of the sea embrace and swarm
with savage life. And high in the no man's land of night   575
torches hang like swords. The hawk on the wing,
the beast astride the fields
can tell of the whirlwind's fury roaring strong.

Oh but a man's high daring spirit,
who can account for that? Or woman's   580
desperate passion daring past all bounds?
She couples with every form of ruin known to mortals.
Woman, frenzied, driven wild with lust,
twists the dark warm harness
of wedded love—tortures man and beast.   585

Well you know, you with a sense of truth
                    recall Althaia,
the heartless mother
who killed her son,
ai! what a scheme she had—   590
                she rushed his destiny,
                        lit the bloody torch
preserved from the day he left her loins with a cry—
                            the life of the torch paced his,
burning on till Fate burned out his life.   595

There is one more in the tales of hate:
                        remember Scylla,
the girl of slaughter
seduced by foes
to take her father's life.   600
            The gift of Minos,
                    a choker forged in gold
turned her head and Nisos' immortal lock she cut
                        as he slept away his breath . . .
ruthless bitch, now Hermes takes her down.   605

Now that I call to mind old wounds that never heal—
   Stop, it's time for the wedded love-in-hate,
for the curse of the halls,
        the woman's brazen cunning
           bent on her lord in arms,   610
  her warlord's power—
              Do you respect such things?
I prize the hearthstone warmed by faith,
a woman's temper nothing bends to outrage.

First at the head of legendary crime stands Lemnos.
   People shudder and moan, and can't forget—   615
each new horror that comes
       we call the hells of Lemnos.
         Loathed by the gods for guilt,
  cast off by men, disgraced, their line dies out.
Who could respect what god detests?   620
What of these tales have I not picked with justice?

      The sword's at the lungs!—it stabs deep,
        the edge cuts through and through
      and Justice drives it—Outrage still lives on,
        not trodden to pieces underfoot, not yet,   625
        though the laws lie trampled down,
          the majesty of Zeus.

      The anvil of Justice stands fast
        and Fate beats out her sword.
      Tempered for glory, a child will wipe clean   630
      the inveterate stain of blood shed long ago—
        Fury brings him home at last,
        the brooding mother Fury!

                [The women leave. Orestes and Py-
                lades approach the house of Atreus.]

ORESTES
                     Slave, the slave!—
where is he? Hear me pounding the gates?

Is there a man inside the house?   635
For the third time, come out of the halls!
If Aegisthus has them welcome friendly guests.

[A voice from inside.]

PORTER
All right, I hear you. . . .
Where do you come from, stranger? Who are you?

ORESTES
Announce me to the masters of the house.   640
I've come for them, I bring them news.
                                        Hurry,
the chariot of the night is rushing on the dark!
The hour falls, the traveler casts his anchor
in an inn where every stranger feels at home.
                                        Come out!
Whoever rules the house. The woman in charge.   645
No, the man, better that way.
No scruples then. Say what you mean,
man to man launch in and prove your point,
make it clear, strong.

[Clytaemnestra emerges from the palace, attended by Electra.]

CLYTAEMNESTRA
                        Strangers, please,
tell me what you would like and it is yours.   650
We've all you might expect in a house like ours.
We have warm baths and beds to charm away your pains
and the eyes of Justice look on all we do.
But if you come for higher things, affairs
that touch the state, that is the men's concern   655
and I will stir them on.

ORESTES

                              I am a stranger,
from Daulis, close to Delphi. I'd just set out,
packing my own burden bound for Argos
(here I'd put my burden down and rest),
when I met a perfect stranger, out of the blue,   660
who asks about my way and tells me his.

                                         Strophios,
a Phocian, so I gathered in conversation.
"Well, my friend," he says, "out for Argos
in any case? Remember to tell the parents
he is dead, Orestes . . .

                              promise me please   665
(it's only right), it will not slip your mind.
Then whatever his people want, to bring him home
or bury him here, an alien, all outcast here
forever, won't you ferry back their wishes?
As it is, a bronze urn is armor to his embers.   670
The man's been mourned so well . . ."

                                        I only tell you
what I heard. And am I speaking now
with guardians, kinsmen who will care?
It's hard to say. But a parent ought to know.

CLYTAEMNESTRA

                                         I, I—
your words, you storm us, raze us to the roots,   675
you curse of the house so hard to wrestle down!
How you range—targets at peace, miles away,
and a shaft from your lookout brings them down.
You strip me bare of all I love, destroy me,
now—Orestes.   680

And he was trained so well, we'd been so careful,
kept his footsteps clear of the quicksand of death.
Just now, the hope of the halls, the surgeon to cure
our Furies' lovely revel—he seemed so close,
he's written off the rolls.

ORESTES

If only I were . . .   685
my friends, with hosts as fortunate as you
if only I *could* be known for better news
and welcomed like a brother. The tie between
the host and stranger, what is kinder?
But what an impiety, so it seemed to me,   690
not to bring this to a head for loved ones.
I was bound by honor, bound by the rights
of hospitality.

CLYTAEMNESTRA

Nothing has changed.
For all that you receive what you deserve,
as welcome in these halls as one of us.   695
Wouldn't another bear the message just as well?
But you must be worn from the long day's journey—
time for your rewards.

[To Electra.]

Escort him in,
where the men who come are made to feel at home.
He and his retinue, and fellow travelers.   700
Let them taste the bounty of our house.
Do it, as if you depended on his welfare.

And we will rouse the powers in the house
and share the news. We never lack for loved ones,
we will probe this turn of fortune every way.   705

LEADER

    Oh dear friends who serve the house,
        when can we speak out, when
    can the vigor of our voices serve Orestes?

CHORUS

    Queen of the Earth, rich mounded Earth,
    breasting over the lord of ships,   710
    the king's corpse at rest,
    hear us now, now help us,
        now the time is ripe—
    Down to the pit Persuasion goes
    with all her cunning. Hermes of Death,   715
    the great shade patrols the ring
    to guide the struggles, drive the tearing sword.

LEADER

And I think our new friend is at his mischief.
Look, Orestes' nurse in tears.

                  [Enter Cilissa.]

Where now, old-timer, padding along the gates?   720
With pain a volunteer to go your way.

NURSE
                                        "Aegisthus,"
your mistress calling, "hurry and meet your guests.
There's news. It's clearer man to man, you'll see."

And she looks at the maids and pulls that long face
and down deep her eyes are laughing over the work   725
that's done. Well and good for her. For the house
it's the curse all over—the strangers make that plain.
But let *him* hear, he'll revel once he knows.

                                        Oh god,
the life is hard. The old griefs, the memories
mixing, cups of pain, so much pain in the halls,   730
the house of Atreus . . . I suffered, the heart within me
always breaking, oh, but I never shouldered
misery like this. So many blows, good slave,
I took my blows.

                        Now dear Orestes—
the sweetest, dearest plague of all our lives!   735

Red from your mother's womb I took you, reared you . . .
nights, the endless nights I paced, your wailing
kept me moving—led me a life of labor,
all for what?

                        And such care I gave it . . .
baby can't think for itself, poor creature.   740
You have to nurse it, don't you? Read its mind,
little devil's got no words, it's still swaddled.
Maybe it wants a bite or a sip of something,
or its bladder pinches—a baby's soft insides
have a will of their own. I had to be a prophet.   745
Oh I tried, and missed, believe you me, I missed,
and I'd scrub its pretty things until they sparkled.
Washerwoman and wetnurse shared the shop.
A jack of two trades, that's me,
and an old hand at both . . .

and so I nursed Orestes,   750
yes, from his father's arms I took him once,
and now they say he's dead,
I've suffered it all, and now I'll fetch that man,
the ruination of the house—give him the news,
he'll relish every word.

LEADER

                      She tells him to come,   755
but how, prepared?

NURSE

                  Prepared, how else?
I don't see . . .

LEADER

              With his men, I mean, or all alone?

NURSE

Oh, she says to bring his bodyguard, his cutthroats.

LEADER

No, not now, not if you hate our master—
tell him to come alone.   760
Nothing for him to fear then, when he hears.
Have him come quickly too, rejoicing all the way!
The teller sets the crooked message straight.

NURSE

                        What,
you're *glad* for the news that's come?

LEADER

                              Why not,
if Zeus will turn the evil wind to good?   765

NURSE
But how? Orestes, the hope of the house is gone.

LEADER
Not yet. It's a poor seer who'd say so.

NURSE
What are you saying?—something I don't know?

LEADER
Go in with your message. Do as you're told.
May the gods take care of cares that come from them.   770

NURSE
Well, I'm off. Do as I'm told.
And here's to the best . . .
some help, dear gods, some help.

[Exit.]

CHORUS

O now bend to my prayer, Father Zeus,
   lord of the gods astride the sky— 775
grant them all good fortune,
the lords of the house who strain to see
       strict discipline return.
Our cry is the cry of Justice,
     Zeus, safeguard it well.

                  Zeus, 780
set him against his enemies in the halls!
   Do it, rear him to greatness—two, threefold
      he will repay you freely, gladly.

Look now—watch the colt of a man you loved,
   yoked to the chariot of pain. 785
Now the orphan needs you—
harness his racing, rein him in,
      preserve his stride so we
can watch him surge in the homestretch,
       storming for the goal. 790

And you who haunt the vaults
where the gold glows in the darkness,
hear us now, good spirits of the house,
    conspire with us—come,
and wash old works of blood   795
in the fresh-drawn blood of Justice.
Let the gray retainer, murder, breed no more.

And you, Apollo, lord of the glorious masoned cavern,
    grant that this man's house lift up its head,
        that we may see with loving eyes   800
    the light of freedom burst from its dark veil!

And lend a hand and scheme
for the rights, my Hermes, help us,
sail the action on with all your breath.
    Reveal what's hidden, please,   805
    or say a baffling word
in the night and blind men's eyes—
when the morning comes your word is just as dark.

Soon, at last, in the dawn that frees the house,
   we sea-widows wed to the winds   810
        will beat our mourning looms of song
             and sing, "Our ship's come in!
        Mine, mine is the wealth that swells her holds—
   those I love are home and free of death."

But you, when your turn in the action comes, be strong.   815
     When she cries "Son!" cry out "My *father's* son!"
          Go through with the murder—innocent at last.

Raise up the heart of Perseus in your breast!
   And for all you love under earth
   and all above its rim, now scarf your eyes   820
             against the Gorgon's fury—
        In, go in for the slaughter now!

                    [*Enter Aegisthus, alone.*]

The butcher comes. Wipe out death with death.

AEGISTHUS
Coming, coming. Yes, I have my summons.
There's news, I gather, travelers here to tell it.   825
No joy in the telling though—Orestes dead.
Saddle the house with a bloody thing like that
and it might just collapse. It's still raw
from the last murders, galled and raw.

But how to take the story, for living truth?   830
Or work of a woman's panic, gossip starting up
in the night to flicker out and die?

[Turning to the leader.]

                         Do you know?
Tell me, clear my mind.

LEADER
                    We've heard a little.
But get it from the strangers, go inside.
Messengers have no power. Nothing like   835
a face-to-face encounter with the source.

AEGISTHUS
—Must see him, test the messenger. Where was he
when the boy died, standing on the spot?
Or is he dazed with rumor, mouthing hearsay?
No, he'll never trap me open-eyed!   840

[Striding through the doors.]

CHORUS

Zeus, Zeus, what can I say?—
how to begin this prayer, call down
    the gods for help? what words
can reach the depth of all I feel?
Now they swing to the work,   845
the red edge of the cleaver
hacks at flesh and men go down.
Agamemnon's house goes down—
    all-out disaster now,
or a son ignites the torch of freedom,   850
wins the throne, the citadel,
    the fathers' realms of gold.
The last man on the bench, a challenger
must come to grips with two. Up,
like a young god, Orestes, wrestle—   855
    let it be to win.

                    [A scream inside the palace.]

—Listen!
            —What's happening?
                            —The house,
what have they done to the house?

LEADER

                            Back,
till the work is over! Stand back—
they'll count us clean of the dreadful business.   860

                    *[The women scatter; a wounded ser-
                    vant of Aegisthus enters.]*

Look, the die is cast, the battle's done.

SERVANT
                              Ai,

Ai, all over, master's dead—Aie,
a third, last salute. Aegisthus is no more.

                    [Rushing at a side door, struggling to
                    work it open.]

Open up, wrench the bolts on the women's doors.
Faster! A strong young arm it takes,   865
but not to save him now, he's finished.
What's the use?
                    Look—wake up!
                              No good,
I call to the deaf, to sleepers . . . a waste of breath.
Where are you, Clytaemnestra? What are you doing?

LEADER
Her head is ripe for lopping on the block.   870
She's next, and justice wields the ax.

                    [The door opens, and Clytaemnestra
                    comes forth.]

CLYTAEMNESTRA
                              What now?
Why this shouting up and down the halls?

SERVANT
The dead are killing the living, I tell you!

CLYTAEMNESTRA

Ah, a riddle. I do well at riddles.
By cunning we die, precisely as we killed.   875
Hand me the man-ax, someone, hurry!

[The servant dashes out.]

Now we will see. Win all or lose all,
we have come to this—the crisis of our lives.

*[The main doors open; Orestes, sword
in hand, is standing over the body of
Aegisthus, with Pylades close behind
him.]*

ORESTES

It's you I want. This one's had enough.

CLYTAEMNESTRA

Gone, my violent one—Aegisthus, very dear.   880

ORESTES

You love your man? Then lie in the same grave.
You can never be unfaithful to the dead.

[Pulling her toward Aegisthus' body.]

CLYTAEMNESTRA

Wait, son—no feeling for this, my child?
The breast you held, drowsing away the hours,
soft gums tugging the milk that made you grow?   885

[Orestes turns to Pylades.]

ORESTES

What will I do, Pylades—I dread to kill my mother!

PYLADES

What of the future? What of the Prophet God Apollo,
the Delphic voice, the faith and oaths we swear?
Make all mankind your enemy, not the gods.

ORESTES

O you win me over—good advice.

[Wheeling on Clytaemnestra, thrusting her toward Aegisthus.]

This way—   890
I want to butcher you—right across his body!
In life you thought he dwarfed my father—*Die!*—
go down with him forever!

You love this man,
the man you should have loved you hated.

CLYTAEMNESTRA

I gave you life. Let me grow old with you.   895

ORESTES

What—kill my father, then you'd live with me?

CLYTAEMNESTRA

Destiny had a hand in that, my child.

ORESTES

This too: destiny is handing you your death.

CLYTAEMNESTRA

You have no fear of a mother's curse, my son?

ORESTES

Mother? You flung me to a life of pain.   900

CLYTAEMNESTRA
Never flung you, placed you in a comrade's house.

ORESTES
—Disgraced me, sold me, a freeborn father's son.

CLYTAEMNESTRA
Oh? then name the price I took for you.

ORESTES
I am ashamed to mention it in public.

CLYTAEMNESTRA
Please, and tell your father's failings too.   905

ORESTES
Never judge him—he suffered, you sat here at home.

CLYTAEMNESTRA
It hurts women, being kept from men, my son.

ORESTES
Perhaps . . . but the man slaves to keep them safe at home.

CLYTAEMNESTRA
—I see murder in your eyes, my child—mother's murder!

ORESTES

You are the murderer, not I—and you will kill yourself.   910

CLYTAEMNESTRA

Watch out—the hounds of a mother's curse will hunt you down.

ORESTES

But how to escape a father's if I fail?

CLYTAEMNESTRA

I must be spilling live tears on a tomb of stone.

ORESTES

Yes, my father's destiny—it decrees your death.

CLYTAEMNESTRA

Ai—you are the snake I bore—I gave you life!

ORESTES

                                        Yes!   915
That was the great seer, that terror in your dreams.
You killed and it was outrage—suffer outrage now.

> *[He draws her over the threshold; the
> doors close behind them, and the
> chorus gathers at the altar.]*

LEADER

I even mourn the victims' double fates.
But Orestes fought, he reached the summit
of bloodshed here—we'd rather have it so.   920
The bright eye of the halls must never die.

CHORUS

Justice came at last to the sons of Priam,
late but crushing vengeance, yes,
but to Agamemnon's house returned
            the double lion,   925
                        the double onslaught
            drove to the hilt—the exile sped by god,
by Delphi's just command that drove him home.

Lift the cry of triumph O! the master's house
        wins free of grief, free of the ones   930
who bled its wealth, the couple stained with murder,
                    free of Fate's rough path.

He came back with a lust for secret combat,
stealthy, cunning vengeance, yes,
but his hand was steered in open fight   935
            by god's true daughter,
                        Right, Right we call her,
            we and our mortal voices aiming well—
she breathes her fury, shatters all she hates.

Lift the cry of triumph O! the master's house   940
        wins free of grief, free of the ones
who bled its wealth, the couple stained with murder,
                    free of Fate's rough path.

Apollo wills it so!—
Apollo, clear from the Earth's deep cleft   945
    his voice came shrill, "Now stealth will master stealth!"
And the pure god came down and healed our ancient wounds,
    the heavens come, somehow, to lift our yoke of grief—
        Now to praise the heavens' just command.

    Look, the light is breaking!   950
    The huge chain that curbed the halls gives way.
        Rise up, proud house, long, too long
        your walls lay fallen, strewn along the earth.

    Time brings all to birth—
soon Time will stride through the gates with blessings,   955
    once the hearth burns off corruption, once
the house drives off the Furies. Look, the dice of Fate
    fall well for all to see. We sing how fortune smiles—
        the aliens in the house are routed out at last!

    Look, the light is breaking!   960
    The huge chain that curbed the halls gives way.
        Rise up, proud house, long, too long
        your walls lay fallen, strewn along the earth.

[The doors open. Torches light Pylades
and Orestes, sword in hand, standing
over the bodies of Clytaemnestra and
Aegisthus, as Clytaemnestra stood
over the bodies of Agamemnon and
Cassandra.]

ORESTES

Behold the double tyranny of our land!
They killed my father, stormed my fathers' house.   965
They had their power when they held the throne.
Great lovers still, as you may read their fate.
True to their oath, hand in hand they swore
to kill my father, hand in hand to die.
Now they keep their word.

[Unwinding from the bodies on the
bier the robes that entangled Agamemnon, he displays them, as Clytaemnestra had displayed them, to the
chorus at the altar.]

                    Look once more on this,   970
you who gather here to attend our crimes—
the master-plot that bound my wretched father,
shackled his ankles, manacled his hands.
Spread it out! Stand in a ring around it,
a grand shroud for a man.

                    Here, unfurl it   975
so the Father—no, not mine but the One
who watches over all, the Sun can behold
my mother's godless work. So he may come,
my witness when the day of judgment comes,
that I pursued this bloody death with justice,   980
mother's death.

                    Aegisthus, why mention him?
The adulterer dies. An old custom, justice.

But she who plotted this horror against her husband,
she carried his children, growing in her womb
and she—I loved her once   985
and now I loathe, I have to loathe—

                    what is she?

[Kneeling by the body of his mother.]

Some moray eel, some viper born to rot her mate
with a single touch, no fang to strike him,
just the wrong, the reckless fury in her heart!

[Glancing back and forth from Clytaemnestra to the robes.]

This—how can I dignify this . . . snare for a beast?—   990
sheath for a corpse's feet?

           This winding-sheet,
this tent for the bath of death!

                No, a hunting net,
a coiling—what to call—?

                    Foot-trap—
woven of robes . . .
why, this is perfect gear for the highwayman   995
who entices guests and robs them blind and plies
the trade of thieves. With a sweet lure like this
he'd hoist a hundred lives and warm his heart.

Live with such a woman, marry *her*? Sooner
the gods destroy me—die without an heir!   1000

CHORUS
  Oh the dreadful work . . .
  Death calls and she is gone.
    But oh, for you, the survivor,
  suffering is just about to bloom.

ORESTES
Did she do the work or not?—Here, come close—   1005
This shroud's my witness, dyed with Aegisthus' blade—
Look, the blood ran here, conspired with time to blot
the swirling dyes, the handsome old brocade.

Now I can praise you, now I am here to mourn.
You were my father's death, great robe, I hail you!   1010
Even if I must suffer the work and the agony
and all the race of man—
                                   I embrace you . . . you,
my victory, are my guilt, my curse, and still—

CHORUS

No man can go through life
and reach the end unharmed.   1015
    Aye, trouble is now,
and trouble still to come.

ORESTES

                              But *still*,
that you may know—
                              I see no end in sight,
I am a charioteer—the reins are flying, look,
the mares plunge off the track—
                                   my bolting heart,   1020
it beats me down and terror beats the drum,
my dance-and-singing master pitched to fury—

And still, while I still have some self-control,
I say to my friends in public: I killed my mother,
not with a little justice. She was stained   1025
with father's murder, she was cursed by god.
And the magic spells that fired up my daring?
One comes first. The Seer of Delphi who declared,
"Go through with this and you go free of guilt.
Fail and—"

I can't repeat the punishment.   1030
What bow could hit the crest of so much pain?

*[Pylades gives Orestes a branch of
olive and invests him in the robes
of Apollo, the wreath and insignia of
suppliants to Delphi.]*

Now look on me, armed with the branch and wreath,
a suppliant bound for the Navelstone of Earth,
Apollo's sacred heights
where they say the fire of heaven can never die.   1035

*[Looking at his hand that still retains
the sword.]*

I must escape this blood . . . it is my own.
—Must turn toward his hearth,
none but his, the Prophet God decreed.

I ask you, Argos and all my generations,
remember how these brutal things were done.   1040
Be my witness to Menelaus when he comes.
And now I go, an outcast driven off the land,
in life, in death, I leave behind a name for—

LEADER
But you've done well. Don't burden yourself
with bad omens, lash yourself with guilt.   1045
You've set us free, the whole city of Argos,
lopped the heads of these two serpents once for all.

*[Staring at the women and beyond,
Orestes screams in terror.]*

ORESTES
No, no! Women—look—like Gorgons,
shrouded in black, their heads wreathed,
swarming serpents!
                    —Cannot stay, I must move on.   1050

PYLADES
What dreams can whirl you so? You of all men,
you have your father's love. Steady,
nothing to fear with all you've won.

ORESTES
                                No dreams,
these torments, not to me, they're clear, real—the hounds
of mother's hate.

LEADER
                        The blood's still wet on your hands.   1055
It puts a kind of frenzy in you . . .

ORESTES
                                God Apollo!
Here they come, thick and fast,
their eyes dripping hate—

LEADER
                        One thing
will purge you. Apollo's touch will set you free
from all your . . . torments.

ORESTES
                        You can't see them—   1060
I can, they drive me on! I must move on—

                                *[He rushes out; Pylades follows close
                                behind.]*

LEADER
Farewell then. God look down on you with kindness,
guard you, grant you fortune.

CHORUS

Here once more, for the third time,
the tempest in the race has struck   1065
the house of kings and run its course.
    First the children eaten,
the cause of all our pain, the curse.
And next the kingly man's ordeal,
the bath where the proud commander,   1070
lord of Achaea's armies lost his life.
And now a third has come, but who?
    A third like Saving Zeus?
Or should we call him death?
Where will it end?—   1075
where will it sink to sleep and rest,
    this murderous hate, this Fury?

AESCHYLUS: THE Oresteia

THE EUMENIDES

FOR MY DAUGHTERS

> *What climbs the stair?*
> *Nothing that common women ponder on*
> *If you are worth my hope! Neither Content*
> *Nor satisfied Conscience, but that great family*
> *Some ancient famous authors misrepresent,*
> *The Proud Furies each with her torch on high.*

—W. B. YEATS, *"To Dorothy Wellesley"*

CHARACTERS

THE PYTHIA, *the priestess of Apollo*

APOLLO

HERMES

ORESTES

THE GHOST OF CLYTAEMNESTRA

CHORUS OF FURIES AND THEIR LEADER

ATHENA

Escorting Chorus of Athenian women

Men of the jury, herald, citizens

TIME AND SCENE: *The Furies have pursued Orestes to the temple of Apollo at Delphi. It is morning. The priestess of the god appears at the great doors and offers up her prayer.*

PYTHIA

First of the gods I honor in my prayer is Mother Earth,
the first of the gods to prophesy, and next I praise
Tradition, second to hold her Mother's mantic seat,
so legend says, and third by the lots of destiny,
by Tradition's free will—no force to bear her down—   5
another Titan, child of the Earth, took her seat
and Phoebe passed it on as a birthday gift to Phoebus,
Phoebus a name for clear pure light derived from hers.
Leaving the marsh and razorback of Delos, landing
at Pallas' headlands flocked by ships, here he came   10
to make his home Parnassus and the heights.
And an escort filled with reverence brought him on,
the highway-builders, sons of the god of fire who tamed
the savage country, civilized the wilds—on he marched
and the people lined his way to cover him with praise,   15
led by Delphos, lord, helm of the land, and Zeus
inspired his mind with the prophet's skill, with godhead,
made him fourth in the dynasty of seers to mount this throne,
but it is Zeus that Apollo speaks for, Father Zeus.
These I honor in the prelude of my prayers—these gods.   20

But Athena at the Forefront of the Temple crowns our legends.
I revere the nymphs who keep the Corycian rock's deep hollows,
loving haunt of birds where the spirits drift and hover.
And Great Dionysos rules the land. I never forget that day
he marshaled his wild women in arms—he was all god,   25
he ripped Pentheus down like a hare in the nets of doom.
And the rushing springs of Pleistos, Poseidon's force I call,
and the king of the sky, the king of all fulfillment, Zeus.
Now the prophet goes to take her seat. God speed me—
grant me a vision greater than all my embarkations past!   30

[Turning to the audience.]

Where are the Greeks among you? Draw your lots and enter.
It is the custom here. I will tell the future
only as the god will lead the way.

*[She goes through the doors and re-
appears in a moment, shaken, thrown
to her knees by some terrific force.]*

Terrors—
terrors to tell, terrors all can see!—
they send me reeling back from Apollo's house.   35
The strength drains, it's very hard to stand,
crawling on all fours, no spring in the legs . . .
an old woman, gripped by fear, is nothing,
a child, nothing more.

*[Struggling to her feet, trying to com-
pose herself.]*

I'm on my way to the vault,   40
it's green with wreaths, and there at the Navelstone
I see a man—an abomination to god—
he holds the seat where suppliants sit for purging;
his hands dripping blood, and his sword just drawn,
and he holds a branch (it must have topped an olive)   45
wreathed with a fine tuft of wool, all piety,
fleece gleaming white. So far it's clear, I tell you.

But there in a ring around the man, an amazing company—
women, sleeping, nestling against the benches . . .
women? No,   50
Gorgons I'd call them; but then with Gorgons
you'd see the grim, inhuman . . .

                       I saw a picture
years ago, the creatures tearing the feast
away from Phineus—
               These have no wings,
I looked. But black they are, and so repulsive.   55
Their heavy, rasping breathing makes me cringe.
And their eyes ooze a discharge, sickening,
and what they wear—to flaunt *that* at the gods,
the idols, sacrilege! even in the homes of men.
The tribe that produced that brood I never saw,   60
or a plot of ground to boast it nursed their kind
without some tears, some pain for all its labor.

Now for the outcome. This is his concern,
Apollo the master of this house, the mighty power.
Healer, prophet, diviner of signs, he purges   65
the halls of others—He must purge his own.

> *[She leaves. The doors of the temple
> open and reveal Apollo rising over
> Orestes; he kneels in prayer at the
> Navelstone, surrounded by the Furies
> who are sleeping. Hermes waits in the
> background.]*

APOLLO
No, I will never fail you, through to the end
your guardian standing by your side or worlds away!
I will show no mercy to your enemies! Now
look at these—

> *[Pointing to the Furies.]*

these obscenities!—I've caught them,   70
beaten them down with sleep.
                              They disgust me.
These gray, ancient children never touched
by god, man or beast—the eternal virgins.
Born for destruction only, the dark pit,
they range the bowels of Earth, the world of death,   75
loathed by men and the gods who hold Olympus.

Nevertheless keep racing on and never yield.
Deep in the endless heartland they will drive you,
striding horizons, feet pounding the earth forever,
on, on over seas and cities swept by tides!   80
Never surrender, never brood on the labor.
And once you reach the citadel of Pallas, kneel
and embrace her ancient idol in your arms and there,
with judges of your case, with a magic spell—
with words—we will devise the master-stroke   85
that sets you free from torment once for all.
I persuaded you to take your mother's life.

ORESTES
Lord Apollo, you know the rules of justice,
know them well. Now learn compassion too.
No one doubts your power to do great things.   90

APOLLO
Remember that. No fear will overcome you.

                              *[Summoning Hermes from the shad-
                              ows.]*

You, my brother, blood of our common Father,
Hermes, guard him well. Live up to your name,
good Escort. Shepherd him well, he is my suppliant,
and outlaws have their rights that Zeus reveres.   95
Lead him back to the world of men with all good speed.

[Apollo withdraws to his inner sanctuary; Orestes leaves with Hermes in the lead. The ghost of Clytaemnestra appears at the Navelstone, hovering over the Furies as they sleep.]

THE GHOST OF CLYTAEMNESTRA
You—how can you *sleep*?
Awake, awake—what use are sleepers now?
I go stripped of honor, thanks to you,
alone among the dead. And for those I killed   100
the charges of the dead will never cease, never—
I wander in disgrace, I feel the guilt, I tell you,
withering guilt from all the outraged dead!

But I suffered too, terribly, from dear ones,
and none of my spirits rages to avenge me.   105
I was slaughtered by his matricidal hand.
See these gashes—

[Seizing one of the Furies weak with sleep.]

        Carve them in your heart!

The sleeping brain has eyes that give us light;
we can never see our destiny by day.

And after all my libations . . . how you lapped   110
the honey, the sober offerings poured to soothe you,
awesome midnight feasts I burned at the hearthfire,
your dread hour never shared with gods.
All those rites, I see them trampled down.
And he springs free like a fawn, one light leap   115
at that—he's through the thick of your nets,
he breaks away!
Mocking laughter twists across his face.

Hear me, I am pleading for my life.
Awake, my Furies, goddesses of the Earth!   120
A dream is calling—Clytaemnestra calls you now.

[The Furies mutter in their sleep.]

Mutter on. Your man is gone, fled far away.
My son has friends to defend him, not like mine.

[They mutter again.]

You sleep too much, no pity for my ordeal.
Orestes murdered his mother—he is gone.   125

[They begin to moan.]

Moaning, sleeping—onto your feet, quickly.
What is your work? What but causing pain?
Sleep and toil, the two strong conspirators,
they sap the mother dragon's deadly fury—

*[The Furies utter a sharp moan and
moan again, but they are still asleep.]*

FURIES
Get him, get him, get him, get him—   130
there he goes.

THE GHOST OF CLYTAEMNESTRA
        The prey you hunt is just a dream—
like hounds mad for the sport you bay him on,
you never leave the kill.
        But what are you *doing?*
Up! don't yield to the labor, limp with sleep.
Never forget my anguish.   135
Let my charges hurt you, they are just;
deep in the righteous heart they prod like spurs.

You, blast him on with your gory breath,
the fire of your vitals—wither him, after him,
one last foray—waste him, burn him out!

[She vanishes. The lead Fury urges on the pack.]

LEADER

Wake up!   140

I rouse you, you rouse her. Still asleep?
Onto your feet, kick off your stupor.
See if this prelude has some grain of truth.

[The Furies circle, pursuing the scent with hunting calls, and cry out singly when they find Orestes gone.]

FURIES

—Aieeeeee—no, no, *no*, they do us wrong, dear sisters.

—The miles of pain, the pain I suffer . . .   145
and all for nothing, all for pain, more pain,
    the anguish, oh, the grief too much to bear.

—The quarry's slipped from the nets, our quarry lost and gone.

    —Sleep defeats me . . . I have lost the prey.

—You—child of Zeus—*you*, a common thief!   150

—Young god, you have ridden down the powers
proud with age. You worship the suppliant,
    the godless man who tears his parent's heart—

—The matricide, you steal him away, and you a god!

    —Guilt both ways, and who can call it justice?   155

—Not I: her charges stalk my dreams,
   yes, the charioteer rides hard,
            her spurs digging the vitals,
      under the heart, under the heaving breast—

—I can feel the executioner's lash, it's searing   160
            deeper, sharper, the knives of burning ice—

—Such is your triumph, you young gods,
   world dominion past all rights.
            Your throne is streaming blood,
      blood at the foot, blood at the crowning head—   165

—I can see the Navelstone of the Earth, it's bleeding,
            bristling corruption, oh, the guilt it has to bear—

Stains on the hearth! The Prophet stains the vault,
   he cries it on, drives on the crime himself.
      Breaking the god's first law, he rates men first,   170
            destroys the old dominions of the Fates.

He wounds me too, yet *him* he'll never free,
   plunging under the earth, no freedom then:
      curst as he comes for purging, at his neck
            he feels new murder springing from his blood.   175

*[Apollo strides from his sanctuary in
full armor, brandishing his bow and
driving back the Furies.]*

APOLLO
Out, I tell you, out of these halls—fast!—
set the Prophet's chamber free!

*[Seizing one of the Furies, shaking an
arrow across her face.]*

Or take
the flash and stab of this, this flying viper
whipped from the golden cord that strings my bow!

Heave in torment, black froth erupting from your lungs,   180
vomit the clots of all the murders you have drained.
But never touch my halls, you have no right.

Go where heads are severed, eyes gouged out,
where Justice and bloody slaughter are the same . . .
castrations, wasted seed, young men's glories butchered,   185
extremities maimed, and huge stones at the chest,
and the victims wail for pity—
spikes inching up the spine, torsos stuck on spikes.

[The Furies close in on him.]

So, you hear your love feast, yearn to have it all?
You revolt the gods. Your look,   190
your whole regalia gives you away—your kind
should infest a lion's cavern reeking blood.
But never rub your filth on the Prophet's shrine.
Out, you flock without a herdsman—out!
No god will ever shepherd you with love.   195

LEADER
Lord Apollo, now it is your turn to listen.
You are no mere accomplice in this crime.
You did it all, and all the guilt is yours.

APOLLO
No, how? Enlarge on that, and only that.

LEADER
You commanded the guest to kill his mother. 200

APOLLO
—Commanded him to avenge his father, what of it?

LEADER
And then you dared embrace him, fresh from bloodshed.

APOLLO
Yes, I ordered him on, to my house, for purging.

LEADER
And we sped him on, and you revile us?

APOLLO
Indeed, you are not fit to approach this house. 205

LEADER
And yet we have our mission and our—

APOLLO
Authority—you? Sound out your splendid power.

LEADER
Matricides: we drive them from their houses.

APOLLO
And what of the wife who strikes her husband down?

LEADER
That murder would not destroy one's flesh and blood.   210

APOLLO
Why, you'd disgrace—obliterate the bonds of Zeus
and Hera queen of brides! And the queen of love
you'd throw to the winds at a word, disgrace love,
the source of mankind's nearest, dearest ties.
Marriage of man and wife is Fate itself,   215
stronger than oaths, and Justice guards its life.
But if one destroys the other and you relent—
no revenge, not a glance in anger—then
I say your manhunt of Orestes is unjust.
Some things stir your rage, I see. Others,   220
atrocious crimes, lull your will to act.
                                        Pallas
will oversee this trial. She is one of us.

LEADER
I will never let that man go free, never.

APOLLO
Hound him then, and multiply your pains.

LEADER

Never try to cut my power with your logic.   225

APOLLO

I'd never touch it, not as a gift—your power.

LEADER

                                        Of course,
great as you are, they say, throned on high with Zeus.
But blood of the mother draws me on—must hunt
the man for Justice. Now I'm on his trail!

> [Rushing out, with the Furies in full
> cry.]

APOLLO

And I will defend my suppliant and save him.   230
A terror to gods and men, the outcast's anger,
once I fail him, all of my own free will.

> [Apollo leaves. The scene changes to
> the Acropolis in Athens. Escorted by
> Hermes, Orestes enters and kneels, ex-
> hausted, before the ancient shrine and
> idol of Athena.]

ORESTES

                                        Queen Athena,
under Apollo's orders I have come.
Receive me kindly. Curst and an outcast,
no suppliant for purging . . . my hands are clean.   235
My murderous edge is blunted now, worn down at last
on the outland homesteads, beaten paths of men.

On and out over seas and dry frontiers,
I kept alive the Prophet's strong commands.
Struggling toward your house, your idol—

                    Goddess,   240

here I keep my watch,
I await the consummation of my trial.

[The Furies enter in pursuit but cannot find Orestes who is entwined around Athena's idol. The leader sees the footprints.]

LEADER

                    At last!

The clear trail of the man. After it, silent
but it tracks his guilt to light. He's wounded—
go for the fawn, my hounds, the splash of blood,   245
hunt him, rake him down.

                    Oh, the labor,

the man-killing labor. My lungs are bursting . . .
over the wide rolling earth we've ranged in flock,
hurdling the waves in wingless flight and now we come,
all hot pursuit, outracing ships astern—and now   250
he's here, somewhere, cowering like a hare . . .
the reek of human blood—it's laughter to my heart!

[Inciting a pair of Furies.]

Look, look again, you two,
scour the ground before he escapes—one dodge
and the matricide slips free.

[Seeing Orestes, one by one they press around him and Athena's idol.]

—There he is! 255
Clutching the knees of power once again,
 twined in the deathless goddess' idol, look,
he wants to go on trial for his crimes.

—Never . . .
 the mother's blood that wets the ground,
 you can never bring it back, dear god, 260
the Earth drinks, and the running life is gone.

—No,
you'll give me blood for blood, you must!
 Out of your living marrow I will drain
 my red libation, out of your veins I suck my food,
 my raw, brutal cups—

—Wither you alive, 265
 drag you down and there you pay, agony
for mother-killing agony!

—And there you will see them all.
Every mortal who outraged god or guest or loving parent:
each receives the pain his pains exact.

—A mighty god is Hades. There 270
 at the last reckoning underneath the earth
 he scans all, he squares all men's accounts
and graves them on the tablets of his mind.

[Orestes remains impassive.]

ORESTES

I have suffered into truth. Well I know
the countless arts of purging, where to speak,   275
where silence is the rule. In this ordeal
a compelling master urges me to speak.

[Looking at his hands.]

The blood sleeps, it is fading on my hands,
the stain of mother's murder washing clean.
It was still fresh at the god's hearth. Apollo   280
killed the swine and the purges drove it off.
Mine is a long story
if I'd start with the many hosts I met,
I lived with, and I left them all unharmed.
Time refines all things that age with time.   285

And now with pure, reverent lips I call
the queen of the land. Athena, help me!
Come without your spear—without a battle
you will win myself, my land, the Argive people
true and just, your friends-in-arms forever.   290
Where are you now? The scorching wilds of Libya,
bathed by the Triton pool where you were born?
Robes shrouding your feet
or shod and on the march to aid allies?
Or striding the Giants' Plain, marshal of armies,   295
hero scanning, flashing through the ranks?
                                              Come—
you can hear me from afar, you are a god.
Set me free from this!

LEADER

                    Never—neither
Apollo's nor Athena's strength can save you.
Down you go, abandoned,   300
searching your soul for joy but joy is gone.
Bled white, gnawed by demons, a husk, a wraith—

                              [She breaks off, waiting for reply, but
                              Orestes prays in silence.]

No reply? you spit my challenge back?
You'll feast me alive, my fatted calf,
not cut on the altar first. Now hear my spell,   305
the chains of song I sing to bind you tight.

FURIES

                              Come, Furies, dance!—
    link arms for the dancing hand-to-hand,
    now we long to reveal our art,
    our terror, now to declare our right
        to steer the lives of men,   310
    we all conspire, we dance! we are
    the just and upright, we maintain.
    Hold out your hands, if they are clean
        no fury of ours will stalk you,
    you will go through life unscathed.   315
    But show us the guilty—one like this
        who hides his reeking hands,
    and up from the outraged dead we rise,
    witness bound to avenge their blood
    we rise in flames against him to the end!   320

Mother who bore me,
　O dear Mother Night,
to avenge the blinded dead
and those who see by day,
　　now hear me! The whelp Apollo   325
spurns my rights, he tears this trembling victim
　　　　　　from my grasp—the one to bleed,
　　to atone away the mother-blood at last.

　　Over the victim's burning head
　this chant this frenzy striking frenzy   330
　　　　　lightning crazing the mind
　　　　　　　　　this hymn of Fury
　chaining the senses, ripping cross the lyre,
　　　　　withering lives of men!

This, this is our right,
　spun for us by the Fates,   335
the ones who bind the world,
and none can shake our hold.
　Show us the mortals overcome,
insane to murder kin—we track them down
　　　　　till they go beneath the earth,   340
and the dead find little freedom in the end.

　　Over the victim's burning head
　this chant this frenzy striking frenzy
　　　　　lightning crazing the mind
　　　　　　　　　this hymn of Fury   345
　chaining the senses, ripping cross the lyre,
　　　　　withering lives of men!

Even at birth, I say, our rights were so ordained.
  The deathless gods must keep their hands far off—
no god may share our cups, our solemn feasts.   350
We want no part of their pious white robes—
    the Fates who gave us power made us free.

  Mine is the overthrow of houses, yes,
  when warlust reared like a tame beast
        seizes near and dear—   355
           down on the man we swoop, aie!
                for all his power black him out!—
for the blood still fresh from slaughter on his hands.

So now, striving to wrench our mandate from the gods,
  we make ourselves exempt from their control,   360
we brook no trial—no god can be our judge.

                [Reaching toward Orestes.]

His breed, worthy of loathing, streaked with blood,
  Zeus slights, unworthy his contempt.

  Mine is the overthrow of houses, yes,
  when warlust reared like a tame beast   365
        seizes near and dear—
           down on the man we swoop, aie!
                for all his power black him out!—
for the blood still fresh from slaughter on his hands.

And all men's dreams of grandeur, 370
        tempting the heavens,
all melt down, under earth their pride goes down—
         lost in our onslaught, black robes swarming,
           Furies throbbing, dancing out our rage.

Yes! leaping down from the heights, 375
   dead weight in the crashing footfall
            down we hurl on the runner
              breakneck for the finish—
cut him down, our fury stamps him down!

Down he goes, sensing nothing, 380
         blind with defilement . . .
darkness hovers over the man, dark guilt,
      and a dense pall overhangs his house,
         legend tells the story through her tears.

Yes! leaping down from the heights, 385
   dead weight in the crashing footfall
            down we hurl on the runner
              breakneck for the finish—
cut him down, our fury stamps him down!

So the center holds. 390
We are the skilled, the masterful,
we the great fulfillers,
memories of grief, we awesome spirits
stern, unappeasable to man,
disgraced, degraded, drive our powers through; 395
banished far from god to a sunless, torchlit dusk,
we drive men through their rugged passage,
blinded dead and those who see by day.

Then where is the man
not stirred with awe, not gripped by fear 400
to hear us tell the law that
Fate ordains, the gods concede the Furies,
absolute till the end of time?
And so it holds, our ancient power still holds.
We are not without our pride, though beneath the earth 405
our strict battalions form their lines,
groping through the mist and sunstarved night.

*[Enter Athena, armed for combat with
her aegis and her spear.]*

ATHENA
From another world I heard a call for help.
I was on the Scamander's banks, just claiming Troy.
The Achaean warlords chose the hero's share 410
of what their spear had won—they decreed that land,
root and branch all mine, for all time to be,
for Theseus' sons a rare, matchless gift.

Home from the wars I come, my pace unflagging,
wingless, flown on the whirring, breasting cape 415
that yokes my racing spirit in her prime.

*[Unfurling the aegis, seeing Orestes
and the Furies at her shrine.]*

And I see some new companions on the land.
Not fear, a sense of wonder fills my eyes.

Who are you? I address you all as one:
you, the stranger seated at my idol,   420
and you, like no one born of the sown seed,
no goddess watched by the gods, no mortal either,
not to judge by your look at least, your features . . .
Wait, I call my neighbors into question.
They've done nothing wrong. It offends the rights,   425
it violates tradition.

LEADER

         You will learn it all,
young daughter of Zeus, cut to a few words.
We are the everlasting children of the Night.
Deep in the halls of Earth they call us Curses.

ATHENA

Now I know your birth, your rightful name—   430

LEADER

But not our powers, and you will learn them quickly.

ATHENA

I can accept the facts, just tell them clearly.

LEADER

Destroyers of life: we drive them from their houses.

ATHENA

And the murderer's flight, where does it all end?

LEADER
Where there is no joy, the word is never used.   435

ATHENA
Such flight for him? You shriek him on to that?

LEADER
                                                                  Yes,
he murdered his mother—called that murder just.

ATHENA
And nothing forced him on, no fear of someone's anger?

LEADER
What spur could force a man to kill his mother?

ATHENA
Two sides are here, and only half is heard.   440

LEADER
But the oath—he will neither take the oath nor give it,
no, his will is set.

ATHENA
                          And you are set
on the name of justice rather than the act.

LEADER
How? Teach us. You have a genius for refinements.

ATHENA
Injustice, I mean, should never triumph thanks to oaths.   445

LEADER
Then examine him yourself, judge him fairly.

ATHENA
You would turn over responsibility to me,
to reach the final verdict?

LEADER
                    Certainly.
We respect you. You show us respect.

                    [Athena turns to Orestes.]

ATHENA
Your turn, stranger. What do you say to this?   450
Tell us your land, your birth, your fortunes.
Then defend yourself against their charge,
if trust in your rights has brought you here to guard
my hearth and idol, a suppliant for purging
like Ixion, sacred. Speak to all this clearly,   455
speak to me.

ORESTES
                    Queen Athena, first,
the misgiving in your final words is strong.
Let me remove it. I haven't come for purging.
Look, not a stain on the hands that touch your idol.
I have proof for all I say, and it is strong.   460

The law condemns the man of the violent hand
to silence, till a master trained at purging
slits the throat of a young suckling victim,
blood absolves his blood. Long ago
at the halls of others I was fully cleansed   465
in the cleansing springs, the blood of many victims.
Threat of pollution, sweep it from your mind.

Now for my birth. You will know at once.
I am from Argos. My father, well you ask,
was Agamemnon, sea-lord of the men-of-war,   470
your partisan when you made the city Troy
a city of the dead.

            What an ignoble death he died
when he came home—Ail my blackhearted mother
cut him down, enveloped him in her handsome net—
it still attests his murder in the bath   475
But I came back, my years of exile weathered—
killed the one who bore me, I won't deny it,
killed her in revenge. I loved my father,
fiercely.

         And Apollo shares the guilt—
he spurred me on, he warned of the pains I'd feel   480
unless I acted, brought the guilty down.
But were we just or not? Judge us now.
My fate is in your hands. Stand or fall
I shall accept your verdict.

ATHENA

            Too large a matter,
some may think, for mortal men to judge.   485
But by all rights not even I should decide
a case of murder—murder whets the passions.
Above all, the rites have tamed your wildness.
A suppliant, cleansed, you bring my house no harm.
If you are innocent, I'd adopt you for my city.   490

[Turning to the Furies.]

But they have their destiny too, hard to dismiss,
and if they fail to win their day in court—
how it will spread, the venom of their pride,
plague everlasting blights our land, our future . . .

So it stands. A crisis either way.   495

[Looking back and forth from Orestes to the Furies.]

Embrace the one? expel the other? It defeats me.

But since the matter comes to rest on us,
I will appoint the judges of manslaughter,
swear them in, and found a tribunal here
for all time to come.

[To Orestes and the Furies.]

        My contestants,   500
summon your trusted witnesses and proofs,
your defenders under oath to help your cause.
And I will pick the finest men of Athens,
return and decide the issue fairly, truly—
bound to our oaths, our spirits bent on justice.   505

[Athena leaves. The Furies form their chorus.]

FURIES
    Here, now, is the overthrow
of every binding law—once his appeal,
    his outrage wins the day,
his matricide! One act links all mankind,
hand to desperate hand in bloody license.   510
    Over and over deathstrokes
      dealt by children wait their parents,
mortal generations still unborn.

    We are the Furies still, yes,
but now our rage that patrolled the crimes of men,   515
    that stalked their rage dissolves—
we loose a lethal tide to sweep the world!
Man to man foresees his neighbor's torments,
    groping to cure his own—
      poor wretch, there is no cure, no use,   520
    the drugs that ease him speed the next attack.

Now when the sudden blows come down,
let no one sound the call that once brought help,
"Justice, hear me—Furies throned in power!"
   Oh I can hear the father now   525
   or the mother sob with pain
      at the pain's onset . . . hopeless now,
   the house of Justice falls.

There is a time when terror helps,
the watchman must stand guard upon the heart.   530
It helps, at times, to suffer into truth.
   Is there a man who knows no fear
   in the brightness of his heart,
      or a man's city, both are one,
   that still reveres the rights?   535

Neither the life of anarchy
nor the life enslaved by tyrants, no,
worship neither.
Strike the balance all in all and god will give you power;
the laws of god may veer from north to south—   540
we Furies plead for Measure.
Violence is Impiety's child, true to its roots,
but the spirit's great good health breeds all we love
and all our prayers call down,
prosperity and peace.   545

All in all I tell you people,
bow before the altar of the rights,
revere it well.
Never trample it underfoot, your eyes set on spoils;
revenge will hunt the godless day and night—   550
the destined end awaits.
So honor your parents first with reverence, I say,
and the stranger guest you welcome to your house,
turn to attend his needs,
respect his sacred rights.   555

All of your own free will, all uncompelled,
    be just and you will never want for joy,
you and your kin can never be uprooted from the earth.
    The reckless one—I warn the marauder
    dragging plunder, chaotic, rich beyond all rights: 560
        he'll strike his sails,
                harried at long last,
stunned when the squalls of torment break his spars to bits.

He cries to the deaf, he wrestles walls of sea
    sheer whirlpools down, down, with the gods' laughter   565
breaking over the man's hot heart—they see him flailing, crushed.
    The one who boasted never to shipwreck
    now will never clear the cape and steer for home;
        he lived for wealth,
                golden his life long—   570
he rams on the reef of law and drowns unwept, unseen.

> *[The scene has shifted to the Areo-
> pagus, the tribunal on the Crag of
> Ares. Athena enters in procession with
> a herald and ten citizens she has
> chosen to be judges.]*

ATHENA
Call for order, herald, marshal our good people.
Lift the Etruscan battle-trumpet,
strain it to full pitch with human breath,
crash out a stabbing blast along the ranks.   575

> *[The trumpet sounds. The judges take
> up positions between the audience and
> the actors. Athena separates the Furies
> and Orestes, directing him to the
> Stone of Outrage and the leader to
> the Stone of Unmercifulness, where
> the Furies form their chorus. Then
> Athena takes her stand between two
> urns that will receive the ballots.]*

And while this court of judgment fills, my city,
silence will be best. So that you can learn
my everlasting laws. And you too,

> *[To Orestes and the Furies.]*

that our verdict may be well observed by all.

[Apollo enters suddenly and looms be-
hind Orestes.]

Lord Apollo—rule it over your own sphere!   580
What part have you in this? Tell us.

APOLLO

                              I come
as a witness. This man, according to custom,
this suppliant sought out my house and hearth.
I am the one who purged his bloody hands.
His champion too, I share responsibility   585
for his mother's execution.
                              Bring on the trial.
You know the rules, now turn them into justice.

[Athena turns to the Furies.]

ATHENA

The trial begins! Yours is the first word—
the prosecution opens. Start to finish,
set the facts before us, make them clear.   590

LEADER

Numerous as we are, we will be brief.

[To Orestes.]

Answer count for count, charge for charge.
First, tell us, did you kill your mother?

ORESTES

I killed her. There's no denying that.

LEADER

Three falls in the match. One is ours already.   595

ORESTES

You exult before your man is on his back.

LEADER

But *how* did you kill her? You must tell us that.

ORESTES

I will. I drew my sword—more, I cut her throat.

LEADER

And who persuaded you? who led you on?

ORESTES

This god and his command.

[Indicating Apollo.]

He bears me witness.   600

LEADER

The Seer? He drove you on to matricide?

ORESTES

Yes,
and to this hour I have no regrets.

LEADER

If the verdict
brings you down, you'll change your story quickly.

ORESTES

I have my trust; my father will help me from the grave.

LEADER
Trust to corpses now! You made your mother one.   605

ORESTES
I do. She had two counts against her, deadly crimes.

LEADER
How? Explain that to your judges.

ORESTES
She killed her husband—killed my father too.

LEADER
But murder set her free, and you live on for trial.

ORESTES
She lived on. You never drove *her* into exile—why?   610

LEADER
The blood of the man she killed was not her own.

ORESTES
And I? Does mother's blood run in my veins?

LEADER
How could she breed you in her body, murderer?
Disclaim your mother's blood? She gave you life.

ORESTES

Bear me witness—show me the way, Apollo!   615
Did I strike her down with justice?
Strike I did, I don't deny it, no.
But how does our bloody work impress you now?—
Just or not? Decide.
I must make my case to them.

[Looking to the judges.]

APOLLO

                     Just,   620
I say, to you and your high court, Athena.
Seer that I am, I never lie. Not once
from the Prophet's thrones have I declared
a word that bears on man, woman or city
that Zeus did not command, the Olympian Father.   625
This is *his* justice—omnipotent, I warn you.
Bend to the will of Zeus. No oath can match
the power of the Father.

LEADER

                  Zeus, you say,
gave that command to your oracle? He charged
Orestes here to avenge his father's death   630
and spurn his mother's rights?

APOLLO

                   —Not the same
for a noble man to die, covered with praise,
his scepter the gift of god—murdered, at that,
by a woman's hand, no arrows whipping in
from a distance as an Amazon would fight.   635
But as you will hear, Athena, and your people
poised to cast their lots and judge the case.

Home from the long campaign he came, more won
than lost on balance, home to her loyal, waiting arms,
the welcome bath . . .

                  he was just emerging at the edge,   640
and there she pitched her tent, her circling shroud—
she shackled her man in robes,
in her gorgeous never-ending web she chopped him down!

Such was the outrage of his death, I tell you,
the lord of the squadrons, that magnificent man.   645
Her I draw to the life to lash your people,
marshaled to reach a verdict.

LEADER

                  Zeus, you say,
sets more store by a father's death? He shackled
his own father, Kronos proud with age.
Doesn't that contradict you?   650

              [To the judges.]

Mark it well. I call you all to witness.

APOLLO
You grotesque, loathsome—the gods detest you!
Zeus can break chains, we've cures for that,
countless ingenious ways to set us free.
But once the dust drinks down a man's blood,   655
he is gone, once for all. No rising back,
no spell sung over the grave can sing him back—
not even Father can. Though all things else
he can overturn and never strain for breath.

LEADER

                  So
you'd force this man's acquittal? Behold, Justice!   660

Can a son spill his mother's blood on the ground,
then settle into his father's halls in Argos?
Where are the public altars he can use?
Can the kinsmen's holy water touch his hands?

APOLLO

Here is the truth, I tell you—see how right I am.   665
The woman you call the mother of the child
is not the parent, just a nurse to the seed,
the new-sown seed that grows and swells inside her.
The *man* is the source of life—the one who mounts.
She, like a stranger for a stranger, keeps   670
the shoot alive unless god hurts the roots.

I give you proof that all I say is true.
The father can father forth without a mother.
Here she stands, our living witness. Look—

[Exhibiting Athena.]

Child sprung full-blown from Olympian Zeus,   675
never bred in the darkness of the womb
but such a stock no goddess could conceive!

And I, Pallas, with all my strong techniques
will rear your host and battlements to glory.
So I dispatched this suppliant to your hearth   680
that he might be your trusted friend forever,
that you might win a new ally, dear goddess.
He and his generations arm-in-arm with yours,
your bonds stand firm for all posterity—

ATHENA

           Now
have we heard enough? May I have them cast   685
their honest lots as conscience may decide?

LEADER
For us, we have shot our arrows, every one.
I wait to hear how this ordeal will end.

ATHENA
                                        Of course.
And what can I do to merit your respect?

APOLLO
You have heard what you have heard.   690

                    [To the judges.]

Cast your lots, my friends,
strict to the oath that you have sworn.

ATHENA
                              And now
if you would hear my law, you men of Greece,
you who will judge the first trial of bloodshed.

Now and forever more, for Aegeus' people   695
this will be the court where judges reign.
This is the Crag of Ares, where the Amazons
pitched their tents when they came marching down
on Theseus, full tilt in their fury, erecting
a new city to overarch his city, towers thrust   700
against his towers—they sacrificed to Ares,
named this rock from that day onward Ares' Crag.

Here from the heights, terror and reverence,
my people's kindred powers
will hold them from injustice through the day   705
and through the mild night. Never pollute
our law with innovations. No, my citizens,
foul a clear well and you will suffer thirst.

Neither anarchy nor tyranny, my people.
Worship the Mean, I urge you, 710
shore it up with reverence and never
banish terror from the gates, not outright.
Where is the righteous man who knows no fear?
The stronger your fear, your reverence for the just,
the stronger your country's wall and city's safety, 715
stronger by far than all men else possess
in Scythia's rugged steppes or Pelops' level plain.
Untouched by lust for spoil, this court of law
majestic, swift to fury, rising above you
as you sleep, our night watch always wakeful, 720
guardian of our land—I found it here and now.

So I urge you, Athens. I have drawn this out
to rouse you to your future. You must rise,
each man must cast his lot and judge the case,
reverent to his oath. Now I have finished. 725

*[The judges come forward, pass be-
tween the urns and cast their lots.]*

LEADER
Beware. Our united force can break your land.
Never wound our pride, I tell you, never.

APOLLO
The oracles, not mine alone but Zeus's too—
dread them, I warn you, never spoil their fruit.

[The leader turns to Apollo.]

LEADER
You dabble in works of blood beyond your depth. 730
Oracles, your oracles will be stained forever.

APOLLO
Oh, so the Father's judgment faltered when Ixion,
the first man-slayer came to him for purging?

LEADER
Talk on, talk on. But if I lose this trial
I will return in force to crush the land.   735

APOLLO
Never—among the gods, young and old,
you go disgraced. I will triumph over you!

LEADER
Just as you triumphed in the house of Pheres,
luring the Fates to set men free from death.

APOLLO
What?—is it a crime to help the pious man,   740
above all, when his hour of need has come?

LEADER
You brought them down, the oldest realms of order,
seduced the ancient goddesses with wine.

APOLLO
You will fail this trial—in just a moment
spew your venom and never harm your enemies.   745

LEADER
You'd ride me down, young god, for all my years?
Well here I stand, waiting to learn the verdict.
Torn with doubt . . . to rage against the city or—

ATHENA
My work is here, to render the final judgment.
Orestes,

*[Raising her arm, her hand clenched
as if holding a ballot-stone.]*

      I will cast my lot for you.   750
No mother gave me birth.
I honor the male, in all things but marriage.
Yes, with all my heart I am my Father's child.
I cannot set more store by the woman's death—
she killed her husband, guardian of their house.   755
Even if the vote is equal, Orestes wins.

Shake the lots from the urns. Quickly,
you of the jury charged to make the count.

*[Judges come forward, empty the urns,
and count the ballot-stones.]*

ORESTES
O God of the Light, Apollo, how will the verdict go?

LEADER
O Night, dark mother, are you watching now?   760

ORESTES
Now for the goal—the noose, or the new day!

LEADER
Now we go down, or forge ahead in power.

APOLLO
Shake out the lots and count them fairly, friends.
Honor Justice. An error in judgment now
can mean disaster. The cast of a single lot   765
restores a house to greatness.

*[Receiving the judges' count, Athena
lifts her arm once more.]*

ATHENA

The man goes free,
cleared of the charge of blood. The lots are equal.

ORESTES
O Pallas Athena—you, you save my house!
I was shorn of the fatherland but you
reclaim it for me. Now any Greek will say,   770
"He lives again, the man of Argos lives
on his fathers' great estates. Thanks to Pallas,
Apollo and Zeus, the lord of all fulfillment,
Third, Saving Zeus." He respected father's death,
looked down on mother's advocates—

[Indicating the Furies.]

he saved me.   775

And now I journey home. But first I swear
to you, your land and assembled host, I swear
by the future years that bring their growing yield
that no man, no helmsman of Argos wars on Athens,
spears in the vanguard moving out for conquest.   780
We ourselves, even if we must rise up from the grave,
will deal with those who break the oath I take—
baffle them with disasters, curse their marches,
send them hawks aloft on the left at every crossing—
make their pains recoil upon their heads.   785
But all who keep our oath, who uphold your rights
and citadel forever, comrade spear to spear,
we bless with all the kindness of our heart.

Now farewell, you and the people of your city.
Good wrestling—a grip no foe can break.   790
A saving hope, a spear to bring you triumph!

[Exit Orestes, followed by Apollo. The Furies reel in wild confusion around Athena.]

FURIES

You, you younger gods!—you have ridden down
    the ancient laws, wrenched them from my grasp—
and I, robbed of my birthright, suffering, great with wrath,
    I loose my poison over the soil, aieee!   795
poison to match my grief comes pouring out my heart,
        cursing the land to burn it sterile and now
rising up from its roots a cancer blasting leaf and child,
    now for Justice, Justice!—cross the face of the earth
the bloody tide comes hurling, all mankind destroyed.   800
. . . Moaning, only moaning? What will I do?
    The mockery of it, Oh unbearable,
mortified by Athens,
we the daughters of Night,
our power stripped, cast down.

ATHENA

                  Yield to me.   805
No more heavy spirits. You were not defeated—
the vote was tied, a verdict fairly reached
with no disgrace to you, no, Zeus brought
luminous proof before us. He who spoke
god's oracle, he bore witness that Orestes   810
did the work but should not suffer harm.

And now you'd vent your anger, hurt the land?
Consider a moment. Calm yourself. Never
render us barren, raining your potent showers
down like spears, consuming every seed.   815
By all my rights I promise you your seat
in the depths of earth, yours by all rights—
stationed at hearths equipped with glistening thrones,
covered with praise! My people will revere you.

FURIES

You, you younger gods!—you have ridden down   820
    the ancient laws, wrenched them from my grasp—
and I, robbed of my birthright, suffering, great with wrath,
    I loose my poison over the soil, aieee!—
poison to match my grief comes pouring out my heart,
        cursing the land to burn it sterile and now   825
rising up from its roots a cancer blasting leaf and child,
      now for Justice, Justice!—cross the face of the earth
the bloody tide comes hurling, all mankind destroyed.
. . . Moaning, only moaning? What will I do?
   The mockery of it, Oh unbearable,   830
mortified by Athens,
we the daughters of Night,
our power stripped, cast down.

ATHENA

               You have your power,
you are goddesses—but not to turn
on the world of men and ravage it past cure.   835
I put my trust in Zeus and . . . must I add this?
I am the only god who knows the keys
to the armory where his lightning-bolt is sealed.
No need of that, not here.
             Let me persuade you.
The lethal spell of your voice, never cast it   840
down on the land and blight its harvest home.
Lull asleep that salt black wave of anger—
awesome, proud with reverence, live with me.
The land is rich, and more, when its first fruits,
offered for heirs and the marriage rites, are yours   845
to hold forever, you will praise my words.

FURIES

But for me to suffer such disgrace . . . I,
the proud heart of the past, driven under the earth,
condemned, like so much filth,
    and the fury in me breathing hatred—   850
O good Earth,
      what is this stealing under the breast,
what agony racks the spirit? . . . Night, dear Mother Night!
All's lost, our ancient powers torn away by their cunning,
ruthless hands, the gods so hard to wrestle down   855
obliterate us all.

ATHENA

              I will bear with your anger.
You are older. The years have taught you more,
much more than I can know. But Zeus, I think,
gave me some insight too, that has its merits.
If you leave for an alien land and alien people,   860
you will come to love this land, I promise you.
As time flows on, the honors flow through all
my citizens, and you, throned in honor
before the house of Erechtheus, will harvest
more from men and women moving in solemn file   865
than you can win throughout the mortal world.

Here in our homeland never cast the stones
that whet our bloodlust. Never waste our youth,
inflaming them with the burning wine of strife.
Never pluck the heart of the battle cock   870
and plant it in our people—intestine war
seething against themselves. Let our wars
rage on abroad, with all their force, to satisfy
our powerful lust for fame. But as for the bird
that fights at home—my curse on civil war.   875

This is the life I offer, it is yours to take.
Do great things, feel greatness, greatly honored.
Share this country cherished by the gods.

FURIES

    But for me to suffer such disgrace . . . I,
the proud heart of the past, driven under the earth,   880
condemned, like so much filth,
    and the fury in me breathing hatred—
O good Earth,
      what is this stealing under the breast,
what agony racks the spirit? . . . Night, dear Mother Night!   885
All's lost, our ancient powers torn away by their cunning,
ruthless hands, the gods so hard to wrestle down
obliterate us all.

ATHENA

              No, I will never tire
of telling you your gifts. So that you,
the older gods, can never say that I,   890
a young god and the mortals of my city
drove you outcast, outlawed from the land.

But if you have any reverence for Persuasion,
the majesty of Persuasion,
the spell of my voice that would appease your fury—   895
Oh please stay . . .
            and if you refuse to stay,
it would be wrong, unjust to afflict this city
with wrath, hatred, populations routed. Look,
it is all yours, a royal share of our land—
justly entitled, glorified forever.

LEADER

              Queen Athena,   900
where is the home you say is mine to hold?

ATHENA

Where all the pain and anguish end. Accept it.

LEADER

And if I do, what honor waits for me?

ATHENA

No house can thrive without you.

LEADER

You would do that—
grant me that much power?

ATHENA

Whoever reveres us—   905
we will raise the fortunes of their lives.

LEADER

And you will pledge me that, for all time to come?

ATHENA

Yes—I must never promise things I cannot do.

LEADER

Your magic is working . . . I can feel the hate,
the fury slip away.

ATHENA

At last! And now take root   910
in the land and win yourself new friends.

LEADER

A spell—
what spell to sing? to bind the land forever? Tell us.

ATHENA

Nothing that strikes a note of brutal conquest. Only peace—
blessings, rising up from the earth and the heaving sea,
and down the vaulting sky let the wind-gods breathe   915
a wash of sunlight streaming through the land,
and the yield of soil and grazing cattle flood
our city's life with power and never flag
with time. Make the seed of men live on,
the more they worship you the more they thrive.   920
I love them as a gardener loves his plants,
these upright men, this breed fought free of grief.
All that is yours to give.

             And I,
in the trials of war where fighters burn for fame,
will never endure the overthrow of Athens—   925
all will praise her, victor city, pride of man.

          [The Furies assemble, dancing around
          Athena, who becomes their leader.]

FURIES

I will embrace
one home with you, Athena,
never fail the city
you and Zeus almighty, you and Ares   930
hold as the fortress of the gods, the shield
of the high Greek altars, glory of the powers.
Spirit of Athens, hear my words, my prayer
like a prophet's warm and kind,
that the rare good things of life   935
come rising crest on crest,
sprung from the rich black earth and
gleaming with the bursting flash of sun.

ATHENA

These blessings I bestow on you, my people, gladly.
I enthrone these strong, implacable spirits here   940
and root them in our soil.
                            Theirs,
theirs to rule the lives of men,
   it is their fated power.
But he who has never felt their weight,
or known the blows of life and how they fall,   945
the crimes of his fathers hale him toward their bar,
and there for all his boasts—destruction,
   silent, majestic in anger,
crushes him to dust.

FURIES

$$\text{Yes and I ban}$$
$$\text{the winds that rock the olive—} \qquad 950$$
$$\text{hear my love, my blessing—}$$
$$\text{thwart their scorching heat that blinds the buds,}$$
$$\text{hold from our shores the killing icy gales,}$$
$$\text{and I ban the blight that creeps on fruit and withers—}$$
$$\text{God of creation, Pan, make flocks increase} \qquad 955$$
$$\text{and the ewes drop fine twin lambs}$$
$$\text{when the hour of labor falls.}$$
$$\text{And silver, child of Earth,}$$
$$\text{secret treasure of Hermes,}$$
$$\text{come to light and praise the gifts of god.}$$

ATHENA

Blessings—now do you hear, you guards of Athens,   960
   all that she will do?
Fury the mighty queen, the dread
of the deathless gods and those beneath the earth,
deals with mortals clearly, once for all.   965
She delivers songs to some, to others
   a blinding life of tears—
Fury works her will.

FURIES

> And the lightning stroke
> that cuts men down before their prime, I curse,
> but the lovely girl who finds a mate's embrace,   970
> the deep joy of wedded life—O grant that gift, that prize,
> you gods of wedlock, grant it, goddesses of Fate!
> Sisters born of the Night our mother,
> spirits steering law,
> sharing at all our hearths,   975
> at all times bearing down
> to make our lives more just,
> all realms exalt you highest of the gods.

ATHENA

> Behold, my land, what blessings Fury kindly,
> gladly brings to pass—   980
> I am in my glory! Yes, I love Persuasion;
> she watched my words, she met their wild refusals.
> Thanks to Zeus of the Councils who can turn
> dispute to peace—he won the day.

[To the Furies.]

> Thanks to our duel for blessings;   985
> we win through it all.

FURIES

> And the brutal strife,
> the civil war devouring men, I pray
> that it never rages through our city, no,
> that the good Greek soil never drinks the blood of Greeks,
> shed in an orgy of reprisal life for life—   990
> that Fury like a beast will never
> rampage through the land.
> Give joy in return for joy,
> one common will for love,
> and hate with one strong heart: 995
> such union heals a thousand ills of man.

ATHENA

Do you *hear* how Fury sounds her blessings forth,
   how Fury finds the way?
Shining out of the terror of their faces
I can see great gains for you, my people.   1000
Hold them kindly, kind as they are to you.
Exalt them always, you exalt your land,
   your city straight and just—
its light goes through the world.

FURIES

> Rejoice,
>> rejoice in destined wealth,   1005
>> rejoice, Athena's people—
>> poised by the side of Zeus,
>> loved by the loving virgin girl,
>> achieve humanity at last,
>> nestling under Pallas' wings   1010
>> and blessed with Father's love.

ATHENA

You too rejoice! and I must lead the way
to your chambers by the holy light of these,
    your escorts bearing fire.

> *[Enter Athena's entourage of women,
> bearing offerings and victims and
> torches still unlit.]*

Come, and sped beneath the earth   1015
    by our awesome sacrifices,
keep destruction from the country,
bring prosperity home to Athens,
triumph sailing in its wake.
              And you,
my people born of the Rock King,   1020
lead on our guests for life, my city—
May they treat you with compassion,
compassionate as you will be to them.

FURIES

Rejoice!—
rejoice—the joy resounds—
all those who dwell in Athens,   1025
spirits and mortals, come,
govern Athena's city well,
revere us well, we are your guests;
you will learn to praise your Furies,
you will praise the fortunes of your lives.   1030

ATHENA

My thanks! and I will speed your prayers, your blessings—
lit by the torches breaking into flame
I send you home, home to the core of Earth,
escorted by these friends who guard my idol
duty-bound.

> *[Athena's entourage comes forward,
> bearing crimson robes.]*

Bright eye of the land of Theseus,   1035
come forth, my splendid troupe. Girls and mothers,
trains of aged women grave in movement,
dress our Furies now in blood-red robes.
Praise them—let the torch move on!
So the love this family bears toward our land   1040
will bloom in human strength from age to age.

> *[The women invest the Furies and sing
> the final chorus. Torches blaze; a pro-
> cession forms, including the actors and
> the judges and the audience. Athena
> leads them from the theater and es-
> corts them through the city.]*

THE WOMEN OF THE CITY

On, on, good spirits born for glory,
Daughters of Night, her children always young,
                    now under loyal escort—
Blessings, people of Athens, sing your blessings out.   1045

Deep, deep in the first dark vaults of Earth,
sped by the praise and victims we will bring,
                    reverence will attend you—
Blessings now, all people, sing your blessings out.

You great good Furies, bless the land with kindly hearts,   1050
you Awesome Spirits, come—exult in the blazing torch,
                    exultant in our fires, journey on.
Cry, cry in triumph, carry on the dancing on and on!

This peace between Athena's people and their guests
must never end. All-seeing Zeus and Fate embrace,   1055
                    down they come to urge our union on—
Cry, cry in triumph, carry on the dancing on and on!

AESCHYLUS: THE Oresteia

NOTES AND GLOSSARY

THE GENEALOGY OF ORESTES
According to Aeschylus

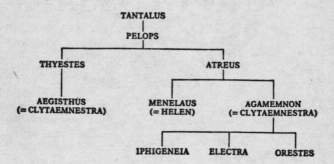

NOTES

The factual notes on mythology, history and language are mainly by WBS, those on imagery and symbolism mainly by RF. Only samples of themes and image-patterns have been cited. Our choice of variant readings in the text has not been specified in the notes. We hope that in most places it will be clear from the translation. As in the introduction, we have drawn from the work of others, and a brief list of their writings may be useful to the general reader. The list is limited to books; separate articles have been omitted, though several of the most important (by Hammond, Goheen and Herington) may be found in the McCall collection, and others are referred to in the notes.

Commentaries

Denniston, J. W. and Denys Page. Ed., *Agamemnon*. Oxford: Clarendon Press, 1957.

Fraenkel, Eduard. Ed. with a Commentary, *Agamemnon*. 3 vols. Oxford: Clarendon Press, 1950.

Lloyd-Jones, Hugh. Trs. with Commentary, *Agamemnon, The Libation Bearers, The Eumenides*. 3 vols. Englewood Cliffs, N.J.: Prentice-Hall, 1970.

Rose, H. J. *A Commentary on the Surviving Plays of Aeschylus*. 2 vols. Amsterdam: N. V. Noord-Hollandsche Uitgevers Maatschappij, 1958.

Sidgwick, A. Ed. with Introduction and Notes, *Agamemnon, Choephoroi, Eumenides*. 3 vols. Oxford: Clarendon Press, 1900–05.

Thomson, George. Ed. *The Oresteia*, with an Introduction and Commentary, in which is included the work of the late Walter Headlam. New Ed., Amsterdam: Adolf M. Hakkert, 1966.

Critical Works

Burke, Kenneth. *The Philosophy of Literary Form: Studies in Symbolic Action.* 3rd ed. Berkeley and Los Angeles: University of California Press, 1973.

Dodds, E. R. *The Greeks and the Irrational.* Sather Classical Lectures, Vol. 25. Berkeley and Los Angeles: University of California Press, 1964.

Earp, Frank Russell. *The Style of Aeschylus.* Cambridge, Eng.: Cambridge University Press, 1948.

Else, Gerald F. *The Origin and Early Form of Greek Tragedy.* Martin Classical Lectures, Vol. 20. Cambridge, Mass.: Harvard University Press, 1965; London: Oxford University Press, 1965.

Fergusson, Francis. *The Idea of a Theater: A Study of Ten Plays, the Art of Drama in Changing Perspective.* London: Oxford University Press, 1949; New York: Doubleday, 1953.

Finley, J. H., Jr. *Pindar and Aeschylus.* Martin Classical Lectures, Vol. 14. Cambridge, Mass.: Harvard University Press, 1955.

Harrison, Jane. *Prolegomena to the Study of Greek Religion.* 2nd ed. Cambridge, 1908; rpt. London: The Merlin Press, 1961.

————. *Themis: A Study of the Social Origins of Greek Religion.* 2nd ed. Cambridge, 1927; rpt. London: The Merlin Press, 1963.

Jaeger, Werner. *Paideia: The Ideals of Greek Culture,* trs. Gilbert Highet. 3 vols. Oxford: Basil Blackwell and Matt, Ltd., 1939–44; New York: Oxford University Press, 1945.

Jones, John. *On Aristotle and Greek Tragedy.* New York: Oxford University Press, 1962; London: Chatto and Windus, 1962.

Kaufmann, Walter. *Tragedy and Philosophy.* New York: Doubleday, 1968.

Kitto, H. D. F. *Form and Meaning in Drama: A Study of Six Greek Plays and of Hamlet.* 2nd ed. London: Methuen, 1964; New York: Barnes and Noble, 1968.

————. *Greek Tragedy: A Literary Study.* 2nd ed. New York: Doubleday, 1954; 3rd ed. London: Methuen, 1966.

Kuhns, Richard. *The House, the City, and the Judge: The Growth of Moral Awareness in the Oresteia.* Indianapolis: Bobbs-Merrill, 1962.

Lattimore, Richmond. Trs. and Introduction, *The Oresteia,* in *The Complete Greek Tragedies: Volume I, Aeschylus,* ed. David Grene and Richmond Lattimore. Chicago: The University of Chicago Press, 1953.

Lebeck, Anne. *The Oresteia: A Study in Language and Structure.* Cambridge, Mass.: Harvard University Press, 1971.

Lloyd-Jones, Hugh. *The Justice of Zeus.* Sather Classical Lectures, Vol. 41. Berkeley and Los Angeles: University of California Press, 1971.

McCall, Marsh H., Jr. *Aeschylus: A Collection of Critical Essays.* Englewood Cliffs, N.J.: Prentice-Hall, 1972.

Méautis, Georges. *Eschyle et la trilogie.* Paris, 1936.

Murray, Gilbert. *Aeschylus: The Creator of Tragedy.* Oxford: Clarendon Press, 1940.

Owen, E. T. *The Harmony of Aeschylus.* Toronto: Clark, Irwin, 1952; London: G. Bell, 1952.

Podlecki, Anthony J. *The Political Background of Aeschylean Tragedy.* Ann Arbor: University of Michigan Press, 1966.

Romilly, Jacqueline de. *La crainte et l'angoisse dans le théâtre d'Eschyle.* Paris: "Les Belles Lettres," 1958.

Rosenmeyer, Thomas G. *The Masks of Tragedy: Essays on Six Greek Dramas.* Austin, Texas: University of Texas Press, 1963.

Sheppard, John T. *Aeschylus and Sophocles.* New York: Longmans, Greene, 1927; London: G. G. Harrap, 1927.

Smyth, Herbert Weir. *Aeschylean Tragedy.* Berkeley: University of California Press, 1924.

Solmsen, Friedrich. *Hesiod and Aeschylus.* Ithaca: Cornell University Press, 1949.

Stanford, W. B. *Aeschylus in His Style: A Study in Language and Personality*. Dublin, 1942; rpt. New York: Johnson Reprint, 1972.

———. *Ambiguity in Greek Literature: Studies in Theory and Practice*. Oxford, 1939; rpt. New York: Johnson Reprint, 1972.

———. *Greek Metaphor: Studies in Theory and Practice*. Oxford, 1936; rpt. New York: Johnson Reprint, 1972.

Steiner, George. *The Death of Tragedy*. New York: Knopf, 1961; London: Faber and Faber, 1961.

Thomson, George. *Aeschylus and Athens: A Study in the Social Origins of Drama*. 2nd ed. London: Lawrence & Wishart, 1946.

AGAMEMNON

SCENE: THE HOUSE OF ATREUS IN ARGOS. When Aeschylus refers to Argos he may mean the entire Argolid in the northeastern Peloponnese (including the cities of Argos and Mycenae) or the city of Argos in particular. The first is the more frequent meaning of "Argos" in the Homeric poems; the second is the usual meaning in classical Greek. The Homeric poems specifically locate the murder of Agamemnon in Mycenae. But this city had been destroyed by its rival, Argos, about four years before the *Oresteia* was produced; and soon after its destruction Argos had become an ally of Athens (as alluded to elsewhere in the trilogy; see *Eumenides* n. 289). Probably, then, Aeschylus deliberately used "Argos" ambiguously so that modernists in his audience might take the scene of the tragedy to be the city of Argos and traditionalists could continue to place it in Mycenae, then, no doubt, as now, much the more awesome setting for the terrible crimes of the house of Atreus. Vincent Scully has described the citadel and its surroundings eloquently: "To left and right the flanking peaks form one huge pair of horns, so that the site as a whole rises as a mighty bull's head above the valley. Yet the horns also suggest here the raised arms of the Mycenaean goddess as she is shown in the many terracotta figurines found at Mycenae and elsewhere . . . . the formation as a whole can be seen as rising out of the earth like the goddess herself appearing in majesty: the mounded hill, the now terrible horns or arms above it, and in the place of the goddess' head the fortress of the lords. . . . Upon this most devouring of thrones the king dares to put himself, and the built-up cone of his citadel occupies its center." (*The Earth, the Temple, and the Gods: Greek Sacred Architecture* [New Haven and London: Yale University Press, 1962], pp. 37–38.) See n. 309.

WATCHMAN. A figure drawn from Homer, but in the *Odyssey* (4.524-28) he serves as a simple hireling of Aegisthus; here, an unwitting agent of the assassins, he is loyal to his king.

Throughout the introduction and the notes we refer to the Homeric background of the *Oresteia*, especially to those events from the house of Atreus which Homer narrates in the *Odyssey*. Taken in sequence, these passages begin with the successful vengeance of Orestes: chosen by Zeus as a strong example of justice (1.29-43), then used by Athena to raise the spirits of Telemachus (1.298-302), then by Nestor (3.248-316) not only to encourage him but also to caution him with the added stories of Clytaemnestra's infidelity and the wanderings of Menelaus, absent from Argos when Agamemnon was assassinated. Next Menelaus tells Telemachus how Proteus informed him of his brother's murder by Aegisthus (4.511-47); and the crime expands when the ghost of Agamemnon tells Odysseus how both he and Cassandra were murdered by his wife together with her lover (11.385-439). However optimistic the sequel of Orestes' vengeance, in other words, each version of Agamemnon's death presents a greater darkness, and so a starker foil for the luminous reunion of Odysseus and Penelope; until, at the end of the *Odyssey* (24.191-202), Agamemnon's ghost calls for a song to immortalize Penelope and another for the notorious Clytaemnestra. Homer has provided the first, and Aeschylus, in effect, the second. Adapting Homer more and more freely throughout the *Oresteia*, he reverses the events and carries them from the darkness to the light—from the bloody return of Agamemnon to the triumphant return of Athena to Athens. The last is Aeschylus' ultimate expansion of Homer and departure from his master. See Intro., pp. 4, 16f., 21, 30, 34, 47f., 64, 94f.

1 *Dear gods, set me free from all the pain:* for relationships between the Mysteries of Eleusis and the *Oresteia*, see Intro., pp. 69ff., 97f. The watchman's appeal for deliverance—the typical appeal of the candidate for initiation—is answered by increased anxiety; see 1059, n. 1605; *Libation Bearers* n. 950, *Eumenides* n. 494.

8 *Our great kings:* dominant stars or constellations that demarcate the seasons. According to tradition Troy fell in the tenth year of the siege, at the setting of the Pleiades (812) that occurs before sunrise in the late autumn and signals the approach of winter, storms at sea and danger to human health.

18 *I mustn't sleep:* a sentry's Nemesis, death for sleeping at the post.

25 *Dawn of the darkness:* the watchman's word for light, *phaos,* can mean hope and safety and may recall the word for man, *phôs,* though here the man is about to be eclipsed. Solar imagery will recur throughout the trilogy and reflect the light of human achievement emerging from the night of barbarism, but in A appeals to the sun will usher in a greater darkness, while the dawn of Orestes' coming remains a distant possibility; see 264f., 596ff., 657ff., 970f., 1183ff., 1605ff.; *LB* n. 950, *E* n. 7.

Destructive images and themes in A will often find a positive expression in Cassandra, as if she had a redemptive power over them and could foresee their eventual regeneration; see 1346ff., where she invokes the sun as the source of future retribution.

30 *Lift a cry of triumph:* see 580, 1121, 1246; *LB* n. 383, *E* n. 1053.

35 *Triple-sixes:* in the game of *petteia* or "falls," an ancient version of backgammon, a throw of triple-sixes allowed the player to occupy the board and win.

45 *Great avenger:* Aeschylus describes Menelaus and Agamemnon as Priam's "adversary in a suit," using the singular to unify the brothers. He breaks with tradition by removing Menelaus from Sparta to Argos, where he and Agamemnon share a common residence and so a common legal claim against the Trojans. The legal metaphor controls the *Oresteia.* It informs the punishment of Troy, the execution of Agamemnon, the indictment of Clytaemnestra and Aegisthus by the chorus, and their subsequent execution by Orestes in *LB*. The metaphor will materialize when Orestes is acquitted in *E* and Athena establishes the Areopagus in Athens.

49 *Atreus' sturdy yoke of sons*: the metaphor is drawn from animal husbandry and joins the Atreidae in mutual power, conjugal hardship, and the destiny they must shoulder. Images from husbandry have a brutalizing effect in *A* (653ff., 1671ff.); the yoke is associated with the yoke of necessity (217) and slavery (951), with the hunt and the net (129 and n.), and every form of taming and suppression in the play (133f., 1066f.). Like its fellows, the yoke has a recoiling force; it will oppress Agamemnon's daughter Iphigeneia (235f.), his enemies (331) and himself (1524). Cassandra ultimately rejects her yoke; see 1280ff.; *LB* n. 74, *E* n. 116.

61 *Someone hears on high*: Apollo presumably as god of prophecy, Pan as god of the natural world, Zeus as god of the sky and universal justice.

63 *These guests*: Metics, resident aliens; the term will apply to Orestes and the Furies; see *LB* n. 959, *E* n. 1021.

65 *Fury*: Clytaemnestra is its embodiment, and perhaps at this moment, as if evoked by mention of the Fury sent to punish Troy, she enters and performs her rites preliminary to her punishment of Agamemnon. (Aeschylus was known in antiquity, and ridiculed by Aristophanes, for his use of the "silent actor.")

66 *Zeus the god of guests*: Zeus *Xenios* presides over the rites of hospitality; these were violated by Paris who abducted Helen while he was the guest of Menelaus.

68 *A woman manned by many*: Helen, who was won by Theseus, Menelaus and Paris among others, and many more pursued her to their graves (1484f.). She was also Clytaemnestra's half-sister, and these lines may include a glance toward the queen.

71f *First blood rites*: the *proteleia* were sacrifices preliminary to the consummation of a rite, often that of marriage; see n. 226. A suggestive word-family in Aeschylus associates *teleia* (the rituals fulfilled) and *teleios* (an adjective for the perfect victim, or as applied to Zeus, the god who brings all things, especially all rituals, to perfection) with the noun *telos* (culmination) and cognate verbs for "consummations" that bring to birth or bring to an end, destroy; see 629, 740, 791, 924, 974ff., 1000ff. Cassandra turns her death into a ritual with prophetic powers. The blasphemous rituals of Agamemnon and his diabolic queen will yield to the magnificent civic rites of Athens. The deadly "ends" that begin the trilogy will culminate in the perfect "ends" of humanity, the marriage of our supernatural and our human powers, the inception of our culture. See Froma Zeitlin, "The Motif of the Corrupted Sacrifice in Aeschylus' *Oresteia, Transactions and Proceedings of the American Philological Association,* xcvi (1965), 463–508.

75ff The subject is left indefinite in the Greek, "anybody." It could include a reference to Paris; Agamemnon who sacrificed Iphigeneia; and Clytaemnestra who is sacrificing now before she kills her husband.

89 *Three legs at a time:* a reference to the notion that an old man's walking-stick is a third leg (as in the riddle of the Sphinx).

91 A *dream:* dreams in Aeschylus have been the subject of profound studies. Here we can only suggest that in A dreams extend from metaphors for insubstantiality or escapism to states of visionary experience. Such visions are used by Clytaemnestra to manipulate her listeners, to undermine her victim, finally to lead the chorus to their prophetic insights. Her visions, like those of Cassandra, are concentrated versions of reality. They fulfill the nightmare foreseen by Calchas, while subjecting it to the force of individual responsibility; see *LB* n. 42, *E* n. 42.

107 *Heal us:* Aeschylus often uses medical terms for measures that promise cures but only aggravate the illness. See 199ff., and the futility of appealing to Apollo the Healer (1261) or Clytaemnestra here. There are no cures in A (390), merely palliatives (539) or remedies as remote as Orestes (1105) or cruel as the homeopathy of pain that actually intensifies the pain (180f.); see 832ff., 1004ff., 1017ff., 1507f.; *LB* n. 69ff., *E* n. 65f.

109 *Now the hope shines,* etc. The ambivalence of Clytaemnestra's fires, like the light-in-darkness theme, will prove benighting; see n. 25, 281ff., 581ff.; *LB* n. 950, *E* notes 7, 13.

112ff *The gods' command . . . the twin command:* the word *kratos,* "power" or "authority," applies both to the gods' mandate and to the Greek commanders—the omen and its agents act as one.

113f *Power . . . fighting strength: Peitho* or Persuasion, the power to win belief, is what the old men have instead of military prowess; see n. 378ff.

120 *Spearhand right:* the side on which auspicious omens appear.

125 *Cry, cry for death,* etc. The refrain modulates from exultation to anguish (139) to a blend of both, stalwart resignation (160); ironic echoes may be heard at 256, 353, 567.

126 *The loyal seer:* as at the outset of the *Iliad,* Calchas foresees much hardship for the Greeks and Agamemnon. The ambiguities in his vision are heightened by his oracular style. His antecedents are general (the wasted kingdom, 131, may include Argos as well as Troy); his verbs are set in a historical present that unifies the past and future, the legend of the house and the repercussions of the war.

129 *The long hunt nets,* etc. The image of the hunt will associate the vengeance wreaked on Troy (810ff.) with the vengeance wreaked on Agamemnon (1402ff.), as the hunter becomes the hunted. The image will also describe Cassandra's victimization (1047), her pursuit of the origins of the curse (1187f.), and her vindication (1338); see n. 49; *LB* n. 335, *E* n. 116. For the image of the net, see Intro., pp. 45f., 65f., 91f.; *LB* n. 493, *E* n. 116.

131 *Fate: Moira* denotes not fate in general, as Fraenkel observes, "but the particular fate which causes the appropriate penalty to follow inevitably upon every sin. Moira is the goddess who sees to it that this connection between cause and effect, i.e., in the sphere of moral or legal obligations, between debt and payment, or between guilt and atonement, is safeguarded against any disturbance." This moralized conception of fate, and its evolution from a retributive force to a creative challenge—from fate to self-determination, in effect—will dominate the *Oresteia;* see n. 1021, 1025ff.; *E* n. 1055.

135ff *Artemis:* according to the account in the older epic Cycle, later adapted by Sophocles, Artemis was angered when Agamemnon shot one of her sacred deer and boasted that his archery was superior to hers—an act of rashness rather than of tragic destiny and choice. Here Agamemnon's action provokes Artemis as the goddess of childbirth (ironically invoked to fulfill a prophecy that involves the death of children); but it is as *Potnia Thêrôn*, the queen of wild beasts and a representative of Mother Earth, that Artemis will unleash her fury against the Olympians, the powers of the Sky.

138 *The eagles' feast*: the image will unite Thyestes' feast, which precipitated the curse, with the violence that follows in its wake, the murders of Iphigeneia, Cassandra and Agamemnon (242ff., 1475, 1531ff.). The image is consistently perverted: as a sacrament it is a slaughter, as a communal joy it nourishes desires for revenge; see 726ff., 813f., 1226ff.; *LB* n. 261, *E* n. 110.

148f The adjectives for the sacrifice of Iphigeneia make it seem unique; it is "unlawful" or "unaccustomed," but Tantalus and Atreus familiarized Argos with child-murder; it is "unattended by feasting" among the present celebrants, but it is part of the legacy of Thyestes' feast. The second term may also refer to offerings to the dead, presented to them but never consumed by them.

150 *The architect of vengeance*: images of crafts and artistry have a negative effect in A; either the practitioner is distraught (1030f.) or the skill in question makes an art of fear or guilt or death (1154ff., 1189ff., 1594). Orestes the mason (1306) will not have perfected his work until the end of the *Oresteia*; see *LB* n. 233, *E* n. 308.

156 Calchas invokes the muse of the *Iliad*, *Mênis*, Wrath or Fury, but here instead of implementing Zeus and Zeus's will she fights his agent to the death.

158 *Calchas clashed out*: the assonance between the prophet's name and the sound of his cries, suggested in the verb *eklangxen*, is typical of euphonic devices which Aeschylus employs throughout this chorus to give emphasis and solemnity; see n. 688ff.

161 *Zeus*: the Greek phrase, "Zeus, whoever he may be," is a formula that points to a religious mystery: the namelessness of the divinity, the blasphemy of naming him at all, and the incomprehensibility, the all-inclusiveness of his power.

169ff Ouranos, Kronos, and Zeus—grandfather, father and son in the embattled generations of the gods; see Intro., p. 12f. This theme of "the third victor," the one who throws his opponent three times to win the contest, will be exemplified in the fates of Agamemnon, Clytaemnestra and Orestes. For the motif of "three," see n. 245. Athletic imagery, drawn from sports like archery and charioteering that are combat skills as well, generally describes defeat in A, or a victory like Clytaemnestra's in the beacon-relay that spells defeat for her husband; see 346ff., 366ff., 624, 1211f. Archery, a deadlier sport, predominates; see *LB* n. 165, *E* n. 151.

182 *Ripeness:* in A the great ideal of *sôphrosunê* is degraded from the virtue of self-command (356) to discipline in its punitive sense—learning one's place or else (1451, 1652).

185ff *So it was that day,* etc. The responsion between this and the preceding stanza yokes the law of Zeus to its example, Agamemnon's quandary at Aulis. For the relationship between his will and the winds of destiny, see Intro., p. 18. The word *pneuma* means both the force of a wind and the vital spirit of a man; their "conspiracy" here may generate not only the present storm (189ff., 218ff.) but all the storms that follow (646ff., 804ff., 1410ff.), ending in the deluge that engulfs the house (1561ff.). In contrast see Cassandra's inspiration and its effects, 1182ff., 1302ff.; n. 1004; *LB* n. 203, *E* n. 250.

217 *The strap of Fate: Anangke* or Necessity as a universal force, though it may also be a compulsion designed to fit the individual. Attempts to derive the word from the verb "to strangle" find support in the traditional metaphor for Necessity, the harness, or as Aeschylus refines it, the strap that fastens the yoke to the neck.

226 *A bridal rite: proteleia;* see n. 71f. In Iphigeneia's sacrifice Lucretius saw a blood-wedding typical of barbaric religion:

> All too often Religion herself has wrought
> Unholy crimes. Elite captains of Greece
> Made foul the altar of the virgin goddess,
> Diana of the Crossways, when these princes
> Drew Iphigeneia's blood. As she stood there,
> Her virgin tresses neatly bound in place,
> With two ribbons outlining either cheek,

> *She saw her melancholy father, there,*
> *Before the altar, saw his ministers*
> *Hiding their knives; she saw her countrymen*
> *Crying at the sight of her. Speechless with fear,*
> *She sank down to the ground on bended knees.*
> *Little good it did her in this crisis,*
> *That she, Iphigeneia, had been his first-born child*
> *And conferred the name of "father" on the king.*
> *The heroes lifted and escorted her*
> *To the altar trembling, not that she should*
> *Be attended by the joyous wedding hymn—*
> *But be handled foully, an innocent girl*
> *At the due time of marriage, a sacrifice,*
> *Pitiful victim of the coup de grâce*
> *Delivered by her father—the good omen*
> *Of an auspicious sailing for the fleet.*
> *Such evil can Religion bring men to!*

—*De Rerum Natura*, I.82-101, trs. Palmer Bovie

In his "Dream of Fair Women" Tennyson describes the victim's feelings:

> *"I was cut off from hope in that sad place,*
> *Which men call'd Aulis in those iron years:*
> *My father held his hand upon his face;*
> *I, blinded with my tears,*
>
> *"Still strove to speak: my voice was thick with sighs*
> *As in a dream. Dimly I could descry*
> *The stern black-bearded kings with wolfish eyes,*
> *Waiting to see me die.*
>
> *"The high masts flicker'd as they lay afloat;*
> *The crowds, the temples, waver'd, and the shore;*
> *The bright death quiver'd at the victim's throat;*
> *Touch'd; and I knew no more."*

232 *Like a yearling:* a yearling kid was customarily sacrificed to Artemis for victory.

245 *Third libations, sang to Saving Zeus:* the first libation was offered to the Olympians, the second to the spirits of the dead, and the third to Zeus the Savior, invoked to harmonize the first two groups of deities. See n. 169ff. In A the motif of "three" or "triads" is perverted. Its nadir occurs in Clytaemnestra's murder of the king, accomplished with three blows (1407ff.) and offered to a trinity of gods (1459ff.). The salvation she administers is death (598, 1249); see *LB* n. 61, *E* n. 4.

248 *I cannot see it, cannot say:* there was a tradition, adopted by Euripides, Goethe, and Gerhart Hauptmann,

that Artemis intervened to save Iphigeneia, as God intervened to save Isaac from his father's knife, and spirited
her off to the Tauri on the Black Sea, where she served as
a priestess of the goddess. This tradition forms an alter-
native to the *Oresteia*, for according to it Iphigeneia, rather
than Athena, later absolves Orestes of his bloodguilt. She
represents the darker, sacrificial aspect of Artemis in Euripides' *Iphigeneia in Tauris*, restoring Orestes to his throne
in Argos, while migrating to Brauron in Attica, where she
continues to safeguard the image of the goddess and conduct a modified version of her bloody rites. Goethe's
Iphigeneia, however, represents the Olympian aspect of
the goddess; a child of the Enlightenment who has rejected Artemis' rites entirely, she redeems Orestes through
the gentle, beneficent arts of neoclassical humanism. As
an archetypal figure, then, Iphigeneia can represent either
of the two great powers dramatized by Aeschylus, the
Olympians or the Earth, though she gradually inclines
toward the gods. In Hauptmann's modern tetralogy on the
house of Atreus, she finally consigns the image of Artemis
to Apollo's shrine at Delphi, and through her own self-
sacrifice prepares the way for a total Olympian victory,
purged of the Fates and the forces of the Earth, and in
marked contrast to the *Oresteia*, where those forces un-
dergo a mutual struggle with the gods and ultimately enjoy
a mutual triumph; see Intro., pp. 87ff.; and Theodore Ziolkowski, "Hauptmann's *Iphigenie in Delphi*: A Travesty?"
The Germanic Review, xxxiv (1959), 105–23.

257 *Our midnight watch:* the motif will evolve from
Clytaemnestra's surveillance over Argos to the Areopagus
in *E* (720), the court whose night sessions keep eternal
vigilance over Athens.

265 *The womb of Mother Night:* also the source of the
Furies, who control this day (*E* n. 322). In *A* images of
infertility predominate, fathers bequeath their crimes to
children, and the Olympians derive their lethal power from
the legacy of the curse; see 378ff., 745ff., n. 311; *LB* n.
131ff., *E* n. 322.

271 *Expose your loyal hearts:* more loyal to Agamemnon
than to her.

281ff The beacons illuminate a geography of peril which
includes the Euripos Straits where Agamemnon murdered
Iphigeneia; Mount Kithairon where the infant Oedipus

was exposed; the Corinthian headlands where predators lay in wait for Theseus; the Gorgon-eyed Marsh reflecting the demon that threatened another Argive hero, Perseus (*LB* n. 818); and Spider Mountain which serves as a perfect vantage point for the Black Widow, Clytaemnestra (n. 309). Her beacons may contrast with the beacons set by Hypermnestra, another Argive wife. When the daughters of Danaos were forced to marry their cousins, Danaos instructed them to murder their new husbands on the wedding night. Only Hypermnestra refused. She was in love with Lynkeus, who had spared her virginity, and she helped him escape to the nearby city of Lyrkeia. She asked him to light a beacon when he had reached safety, promising to light a beacon from the heights of Argos in return. It was a testament to their faith, and the Argives commemorated it with a yearly torchlit festival. Clytaemnestra's beacons, in other words, may evoke a more constructive meaning far beyond this play. They will actually have forecast the final torchlit march of the Athenians and the Eumenides; perhaps they will remind us too of the *lampadêphoria* run in honor of Athena at the Panathenaic Festival—as if even now the queen were acting, quite unconsciously, in league with the gods' eventual designs.

Although the locations of some of the later stations in Clytaemnestra's chain are uncertain, the general direction is clear: west from Mount Ida near Troy, to Hermes' Rock on Lemnos, to Mount Athos in northern Greece; then south to Mount Makistos (presumably in Euboea, the large island off the coast of central Greece), over the Straits of Euripos to Mount Messapion (unidentified but evidently on the mainland), across the plain of Asôpos in Boeotia to Mount Kithairon near Thebes, to Mount Aigiplankton (presumably near the Isthmus of Corinth), and down the Saronic Gulf to Argos.

281 *Ida*: a mountain range which forms the southern boundary of the Troad; from its summit Zeus surveyed the Trojan war.

286 *The Saving Father's face*: Mount Athos, the weather mountain at the tip of a rocky peninsula in northern Greece, was a seat of Zeus. Its third position in the circuit may suggest it was the seat of Zeus the Savior, and the beacons may begin, ironically, as an auspicious omen.

303 *Marsh, the Gorgon's Eye:* like Mount Makistos ("Tremendous") and Mount Aigiplankton ("Where-the-Goats-Range"), the marsh has been variously identified, but each site reflects Clytaemnestra's imaginative power over geography.

307f *The headland beetling down the Saronic Gulf:* perhaps the lower foothills sloping down to the sea near Krommyon in the Megarid.

309 *The Black Widow's face:* Mount Arachnaion, "Spider Mountain," probably now Mount Saint Elias, the peak of the great ridge Arna north of Argos; see 1520. If Aeschylus locates the action in Mycenae, however, "Spider Mountain" may refer to the citadel itself, or to one of the two rocky horns that rise immediately above it. The heights, at any rate, might form a perfect observation post from which to ambush an unsuspecting enemy—hence, perhaps, the association with the spider and its web. Dorothy Thompson tells how she and the Greek foreman of their excavation "were walking back from the Argive Heraion when the citadel of Mycenae suddenly loomed up at the end of a gorge. Only the sunlight touching the acropolis when the rest was in shadow brought it out clearly in a menacing light. He remarked [in modern Greek] 'Mycenae is like a spider-web; it sees, but is not seen.'"

311 *The true son,* etc. The genealogical metaphor binds Agamemnon to his fathers' crimes and punishments. For the generative, sexual force of this entire passage, see P. G. Maxwell-Stuart, "Clytaemnestra's Beacon Speech: *Agamemnon,* 281–316," *La parola del passato,* cliii (1973), 445–52.

316 *First in the laps and last,* etc. Applied to the Torch Race this is almost a platitude. But perhaps Clytaemnestra has in mind another race still to be run—a race in which she hopes herself to be the final runner; see 346ff.

339 *Off guard at last:* Clytaemnestra's adjective can mean "unprotected," even "indefensible," as well as "released from standing guard," and so prepares us for her warnings that follow.

350 *The avenging dead:* her rhetorical plural may refer equally to the dead at Troy and to her daughter.

351 Clytaemnestra's ironies here may be prophetic not only of Agamemnon but of herself—driven to kill her husband yet somehow reluctant—but her personal torment will not emerge until she meets him at the gates; see Intro., pp. 23f.

378ff The passage is corrupt in Greek, but the general sense is that the gods repay the fathers' crimes by visiting them upon their children's heads. Such inherited guilt will bring down Agamemnon as well as Paris. Indeed the same forces overwhelm both men. "*Atê* is Harm or Ruin," as George Thomson explains, "or the blind infatuation . . . that leads man to commit some rash act which causes ruin. . . . When *Atê* is minded to destroy a man, she lays temptation [*Peitho*, Persuasion, Allurement] in his path to induce him to commit some definite and overt act of *hubris*—to play in fact the part of an *agent provocateur*." There is a strange equivalence between Iphigeneia and Helen as such agents (see the metaphor for their glances, 238f., 737f.). The sacrifice of his daughter was as irresistible to Agamemnon as the abduction of Helen was to Paris (see 220ff., 387ff.). He and Agamemnon become equal targets of the gods, while the king's offense—violating the sheer innocence of Iphigeneia—becomes that much worse.

Peitho recurs throughout the *Oresteia* in a range of personifications: the persuasive power of the chorus (n. 113), Helen's and Clytaemnestra's power to seduce and ruin, Orestes' power to deceive his enemies and avenge his father in *LB*, and finally Athena's power to reconcile the Furies in *E*. As a moral concept *Peitho* gradually evolves from a destructive to a constructive force; see Intro., pp. 16, 26, 33, 84; *LB* n. 714, *E* n. 893.

408ff *Prophets of the house*, etc. In describing Helen they recall the Trojan elders in the *Iliad* (3.146ff.), but are they at the gates as she arrives in Troy, or are they Argives watching what she leaves behind, the harried preparations for the war? Both, perhaps, and Helen's victims either way.

436 *The balance*: contrast the balance scales of justice, in which the elders have placed their hopes (250ff.); see 165, 567; *LB* n. 61, *E* n. 539.

474f *Just like a woman*, etc. A refrain that increases the shock of the queen's defiance later; see 587f.

479–92 Here we follow the majority of modern editors, against the ms. tradition, by giving these lines to the leader of the chorus.

483ff A *herald running*, etc. Aeschylus places time at the service of dramatic time; he telescopes the action to make the climax swifter.

500ff *No more arrows*, etc. Perhaps a specific allusion to the plague which Apollo visited on the Greeks when Agamemnon refused to release the daughter of Apollo's priest (*Iliad* 1.43ff.).

505 *Hermes*: invoked as the patron of heralds, who carries messages and in particular the word of Zeus. Some hint of his chthonic power as the Escort of the Dead, specified in *LB*, may also be implicit; see *LB*, notes 1, 126, 803; *E* n. 93.

516 *Zeus who brings revenge*: Zeus *Dikêphoros*, who brings vengeance to completion.

517 *Dug Troy down*, etc. Images of agriculture, like those of husbandry, have a destructive force in A. The breaking of Trojan soil will yield to the harvest of Agamemnon's house (1688f.), inexhaustible (959f.) and a perversion of the earth (1413ff.); see 197f., 491f., 658f., 967ff., 1043f.; *LB* n. 205, *E* n. 494.

518 *The shrines of her gods*, etc. Some editors would delete the line, which resembles a line in Aeschylus' *Persians* (811) spoken by Darius when he condemns the Persians for their desecration of the Greek shrines. The present line, to any members of the audience who remembered its earlier context, would have stressed the brutality of Agamemnon, while fulfilling Clytaemnestra's warning (342) and preparing for the king's demise.

528 *Pay the price twice over*: while Paris pays doubly with the loss of Helen and his home, the destruction is so complete that Troy pays double damages, the penalty for theft according to ancient Greek law. For the theme of "double-ness," see Intro., p. 44, 66f., 90ff.; A 820, 871, 1497ff.; *LB* notes 61, 373; *E* n. 4.

580 *I can taste the riches*: according to custom, the bearer of good tidings was rewarded; cf. *LB* 685ff.

598 *Open wide the gates*: which Cassandra will identify with the Gates of Hell (1314).

600 *The people's darling:* an erotic word in Greek and offensive when applied to the returning commander-in-chief.

606 *Our seal:* perhaps a reference to the royal treasures sealed up during the king's absence; but an erotic symbolism may also be implied—a denial of adultery with Aegisthus, which the chorus knows to be a fact; see 1660.

608 *Dyeing bronze,* etc. See 960, and Intro., p. 21.

609 *That is my boast:* in distinction to the herald's (568ff.).

613 *She only says what's right:* an intentional irony (the queen's words are appropriate but false), yet a modest one compared to hers.

620 *He's lost:* for Menelaus' subsequent adventures, see Intro., pp. 95f.; *LB* n. 1041.

632ff The herald's incoherence reflects his anguish and may indicate the confusion between the public purpose of the war and its heavy private toll.

648 *Fire and water:* lightning and the sea. The elemental opposites may also serve, though this is doubtful, as symbols for Athena (entrusted with Zeus's lightning-bolt) and Poseidon, who fought on behalf of the victorious Greeks throughout the war and now unite against them.

688ff *Helen . . . hell:* see Intro., p. 22. The Greek exemplifies the "etymological figure of speech" by which two similar words (one of them often a proper name) were taken to be similar in meaning. This belief was sanctioned by the superstition that a proper name could contain an omen of its owner's destiny (the *nomen-omen* principle, this Latin phrase itself being a *nomen-omen*): so in other Greek tragedies *Ai-as* (=Ajax) is compelled by fate to cry out *ai! ai!* in agony, and Pentheus is reduced to tragic grief (*penthos*). The belief is critically scrutinized by Plato in his *Cratylus.*

Here as elsewhere there is an implicit comparison between Clytaemnestra and Helen and, less obviously, Penelope. They form a curious pattern of contrasting and combining qualities: Helen abandoned her home and husband but returned in the end to live affectionately with him, as described in the *Odyssey*; Penelope was left at home by her husband and remained faithful to him through many trials; Clytaemnestra also was left at home but finally betrayed him. So Penelope and Clytaemnestra stand at the two extremes of loyalty and disloyalty, while Helen shares the qualities of both.

723ff It was the custom for children when they reached maturity to make a thank offering to their parents.

744ff *An ancient saying,* etc. Wealth and its dangers recur (457ff., 525, 804ff., 943ff.), until *E* 543ff., where the positive effects of legitimate prosperity are praised.

769ff *How to salute you,* etc. The chorus is apparently (the text is very uncertain in places) hinting to Agamemnon that he must be on his guard against hypocritical expressions of loyalty, primarily of course from Clytaemnestra. Many commentators have looked on Agamemnon as an admirable, though somewhat limited character— courteous, magnanimous, majestic, all in all a good man done to death by an evil woman. But others have questioned this, more persuaded by Agamemnon's background and his presentation here. He may be a brave man in the *Iliad* but not a man of self-control; he is a reckless monarch who vacillates between professions of piety and self-aggrandizement, a general who risks defeat by refusing sound advice; see Intro., pp. 16ff., 22ff., 38.

779ff *The good shepherd:* a trope, traditional since the time of Homer, for a defender of the people, but as applied to Agamemnon it may recall his husbandry as well—he sacrificed his daughter as he would a yearling kid (232) or lamb (1441f.).

796 *My accomplices,* etc. *Metaitioi;* see Intro., p. 23; *LB* n. 100, *E* n. 102. Clytaemnestra is *sunaitia,* responsible for Agamemnon's murder (1118); Zeus is *Panaitios,* responsible for all the violence in the play (1514).

799 *Their lots:* in the Athenian law courts each voter, having been given his voting-pebble, placed one hand over each of two urns (one to receive votes of acquittal, the other, condemnation). In this case the urn for acquittal, personified as a sentient being, is disappointed at not receiving the voting-pebble from the hand placed over it; see n. 45.

810 *The wild mare:* an allusion to the Greek warriors in the Trojan horse. Animal imagery, like that of husbandry, illustrates the brutalization of a victim and occasionally of the victimizer too; see 54ff., 604, 1063, 1127ff., 1237ff., 1500ff., 1694, and n. 49; *LB* n. 252, *E* n. 94.

827 *I dragged that man to the wars:* Odysseus tried to evade conscription for the Trojan War—out of prudence, more likely, than from any cowardice. Agamemnon is priding himself on his own prudence; society holds out a flattering mirror to the proud, but he knows a hypocrite when he sees one. The one loyal man he saw at Troy was Odysseus, and Agamemnon sings his praises—but as anyone in Athens would have known, Odysseus was an archdeceiver.

828 *Trace-horse:* stronger and better fed than the yoked horses at the center of the team, the trace-horse was depended on for effort in a crisis, as when the chariot would swerve around the post; see 1673.

838 *Right hand:* the customary gesture of worship.

859 *Geryon:* the tenth labor of Heracles was to fetch the cattle of Geryon, a mythical giant who, because he had three bodies, had to be killed three times before he died. As described in an Aeschylean fragment (37[74]): "he brandi␣ d three spears in his [right] hands, and, holding out tl␣ shields in his left and shaking his three crests, came ␣ like Ares in his power."

869ff *Our loyal brother-in-arms will take good care of him:* Clytaemnestra has sent Orestes away to give herself and Aegisthus freer rein, but she may also have wished to insure the safety of her son. Her agent "Strophios" (the name perhaps implies "a man of turns") lives in the deme of Delphi, and his words are Delphic indeed. As Clytaemnestra repeats his ambiguous warning here, his subject "you" may apply to herself and Aegisthus or to herself and Agamemnon; her hint of treason may also stir with lingering loyalty to her husband; see Intro., pp. 23f., *LB* n. 661f.

902 *Let the red stream flow:* as Robert Goheen reports, "For the performance of the *Agamemnon* at Syracuse shortly after World War I, Ettore Romagnoli as director sought the effect by having the carpet represent blood almost as literally as possible. The color was attained by dyeing material in the blood of an ox, producing a dark reddish brown. Instead of running the carpet straight back to the palace door, it was unrolled to form a sinuous track 'like a vein running down a muscular arm.'" ("Aspects of Dramatic Symbolism: Three Studies in the *Oresteia*," *American Journal of Philology*, lxxvi [1955], 116n.)

903 *The home he never hoped to see:* his fathers' house, which is the house of death.

908 *Leda:* Agamemnon's association of Leda with her daughter Clytaemnestra may remind us of Leda's legendary surrender to Zeus.

957ff With this speech Clytaemnestra not only avoids a sinister silence in which Agamemnon might reconsider his choice; she empowers him to pursue it; see Intro., p. 27, and notes following.

964 *I would have sworn to tread,* etc. In contrast to him (928f.).

966 *To bring that dear life back!* A strong encouragement if the life is Agamemnon's, a death sentence if it is Iphigeneia's.

967ff He is like the root of a tree returned to leaf, shading the house against the Dog Star's heat, but he is actually the root of crime that reinvigorates the bloodlust in the race.

972 *The bitter virgin grape:* a reference to the blood of Iphigeneia, the unripe virgin girl, that may also imply a reversal of the natural order of things; see 1410ff.

995 *Not fit for the lyre:* morbid, not associated with festive songs inspired by the lyre-god Apollo; see n. 1077.

1004ff *Even exultant health,* etc. According to the doctrine of the Golden Mean, the ancient Greeks believed that excess and deficiency should be avoided (see 748ff.), even in matters of health (i.e., too much health was dangerous, or in terms of Shakespeare's pun: "goodness, growing to a plurisy, / Dies in his own too-much"). One should reduce such excess, as the wise sea-captain (in the following lines) jettisons some of his excessive freight. Behind the passage may lie the metaphor of the ship of state (see 185ff., 786ff.), but Agamemnon's role as captain is undermined by his association with another metaphor, the storm; see n. 185ff.; *LB* n. 203, *E* n. 250.

1017ff *A man's lifeblood,* etc. A recurrent theme that stresses not only the fragility of life but the futility of vengeance as a way of life. It will contrast with the rejuvenation that men enjoy under the new dispensation of Athenian justice; see *LB* 66ff., *E* 655ff.

1021 *The master-healer*: Asclepios acquired such skill as a physician that he restored a dead man to life, and was consequently struck dead by Zeus with a thunderbolt because his action disturbed the natural order, personified as *Moira*, Fate, who dominates the remainder of this chorus. The notion of a kind of settled "departmentalization" of the functions of gods and men is a logically necessary element in polytheism. Asclepios trespassed on "the department" of *Thanatos*, god of death (as his father, Apollo, does in Euripides' *Alcestis*), and being mortal, is sacrificed to *Thanatos* for his transgression. Similarly (in the following lines) it is not within the "departmental" powers of the human heart to speak out for itself; the principle of *Moira* forbids it.

1036f *The god who guards our dearest treasures*: apparently a reference to Zeus *Ktêsios*, who protects the house and its possessions. Later, as Clytaemnestra's intentions become clearer, the god will yield his domestic authority to the ancestral spirit of revenge.

1038 *Heracles*, etc. Heracles was sold in bondage by Hermes to Omphale, queen of Lydia. Gourmandizer that he was, he accepted his slave's rations and served his mistress well by ridding her kingdom of the dangers that beset it.

1056 Clytaemnestra's hearthstone rivals Apollo's Navelstone at Delphi.

1066 *The cutting bridle*: a sharp-edged bit used in the breaking-in of high-spirited horses.

1077 *Who wants no part of grief*: Apollo required songs of joy, not mourning and the dirge.

1079 *Apollon = apollon* ("destroying"); an example of *nomen-omen*; see n. 688ff.

1085 *Where have you led me now?* Apollo *Aguiatês*, Guardian of the Highways, has led her to her death.

1105 *Rescue's far away*: probably a reference to Orestes; see 1679ff.

1115ff Cassandra's broken utterances draw the chorus into her train of thought, forcing them to supplement her fragmentary vision; see Intro., pp. 29f., and the comparable power of Ophelia's broken utterances in *Hamlet* (IV.v.7-13):

> "Her speech is nothing,
> Yet the unshapèd use of it doth move
> The hearers to collection; they aim at it,
> And botch the words up fit to their own thoughts,
> Which, as her winks and nods and gestures yield them,
> Indeed would make one think there might be thought,
> Though nothing sure, yet much unhappily."

1120 *Stone them dead:* a death reserved for the most infamous criminals, since it denoted an expiation of their crime by the entire community; see 1648f.

1145 *Her son:* Itys, son of Philomela (or in another version, Procne). Philomela was turned into a nightingale after she had inadvertently tricked her husband, Tereus, into eating his son's flesh. The allusion reinforces the earlier allusion to Thyestes' feast, but it also distinguishes Philomela from Cassandra, and she insists upon the difference. Philomela was saved by the gods from internecine strife and made immortal with her song—in Keats's words, "thou wast not born for death, immortal Bird! / No hungry generations tread thee down." But Cassandra is condemned to the house of Atreus, her god will abandon her and make her sing in hell.

1182f *Clear and sharp,* etc. As the wind drives a wave toward the rising sun, so Cassandra's prophetic powers bring catastrophe to light. *Lampros* can mean "keen" for wind and "clear" for oracles.

1196 *The frenzy that began it all:* see 222, 387f., 808f., Intro., pp. 30ff., and D. H. Lawrence's observation to Lady Ottoline Morell, March 1(?), 1915 (*Collected Letters,* ed. Harry T. Moore [New York: The Viking Press, 1962], I, 326): "Do you know Cassandra in Aeschylus and Homer? She is one of the world's great figures, and what the Greeks and Agamemnon did to her is symbolic of what mankind has done to her since—raped and despoiled and mocked her, to their own ruin. It is not your brain you must trust to, nor your will—but to that fundamental pathetic faculty for receiving the hidden waves that come from the depths of life, and for transferring them to the unreceptive world. It is something which happens below the consciousness, and below the range of the will—it is something which is unrecognized and frustrated and destroyed."

1218 *Once I betrayed him I could never be believed:* possibly too (but this is only a conjecture) Apollo then added the cruel condition that if anyone did say he believed her, it would be a sign that she was about to suffer a violent death: this would explain her outburst of woe when the chorus accepts the truth of her divinations shortly afterward.

1232 A *lion,* etc. Aegisthus.

1237ff *That detestable hellhound:* like Cerberus (*Theogony* 769–74), the warder of Hell, but Cerberus could be drugged and so eluded; no one returns from Clytaemnestra's "Gates of Death" (1314).

1243 *Viper,* etc. The *amphisbaina,* a terrifying mythical snake with a head at both ends of its body. Its name means "going backward or forward," and it has been seen as a symbol of inconstancy and adultery.

1244 *Scylla:* a female monster with six ravenous doglike heads and twelve feet, lurking in a cave above a narrow strait of the sea, as described in the *Odyssey* (12.85–100). Aeschylus relocates the outlandish, superhuman dangers of the *Odyssey* within the confines of Agamemnon's hearth and personifies them in his wife; see n. 1391ff.

1261 *The Healer:* presumably Apollo. Agamemnon is now apportioned to *Thanatos,* Death.

1266 *I don't see who,* etc. The leader is reluctant, perhaps obtuse, but Agamemnon may seem well defended, and his only male opponent, Aegisthus, is inept.

1279 *Trappings:* over Cassandra's body she might have worn the *agrênon,* the netlike woolen robe worn by soothsayers; its resemblance to a hunting-net would reinforce her image as a victim (n. 129).

1297 *Not to serve at my father's altar:* Cassandra, the daughter of Agamemnon's enemy, resembles his own daughter, Iphigeneia: both are his victims; both are brides of death and prophets in effect, but Cassandra's impact on the future is more constructive.

1299 *The first blood drawn:* the *prosphagma,* the blood-offering to the dead which was preliminary to a hero's funeral, or the victim itself.

1302ff *There will come another*, etc. On the relationship between suffering and regeneration in Cassandra's vision, see Intro., pp. 32f. Agamemnon's body will be *huptiasma*, "laid low" in death and "upturned" like hands in supplication, calling forth his son.

1337ff *I cried out, not from fear*, etc. According to Attic custom, "only if . . . the cry of distress has been raised, can evidence of the deed of violence be later laid before a court of law" (Fraenkel).

1391ff Clytaemnestra's speech is a phantasmagoria of Homeric images, distorted as in a witch's mirror that turns the queen from a triumphant warrioress in the *Iliad* to a hostess more sinister than any in the *Odyssey*. Agamemnon resembles both Greek and Trojan warriors in their agonies (Diomedes, *Iliad*, 5.113; Hippodamas, 20.403f.)—as if he were vulnerable to friend and foe alike. Vaunting over his body Clytaemnestra travesties the delight of Menelaus (the brother Agamemnon needs)when he receives a prize at Patroclus' funeral games: "his anger/was softened, as with dew the ears of corn are softened/in the standing corn growth of a shuddering field" (23.597–99, trs. Lattimore), an image of fresh and unsophisticated joy. As Clytaemnestra revels in Agamemnon's blood she recalls the rains of blood that Zeus hurls down when Hector is about to rout the Greeks (11.52ff.). And each stage in her rites of welcome, her bathing and cloaking of her guest, perverts the rituals of the *Odyssey*. Her "feasting" in revenge is a violation of an Odyssean code that prohibits boasting over one's fallen enemy. Perhaps her greatest perversion overturns the "marvelous simile" which celebrates Odysseus' reunion with his wife, "his dear wife, clear and faithful, in his arms,/longed for/as the sunwarmed earth is longed for by a swimmer/spent in rough waters where his ship went down/under Poseidon's blows, gale winds and tons of sea" (23.232–35, trs. Fitzgerald). Her cup of welcome, customarily sacred to the gods, is a vessel of the curse (1420ff.); see 1275f., and n. 71f.; *LB* n. 17, *E* n. 110ff.

1431f *What poison*, etc. Madness was often attributed in antiquity to the eating of some noxious plant or mineral.

1456 *Loved ones*: probably her friends and allies in general.

1467 *The golden girls,* etc. Clytaemnestra's sarcastic plural enlarges on Chryseis, whose name derives from the word for gold, the daughter of Apollo's priest. Agamemnon appropriated her and incurred Apollo's anger at the outset of the *Iliad.*

1472 *The swan:* the bird of Apollo, reputed to sing only when about to die.

1497 *The twinborn sons of Tantalus:* here Agamemnon and Menelaus.

1517ff *Oh my king,* etc. Repeated 1542ff.; the second line may echo the elders' greeting of the king (769). In these closing scenes they display the more admirable side of Agamemnon (1575ff.) to dramatize their resistance to Clytaemnestra and their former dependence on the king (1479f.), and perhaps to provide the rites of burial he requires. They are his only hope since, as Rose explains, his successor is an enemy, his son a child and an exile, and his widow his assassin, who will deny him rites and mutilate his body; see *LB* 428ff.

1539 *Black war:* the elders return to the themes of the opening chorus. Here the god of war (53) is internecine, not international, and even harder to appease.

1582ff *Our daughter,* etc. Clytaemnestra's omission of the fact that Agamemnon murdered Iphigeneia only heightens her irony; the dead were thought to find an affectionate welcome in the underworld from the loved ones who had gone before them.

1585 *The ferry:* Charon's ferry across the river Styx.

1588 *Charge meets countercharge:* the chorus' charge that Clytaemnestra murdered Agamemnon has been met by her charge that he murdered Iphigeneia.

1592 *The one who acts must suffer:* the maxim, a commonplace since Hesiod, summarizes the *lex talionis,* the law of retaliation. In A it has a retaliatory force indeed, striking both at Agamemnon's enemies and at himself; see 523f., 1555ff., 1691f.; *LB* n. 320, *E* n. 877.

1603 *Purged,* etc. Perhaps an allusion to the purgations of the Mysteries. *Agamemnon* may be seen as a savage parody of these rites. The queen supplants the king of death, the sacred marriage weds her to the curse, the sacred birth revives her daughter's ghost at the Styx, and men and gods unite in mutual destruction; see A n. 1, LB n. 950, E n. 494.

1610ff *The Furies' tangling robes.* For the interweaving of the Furies and the justice of the gods, see Intro., pp. 12ff., 16f., 22, 37, 47, 66ff., 77f., 86ff. It is a paradoxical relationship, and Aegisthus, ironically, is one of the first to introduce it; as he boasts he wove the fatal plot together, he shuttles from "the Furies' tangling robes" to "the nets of Justice."

1612ff *Atreus, this man's father,* etc. Despite Aegisthus' claims to clarity and precision, his antecedents blur and his ironies are so indiscriminate that one may wonder where his loyalties actually lie—with Thyestes who suffered outrage, or with Atreus who committed it. See Intro., pp. 38f.

1614 *Atreus' brother challenged him,* etc. Thyestes, after seducing Atreus' wife, Aëropê, stole the golden lamb which was the warrant of Atreus' title to the throne.

1623 *A feast for gods:* the precedent for Thyestes' feast was the cannibalistic feast that Tantalus presented to the gods.

1634 *Pleisthenes:* since the name of this unidentified ancestral figure means "having the most strength," it may have been a title of Atreus himself or a dynastic title for the sons of Pelops.

1662ff *Orpheus,* through the power of his song, could enchant the animals and rocks and trees, and they would follow in his footsteps. The irony Aegisthus trains on the chorus is well summarized by Denniston-Page: "Orpheus *led on* all that heard him, you will be *led off* to execution; *he* delighted with the charm of his voice, *you* infuriate me with your barking."

1690 *Our lives are based on pain:* see 961.

1695 A muted echo of her former exultation (352).

1706 *Cock:* the type of swaggerer that fights with his own kind, a figure of licentiousness and strife; see E 870ff.

1708 *Set the house in order,* etc. An echo, perhaps, of the certitude with which the queen invited Agamemnon to his doom (906).

THE LIBATION BEARERS

TIME: SEVERAL YEARS, etc. Ancient commentators took Orestes to be about eighteen or twenty, and Electra to be some years older.

1 "Underground Hermes," the Escort of Souls, controls the spirits of the dead; but Hermes will mediate between the dead and the living and assume his more Olympian aspects as the god of messengers, stratagems and battle— his brother Apollo's agent, hence the comrade of Orestes. Perhaps a "herm" (a statue dedicated to him) was visible on-scene; see notes 126, 803; A n. 505, E n. 93.

2 *The fathers' power*: ambiguous; a reference both to Father Zeus and to 'the domains of Orestes' father, Agamemnon.

7 *Inachos*: the chief river of Argos. Young men in ancient Greece customarily on reaching manhood dedicated a lock of their long, youthful hair to the local river-god. Here Orestes combines this ceremony with another rite of offering a lock to a dearly loved dead person.

11ff *What's this?* etc. The one manuscript in which this play has survived begins here. The previous lines are restored from scattered quotations preserved in the works of other Greek writers. The full speech may have been much longer (like the prologue to *E*).

17 *Bearing cups*: libations will turn from rites of aversion to rites of invocation; see 86ff., 159ff. and n., 347f., 525f., 565 and n.; A n. 1391ff., E n. 110. In *LB* earlier images renew their destructive power, while (as if influenced by Cassandra) they gain a new potential. They are transitional in the *Oresteia*—humanized, often psychologized with an intimacy that carries pain and promise both, before they can be harmonized in the final play.

23 *Pylades*: son of Strophios, prince of Phokis, where Orestes had been in exile since before his father's death. In the legends Pylades plays a variety of roles, from Orestes' host to the future husband of Electra, but here he appears as the spokesman of Apollo, as the austerity of his single utterance (887ff.) will suggest.

28ff The tearing of the cheeks with one's fingernails, the beating of the breast, and the ripping of clothes were signs of violent mourning in the ancient world; see n. 413ff.

42 Clytaemnestra's chambers, perhaps the depths of her conscience, are likened to a prophet's cell; for the "interiorization," the personalization of themes from A, see Intro., pp. 64ff. In *LB* omens are replaced by dreams, and dreams will increase the nightmares of reality, but they will also empower characters to pursue their separate destinies; see 510ff., 915ff., 1053; A n. 91, E n. 42.

61 *Justice . . . turns the scales:* the supreme principle of the *Oresteia* here is reinforced by the theme of light-in-darkness (see n. 137), and the motif of the "triad" (here dawn, dusk and night). In *LB* the "triad" will suggest a totality of retaliation, adding a lethal third blow to Orestes' double onslaught of revenge (321, 1064ff., see n. 373). But while "triads" pervert the harmonizing effects of the third libation poured to Saving Zeus, they may also imply a promise of that harmony, which will be fulfilled in the third, final play; see notes 312ff., 565; A n. 245, E n. 4. Similarly the metaphor of the scales of justice stresses the counterweight, the revenge dealt by Orestes, then felt by him in turn, while it may reflect the rightful balance of opposing claims that he acknowledges (448); see A n. 436, E n. 539.

69ff *Like infection . . . no cure:* the familiar imagery from A, but now the sickness will extend to madness, the cure to matricide. Suffering may be homeopathic, however; Apollo may become a healer; see 285ff., 458ff., 526, 1059f.; A n. 107, E n. 65f.

70ff Violation of virginity is also an example of an irreparable act of aggression. The chorus women are beginning to think of their own suffering as slaves captured in war. They are not born slaves, since born slaves had no fathers (see 75), but gentlewomen, hence their ease and equality with Electra.

74 *Yoke:* the image will suggest not only the oppressions of fate (785) but also conjugal joy (584) and the liberation of society (951), though Orestes must be yoked to further torment at the end; see A n. 49, E n. 116.

86 *I pour*, etc. A ritual mixture of meal, honey and oil offered to the gods and to the dead.

95ff The avoidance of looking back suggests the ritual casting away of the refuse after a propitiatory sacrifice, not simply household cleaning. If Electra treats the libations in this way, she implies that there is something abominable about them.

100 *Join me here:* as *metaitioi*, here partners rather than accomplices; see A n. 796, E n. 102.

107 *Like an altar:* it might be impious to think of a tomb as an altar, and the women demonstrate their reverence at once.

116 Electra's reluctance to name Orestes—as if she had never thought of him as the avenger—is matched by the reluctance of the women (178ff.), who may never have thought he would return.

122 *Judge or avenger, which?* An important moral distinction, too subtle for the chorus, which disregards it here.

123ff Hate and love in equal measure, they seem to say, as if one emotion might reinforce the other.

126ff *Herald king:* like Orestes she prays to Hermes, but here as the god of messengers who mediates between the living and the dead.

130 *The high watch:* perhaps the ancestral powers attached to their house, not the dead in general.

131ff *Earth*, etc. Images of fertility and parenthood waver between destruction and creation. Heredity is both a fatal legacy and a challenge that a person forge his destiny himself; see 211, 382 and n., 529ff., 630ff., 674 and n., 915; A n. 265, E n. 322.

137 *The light that saves our house:* Orestes is the *phôs*, the man who brings the *phaos*, the light of salvation, but his light is plunged in darkness at the last; see 326, 408, 850, 950 and n.; A n. 25, E n. 7.

159ff This difficult passage, a "polar expression," seems to mean, "Let our lamentations, accompanied by libations, have the positive force of preserving what is good and the negative force of preventing what is evil." So the women implement Electra's prayer for good, her curse against the bad (n. 17). Clytaemnestra's offering, meant to soothe the dead, enlivens them and their avengers; the act of mourning becomes a call to action; the grave itself, the region of oblivion, becomes a source of personal identity and power.

165 The *bow of Scythia*, named after the people of South Russia who originated it, was shaped with a double curve, like a Cupid's bow, to give it extra torsion. As Heracles regularly used one, the chorus may be thinking of him here, invoking him in his aspect of the liberator, which he shared with Perseus; see n. 818. Imagery of athletics seems to have an optimistic effect—each sport seems to bring Orestes closer to victory, but his charioteering and his archery will bring him failure in the end. Wrestling seems to predominate in this play about engagement and embrace; see 343, 378, 485f., 676, 853 and n., 1019ff., 1031; A n. 169ff., E n. 151.

195ff The turbulence of Electra's emotions, as Anne Lebeck observes, forecasts those of her brother at the end of the play.

203 *Sailors:* imagery of sailing takes an auspicious course until it meets "the tempest in the race" (1065); see 643f., 810ff.; A notes 185ff., 1004; E n. 250.

205 A *mighty tree:* images from planting and agriculture tend to be personal, genealogical, hopeful. Even when Orestes' pain begins to "bloom" (1004), he is "armed with the branch and wreath" of suppliants to Delphi (1032); see 264ff., 490f.; A n. 517, E n. 494.

206ff *Tracks,* etc. The thick dust around Agamemnon's tomb, where no wise Argive would go for fear of Clytaemnestra's wrath, would take a clear impression. The recognition of special characteristics in a footprint, which Euripides found ludicrous (*Electra*, 503ff.), might have been common practice in an epoch of skilled hunters and trackers. Moreover, Electra finds a resemblance in the contours of her brother's print, not its size.

233 *Work of your own hand:* presumably what Orestes now displays as proof of his identity is a garment woven by Electra with a distinctive design of wild animals, sent to him as a gift during his exile or given to him at birth as a swaddling band. Images of crafts and artistry may have a constructive effect in *LB*—the smith of Fate may counteract his work in *A* (*A* 1564f., *LB* 628ff.); Clytaemnestra's masterwork, the robes, will stimulate Orestes' conscience even as they drive him mad; see Intro., pp. 62ff. *LB* 975ff., A n. 150, E n. 308.

240ff *Four loves in one*, etc. So Andromache praises Hector in the *Iliad* (6.429f.), hoping to persuade him not to fight and jeopardize their family. Electra will stir her brother into combat; he will ultimately reconstitute his family and his people.

244 *My sister*: Iphigeneia, sacrificed by Agamemnon. In other accounts Electra has a living sister, Chrysothemis, who is often seen as her foil, weak, conventional. Here, as Sidgwick says, "Iphigeneia dead, Electra is alone."

248 *Saving Zeus, Third Zeus*: see A n. 245.

252 *Viper*: literally *echidna*, here perhaps like the ravenous monster of that name—half beautiful woman, half grim speckled snake—described by Hesiod. The image of the snake strangling an eagle would seem to reverse the common emblem of the victory of good over evil—an eagle strangling a snake; but see Intro., pp. 66f., 91f.; *LB* n. 514.

Animal imagery will distinguish the children from their parents in *A*, stressing their weakness (Electra as a dog that fawns on hope, *LB* 195, vs. Clytaemnestra who fawned in treachery), their vengefulness (Orestes as the bull, *LB* 280, vs. the cow that gored his father), and their dignity (as the regal lion, *LB* 925, vs. the ravening lion, Agamemnon), but Orestes must be hunted by the hounds of his mother's curse, 1054f., the final revenge of Artemis for the work of Zeus's winged hounds in *A*. The pattern which had a brutalizing effect (*A* n. 810) is more suggestive here of natural energies that can go either way; see *E* n. 94.

261 *Banquets*: the image is now associated with forms of propitiation, even nourishment, as well as with Thyestes' feast and its effects; see 470ff., 531ff., 1067; A n. 138, E n. 110ff.

262 *Destroy the eagle's brood*, etc. Zeus depends on the eagle to embody his auguries and on kings to represent his power among men.

272 *In the fire*: not burning on the funeral pyre, as Rose observes, but burned alive in what the Romans called the *tunica molesta*, the dress of pitch.

282ff This vividly phrased passage describes the two main punishments for those who become polluted by refusing to exact vengeance for a kinsman's murder (a relic of a primitive state of society before the community as a whole punished murderers according to a legal process). The first punishment consists of foul and maddening sicknesses (including a kind of leprosy), and the second, forcible ejection from the community.

312ff The movement of the chant (see Intro., pp. 52ff.) is reflected in its designations: it begins as a *goös*, a wailing lament that carries glory and revenge; as it changes to a *thrênos*, a formal dirge, its vengeance can be felt like a double lash, then a stabbing arrow, yet it has a constructive moral power too; it conveys a *nomos*, a custom of revenge that turns into a *stasis*, a popular revolt in behalf of justice. The goal of the chant is to become a *paiôn*, a battle-song that may be a thanksgiving hymn as well. Its structure, the responsion of its stanzas and its voices, may be "choreographed" as follows:

```
IA. [Chorus]        IB. [Chorus]        II. Chorus—G       III. Orestes
    Orestes—A           Orestes—D           Electra—H          Electra   —J
    Chorus—B            Chorus—E            Orestes—I          Chorus
    Electra—A           Electra—D           Chorus—I           Orestes
    [Chorus]            [Chorus]            Electra—G          Electra   —J
    Orestes—C           Orestes—F           Chorus—H           Chorus
    Chorus—B            Chorus—E                               Chorus—K
    Electra—C           Electra—F                              Chorus—K
```

The growing unity of the celebrants is embodied in this structure. It describes not only a single triad but repeated triads, and each grows tighter, more interlocking as the sense of crisis gathers head. In IA the women act as midwives, instilling energy into the children's unrealistic dreams of glory. In IB they merely reflect the children's changing moods, as Electra asserts her leadership and invokes her mother's force. But in the second, central section Orestes is surrounded by excruciating pressures. The women break into an agony of mourning in response to the agony of Electra, helpless during her father's murder but incensed; while her account of his maimed rites, in turn, provokes the women's urging of Orestes. The stanzas in this section develop a double motion. Taken in responsion, they surround him, tearing him between his father's and his mother's claims; taken in order, the stanzas thrust him on to action. He emerges as the leader, and Electra and the women consolidate behind him in the third, final movement, until the women recoil and leave the children to their coda, their antiphonal fury of revenge.

320 *The one who acts must suffer:* the maxim expounded by the chorus in A that every deed brings its retribution; see A 1592 and n. The maxim leads the law of Zeus—that we must suffer into truth—into its negative, punitive extreme, the *lex talionis;* but it will become a law of compensation—that we may suffer into self-fulfillment and social justice; see E n. 877.

321 *Three generations:* refers in a general sense to venerable antiquity. It may also recall the motif of the three generations of conflict referred to in A, here with special reference to the house of Atreus; see A 169ff. and n.

330 *The fire:* the funeral pyre.

335 *Hunt,* etc. The image returns to hunt the hunters down; it will be turned against Orestes too (911, 1054f.), but not before it acquires more personal, creative senses—the search for vital recognitions, like Electra's "tracking" of her brother (206ff.) and, in effect, the pursuit of one's destiny; see A n. 129, E n. 116.

342 *And the pain is equal, whose is worse?* The construction, like the tragic choice itself, echoes through the *Oresteia;* see A 212, E n. 155.

343 *Third last fall:* see A n. 169ff.

350 The Lycians were Anatolian allies of the Trojans.

359 *The giant kings who judge,* etc. Minos, Rhadamanthos, Aiakos.

371 *The Blest,* etc. The Hyperboreans, a legendary people who worshiped Apollo and were believed by the ancient Greeks to inhabit an earthly paradise in the far north of Europe.

373 *The double lash:* perhaps a reference to the positive and negative reasons for revenge that follow here—the death of Agamemnon, the brutality of Aegisthus and Clytaemnestra; or the double lamentation of Orestes and Electra that will lash their father back to life and lash themselves to fury. In A the pattern of "doubling" suggests retaliation; here it adds a sense of recrimination and perhaps of future restoration too; see n. 61, 925f., 964.

382 *For parents of revenge revenge be done:* this difficult line, as Anne Lebeck observes, "applies to both parents: fulfillment of revenge for the father, for the mother penalty paid in full. And this is the dilemma of Orestes. The task of avenging his father entails wronging his mother; he cannot do one without the other." His reluctance to name his mother as his victim (425ff.) will continue until he drops his disguise and faces Clytaemnestra as her son (886).

383 *Cries of triumph:* Clytaemnestra's former exultation turns against her; see 929; *A* n. 30, *E* n. 1053.

384f The man and the woman here are Aegisthus and Clytaemnestra.

413ff Persian professional mourners were renowned for the violence of their lamentations. The women here accomplish the rites which were denied the king at the time of his death.

428f *Hands lopped,* etc. A reference to the practice of mutilation—cutting off the hands and feet of a dead enemy and tying them on a rope around his neck and under his armpits, to prevent his ghost from pursuing the killer.

443ff *I am calling you, my father:* this and the following lines have the force of an evocation to raise the ghost of a dead person from his tomb as in the evocation of Darius in *Persians,* 640ff. (where Darius' ghost actually appears on the scene).

461 *Their bloody strife:* an echo of the war at Troy (*A* 697) that magnifies the internecine war in Argos and the heroism of Orestes; see notes 884f., 951; *E* n. 771.

470 *The sacred feast:* offered to the earth and providing a kind of sustenance to the dead.

474 *My bridal wine:* presumably Electra was forbidden to marry, lest she bear a son who might avenge her father.

477 *Persephone:* daughter of Demeter and wife of Pluto, ruler of Hades; perhaps because she returns to life each spring, she may be invoked as a source of power from the dead; see Intro., pp. 69f.

493 *Corks to the net:* this dominant symbol begins to emerge in a more optimistic light; see Intro., pp. 65f.

510f *Some terror . . . groping through the night:* the rare Greek word "night-wandering" (or "causing wanderings in the night") is repeated from the opening scene of *A* (15); now Clytaemnestra feels the fear she had induced, and the torches must be lit to give her comfort.

514 *A snake:* the symbol begins to dominate the play. In general the serpent was an emblem of relentless, silent power coming from under the ground, often sinister and harmful, but sometimes, as in its association with the god of healing, Asclepios, it served beneficial purposes. In *LB* it will be associated equally with the Furies and Orestes, vengeance and regeneration, a blend of powers that Aeschylus begins to develop within the dream of Clytaemnestra. In the earlier, lyric account of Stesichorus, she dreams simply that she saw a snake and from its blood-stained head appeared a king of the line of Pleisthenes. Here she bears the snake that is her son, her progeny and her death in one. Like the female viper, according to Greek belief, she kills her mate and then is murdered by their offspring in revenge; see 987ff.

550f *Speak Parnassian . . . the native tones of Delphi:* actually Phokis in Greek, the district in which Delphi lies. Although it is unlikely that Orestes adopts a dialect, much of what he will say at the gates is Delphic indeed— cryptic, charged with moral resonance; see Intro., pp. 56ff.; and notes to lines 657 through 687f.

553 *Ridden by a curse:* and so, like a man possessed, either not capable of courtesy or wary of any visitation. Orestes' ruse of waiting at the doors may help him to determine Aegisthus' whereabouts or rally indignant citizens to his side, but the plan is far-fetched and rendered worthless in the sequel.

565 *Our third libation poured to Saving Zeus:* third after Thyestes' feast and Agamemnon's assassination (1064ff.), or third after Agamemnon's murder of Iphigeneia and Clytaemnestra's murder of the king. That a murder should be a libation is a savage irony, of course, though like a third libation poured to Zeus, it will ultimately mitigate the sufferings of the house.

572ff In all three plays of the *Oresteia* the central chorus involves the relationship between the Furies and the justice of the gods, yet their relationship is slowly changing from one of antagonism to one of mutual dependence. The chorus that ushered home Agamemnon (A 977–1003) conscripted justice beneath the Furies, and the Furies killed the king. The present chorus, that ushers home his son, makes justice depend upon the Furies for success. See E 506–71, and Intro., p. 56.

576 *Torches*: such abnormal and ominous lights in the sky as meteors and comets.

587 *Althaia*: daughter of Thestios and Eurythemis, was a notorious example of an unloving mother: in anger at the death of one of her brothers she caused the death of her son Meleager by burning a log on which his life was magically dependent.

597 *Scylla* of Megara (not the monster with the same name in the *Odyssey*) betrayed her father, Nisos (whose life depended on a magical lock of hair on his head), to Minos, king of Crete, when he was besieging their city. Her motive was love, according to legend, and her crime betrayed her people. Aeschylus, however, makes Scylla the object of a bribe, and her crime remains quite private, in contrast to Clytaemnestra's greater guilt and destructiveness that follow.

614 *Lemnos*: as a third example of feminine ruthlessness and treachery, the chorus cites the abominable massacre of husbands by the women of Lemnos.

645 *Whoever rules the house*: Orestes' preference will recoil; the woman, not the man, will appear first and she will be the master.

649 Electra's presence here is arbitrary, though it may lend ironic point to Clytaemnestra's command (702) and fulfill Orestes' wishes (566f.). There is no stronger evidence for her remaining, however, and her likely disappearance from the action may represent a lapse on Aeschylus' part. Unless, of course, it is suggestive in itself—as if Electra might serve to summon Clytaemnestra to the stage, and then must leave Orestes to his mother for maturing. See Intro., p. 66.

652 *We have warm baths*, etc. Clytaemnestra corrects the porter's manners; she attends to the strangers' needs before determining who they are. The queen may recall the pleasures extended to Odysseus by Alcinous, king of

Phaeacia—"changes of dress, warm baths, and downy beds" (*Odyssey* 8.249, trs. Fitzgerald), though such comforts were simply customary. Clearly Clytaemnestra recalls her lethal welcome of Agamemnon and Cassandra in A.

656 *I will stir them on*: Clytaemnestra's verb can mean to share, or to make common, defile, commit adultery; she repeats it (703).

657 *Daulis*, etc. A precinct in Phokis on the road from Thebes to Delphi. Verrall has made the intriguing suggestion that Orestes met the stranger where Oedipus met his father. So another parent's destiny is sealed, another son's as well, but here the son will suffer and succeed.

661f *Strophios, a Phocian*: "the man of turns" has returned, no longer the queen's ally but an accomplice in her death; see A n. 869ff.

668f *An alien*, etc. Orestes may stress the pains of exile to indict his mother more severely.

671 *The man's been mourned*, etc. By Argos since his father's death, by his sister and the chorus at the outset of this play, now perhaps by himself as he sees what he must do.

674 *A parent ought to know*: a challenge—the parent worth her salt would recognize her son—that conveys a sense of hurt as well: she might even show concern. She answers him in kind; see Intro., p. 57ff.

687f *Known*, etc. *Gnôtos* can mean either known or kindred.

714 *Persuasion: Peitho* in her aspect of cunning deception, here employed in a righteous cause; see A n. 378ff., E n. 893.

762 *Rejoicing all the way!* There is an ambiguity in the syntax here; it implies that both the nurse and Aegisthus are to feel joy at the message. Then Aegisthus' joy should make him come unattended by his bodyguard, eager to hear further details of the good news (cf. A 320f.), and the nurse's joy will give verisimilitude to the message (763). At 764 the nurse naturally expresses surprise that the chorus-leader should tell her to rejoice in reporting Orestes' death, but is reassured, without further explanation, at 767.

798 *Cavern*: the temple of Apollo at Delphi, in particular the chasm in the ground over which his sacred tripod stood, drawing up prophetic vapors from the earth; see *E* n. 29.

803 *Hermes*: here the god of stratagems, especially deceptive messages.

818 *Perseus*: according to tradition, the grandson of an earlier pre-Pelopid king of Argos. He killed the Gorgon, Medusa, whose serpentine hair and lethal glance could petrify a man, by shielding his eyes and using Athena's help. His country, his enemy, his patron goddess, and his role as a liberator all suggest a parallel with Orestes; see n. 1047.

824 *I have my summons*: Aegisthus plays with legal terminology that undoes him.

853 *The last man on the bench*: probably the third wrestler, who, ironically, takes on both contestants here, not simply the winner in the match that went before.

859 *Stand back—*: When Aegisthus' servant rushes in, the women scatter; they want to be counted "clean of the dreadful business," and from now on they are removed from the violence of the action and its meaning. And they are not alone. The servant struggles with Clytaemnestra's doors but cannot wrench them open. She is beyond the reach of all but one, her son Orestes. See Intro., pp. 59ff.

863 *A third, last salute*: traditionally raised for the dead. There is no speaker indicated in the manuscript for these two lines, however, and if three cries of agony were given by Aegisthus they would form another "triad" like the three blows delivered to Agamemnon.

884f Similarly Hecuba exposes her breast to Hector (*Iliad* 22.80) to persuade him not to fight Achilles.

886 For an excellent discussion of Orestes' hesitation and its consequences for the entire *Oresteia*, see William Arrowsmith, "The Criticism of Greek Tragedy," *Tulane Drama Review*, iii (1959), 31–57.

902 *Sold me*: in a manner of speaking, no doubt, but Orestes regards his forced exile as the worst disgrace a freeborn man could suffer.

904 *I am ashamed to mention it in public*: by sending him away from Argos his mother could indulge her adul-

terous love for Aegisthus. In reply she refers to Agamemnon's adulteries with captive women at Troy, especially Cassandra.

912 A *father's [curse]*: the Furies are regarded not simply as avengers of the mother-right in Aeschylus; they can expand their targets, as they have done in A and will do in E.

913 *I must be spilling live tears on a tomb of stone*: Clytaemnestra's tears, in effect, are the last libation poured on Agamemnon's tomb and its extension, the hardening resolution of Orestes. Her dream united her husband and her son in mutual purpose; now her recognition gives their union life. See Intro., p. 61.

915 *I gave you life*: Clytaemnestra comes full circle (895), back to the life that only she can give, but her final words are fraught with tragic awareness and power.

918 *The victims' double fates*: probably Clytaemnestra and Agamemnon or Aegisthus, rather than the queen and Orestes, since the women have a limited understanding of his future.

921 *The bright eye*: a traditional metaphor for the perception, hope and light which a leader offers his society.

925 *Double lion*: Orestes and Pylades.

936f *God's true daughter . . . Right we call her*: a *nomen-omen* deriving *Dikê* (justice) from *Dios kora*, daughter of god; see A n. 688ff.

950 *Look, the light is breaking*: LB may be seen as a tragic parody of the Mysteries of Eleusis. The imagery which has compared Orestes to an athlete struggling for victory—a wrestler, more particularly a charioteer (501)—may be drawn from descriptions of the candidate for initiation who struggles to escape this mortal coil and achieve a spiritual victory of blessings and repose. Orestes the wrestler is about to be cast down, however, the charioteer about to be ridden off the track (1019ff.); the light invoked by the chorus and the torch ignited by the liberator will illuminate a vision of despair; see Intro., pp. 61f.; LB n. 137; A notes 1, 25, 109; E notes 7, 13.

951 *The huge chain that curbed,* etc. The weight of continuous ill fortune that has oppressed the Atreidae—the same metaphor that had described the effect of the Greek army on the Trojans (A 133f.).

959 *The aliens,* etc. Metics; the chorus is probably referring to the usurpers, unaware that Orestes and Pylades must now be treated as aliens too; see A n. 63, E n. 1021.

977 *The Sun:* it was customary to call on this all-seeing deity to witness acts of justice or injustice when the doer or sufferer was certain of being in the right, as Cassandra did before her death in A.

982 *The adulterer dies:* such a killing was allowed, as a crime of passion, by Attic law.

992 *The bath of death:* Orestes' word for bath can mean coffin as well. His mind has begun to leap in free association reminiscent of Cassandra when she is frenzied by Clytaemnestra and her nets; see A 1116ff., 1241ff.

1006 *Aegisthus' blade:* this seems to imply that Clytaemnestra used the sword of Aegisthus to kill Agamemnon, despite the fact that Clytaemnestra's preferred weapon was a battle-ax (876). Seneca in his *Agamemnon* (890ff.) represents Aegisthus as using his sword and Clytaemnestra as using a double ax, but Aeschylus does not say that Aegisthus took part in the murder.

1041 *Menelaus:* according to Homeric tradition, Menelaus would arrive in a day or so, too late to be of help.

1043 *A name for—:* the chorus cuts him short, in effect, before he can utter ill-omened words about his exile and his death.

1047 *Lopped the heads of these two serpents:* as if he were a victorious Hercules or Perseus, though such praises only evoke the Furies in Orestes' mind. Aeschylus was the first Greek writer to describe them as having snakes in their hair (like Gorgons).

1050 *Cannot stay:* the phrase overturns Orestes' declarations at the outset, "I have come home . . . the exile home at last."

THE EUMENIDES

1 *Mother Earth:* man first worships Earth, his source of food, "but before long," as Jane Harrison writes in the Introduction to *Themis*, "he notices that Sky as well as Earth influences his food supply. At first he notes the 'weather,' rain and wind and storm. Next he finds out that the Moon measures seasons, and to her he attributes all growth, all waxing and waning. Then his goddess is Phoebe. When later he discovers that the Sun really dominates his food supply, Phoebe gives place to Phoebus, the Moon to the Sun. The shift of attention, of religious focus, from Earth to Sky, tended to remove the gods from man; they were purged but at the price of remoteness." That is the price of Delphi, as Aeschylus portrays it; for the humanism of Athens and her gods, see Intro., p. 86.

3 *Tradition:* literally *Themis*, the Titaness whose province is established law and custom.

4 *Third by the lots of destiny:* perhaps in the third generation of the gods, as apportioned by Zeus before the birth of Apollo. In *E* the "triad" motif recurs less in explicit statement than as a kind of structural obsession, an *idée fixe* that turns destruction into joy. The Furies' refrains, painfully repeated (*e.g.* 329–34, 342–47), resolve into a third, harmonious song (1004–11, 1023–30). The entire trilogy, as others have observed, recalls the "triad" of stanzas found in choral lyric poetry, like the opening "triad" in *A* (112–60); the turn and counterturn are resolved in a final stand that unifies the partners as a priest presides at a marriage. The basic "triad" of the trilogy itself makes the third play a metaphor for the Mean; *The Eumenides* reconciles the opposites within the *Oresteia* to produce a state of equilibrium; see Intro., pp. 92ff.; *E* 772ff., 1004ff.; *A* n. 245; *LB* n. 61; C. John Herington, "Aeschylus: The Last Phase," *Arion*, iv (1965), 387–403; and Diskin Clay, "Aeschylus' Trigeron Mythos," *Hermes*, xv (1969), 1–9.

7 *Phoebe:* another Titaness, generally associated with the moon, whose name connotes not only radiance but purity. As Apollo's grandmother, it was appropriate for her to bestow her name upon him at birth, Phoebus Apollo.

The note of "purification" in these names, sounded three times over in the Greek, prepares us for the purging of Orestes.

The light-in-darkness theme will now extend into a cosmic conflict between the gods of the Sky and powers of the Earth; see 396ff., 720, 759ff., 937f., 1043ff.; A n. 25, LB n. 137. The imagery of E expands the destructive force of images in A and the human potential of those in LB, while the two extremes are harmonized at last, thanks to a new flexibility of poetic technique in the final play. Earlier images are diffused; they exceed their literal boundaries, blending with other images and often turning into actions that achieve a greater, more positive moral effect; see Intro., pp. 89ff.

9f *Delos . . . Pallas' headlands*: in this account Apollo came to Delphi from Delos (his island birthplace and one of his chief sanctuaries) via Attica, the land of Pallas Athena.

13 *The god of fire*: Hephaistos, whose provinces were fire and mechanical crafts, was the father of Erichthonios, mythical king of Athens. Road-making is probably mentioned here as a symbol of civilization, though it may refer to Apollo's Sacred Way from Athens to Delphi. The reference to his early journey through Attica anticipates his return to Athens later in this play. The reference to Hephaistos and road-making may anticipate the final torchlit procession; see 396, 1039; A n. 109, LB notes 137, 950.

21 *Athena Pronaia*, the "Defender of the Temple," had a notable shrine at the main entrance to the sanctuary at Delphi. Her precinct can still be visited in the valley below the Castalian Spring. Athena *Pronaia* would become conflated with Athena *Pronoia*, the Goddess of Forethought, a power she begins to exercise within this play.

22 *Corycian rock*, etc. A wild district on a plateau of Parnassus, high above Delphi, with a famous cave frequented by Pan and the Nymphs.

24 *Dionysos*: the god traditionally took over control of the Delphic sanctuary during the three months of winter, when Apollo departed for a more genial climate. The viceregency of Dionysos began, as the priestess recalls,

with his savage epiphany at Thebes. Pentheus, the young king of Thebes, was torn in pieces by his mother and other frenzied maenads because he had resisted the god—torn in pieces "like a hare," as Aeschylus phrases it, as if to remind us that the Olympians had been ruthless in the past, and, more specifically, to recall the vivid image of the hare mangled by hunting eagles, a symbol of the destructiveness of war (A 122ff.) and to hint, too, at the fate of Orestes if he is delivered over to the Furies.

27 *Poseidon:* was said to have had a cult at Delphi in earlier times; his sparkling sea lies clearly visible below the sacred mountain.

28 *Zeus:* significantly, perhaps, all the Olympian gods mentioned are male except Athena. The only major male gods who are not mentioned are Ares, god of war and destruction, and Hermes, who will appear later. This "masculinity" may contrast with the more feminine powers who will preside at Athens; see Intro., pp. 87ff.

29 *Seat:* actually a kind of tripod on which the Pythia sat while delivering her oracles in the interior of the temple.

31 *Where are,* etc. Normally there would be a crowd of Greeks and others waiting to enter the temple and ask the oracle their questions. Greeks had precedence over non-Greeks.

37f *Crawling on all fours . . . an old woman,* etc. This rather sensational visual effect embodies a theme stressed by the elders in A: the helplessness of old age in the face of violence and terror. The Pythia in Aeschylus' time had to be a woman of at least fifty years of age. She may symbolize the need for a new, young régime in general, or reflect the poet's failing strength in 458 B.C.

42 *I see,* etc. For the resemblance of this scene, perhaps of the entire play to the world of dreams, see Intro., p. 71f., 92ff. Here dreams will reach their supernatural extreme, prophetic and ordained; at the same time they will lead us from the flux of nightmare to a living, waking vision of individual responsibility and promise—dreams become a dominant culture pattern of the race; see 108f., 131ff., 156ff.; A n. 91, LB n. 42.

51ff *Gorgons . . . Phineus:* the first were the fabulous monsters whose terrifying appearance—tusks, protruding lips, snaky hair—turned people to stone; see LB n. 818.

The winged Harpies, another group of notoriously hideous female demons, persecuted Phineus, a king of a district on the Black Sea, by snatching away or defiling his food.

58 *What they wear*: black, the color of sacrilege and bad omens.

65f *Healer*, etc. For the limits of Apollo's cures and purgations, see Intro., pp. 72ff. Homeopathy—an immersion in poison, plague and their moral analogies: maddening guilt and the agony of failure—becomes the means to individual and social health in the *Oresteia*; see 330ff., 518ff., 543ff., 795ff., 993ff., n. 178; A n. 107, LB n. 69ff.

67 *No, I will never fail you*: that was Apollo's first promise (*LB* 273); must Orestes challenge him to keep his word?

74 *The dark pit*, etc. Tartarus, the underworld to which the Titans were condemned by the Olympians.

83 *Her ancient idol*: the olive-wood figure in the Erechtheum on the Acropolis, the original patroness of Athens, not the colossal statue created (later than this play) by Pheidias for the Parthenon.

93 *Hermes*: the Escort of the Dead emerges here to lead Orestes back to life, a sign of the hopeful, regenerative turn that men and gods will take in this concluding play; see A n. 505, *LB* notes 1, 126, 803.

94 *Shepherd him well*: animal imagery will turn from brutalizing to humane effects. The more savage images (115, 191f.) are abandoned for images which are more sacramental (326ff., 462ff.). The Furies turn from hunting-hounds (132f.) to more domestic creatures (248), foreshadowing the shepherded community, the triumph of civilization (955ff., 991ff., 1009ff.). The serpent, their symbol, will discard its venomous, infernal aspect (493f.) as the Furies assume their powers of regeneration (919f.). The *Oresteia* celebrates the husbandry of heaven; see A n. 810, *LB* n. 252.

102 *Guilt*: aitia, moral responsibility, will turn from a burden to a challenge; see 198, 447f., 585; A n. 796, LB n. 100.

110ff *Libations*, etc. Sacrifices to the spirits of the underworld, always conducted at night, burned close to the earth in a low brazier, consisting of honey, milk and water. The image of the feast will grow horrific as the Furies threaten to banquet on Orestes (262ff.), then august and sacramental as they accept their cult in Athens and the land's first fruits. The image may extend into the atmosphere of health, nurture and the assimilation of our powers that ends the trilogy; see A n. 138, LB n. 261. For the image of libations, see Intro., p. 92; A n. 1391ff., LB n. 17.

116 *Your nets:* this dominant symbol turns from an implement of capture to a symbol of release, finally to an emblem of Athenian culture; see Intro., p. 91. A related image, that of the hunt, is similarly transformed; see A n. 129, LB n. 335. That of the yoke dissolves, in effect, into the responsibilities we shoulder and enjoy, the ballast of our destiny; see A n. 49, LB n. 74.

150 *Child of Zeus:* Apollo.

151 *Ridden down:* imagery of athletics turns more toward riding and racing than the combat skills of archery and wrestling, but these references are less explicit than before, more inclusive of human "pursuits" in general; see 249ff., 375ff., 414ff.; A n. 169ff., LB n. 165.

155 *Guilt both ways,* etc. The grammar of impossible alternatives, the tragic choice of evils, expanded from A 212 and LB 342; see E 495f.

178 *This flying viper:* a striking metaphor for an arrow; it develops the recurrent snake symbolism and perhaps implies a kind of homeopathy—snake-arrow against snake-goddesses.

183ff *Where heads are severed,* etc. Apollo associates the Furies with the worst kinds of "official" cruelty, the ugliest elements in despotic government, which were typical, as the Greeks saw it, of Oriental justice. It is Apollo, however, who has made "Justice and bloody slaughter . . . the same"; the torture-chamber he describes recalls the house of Atreus, to which he condemned Cassandra (see A 1088ff.) and dispatched Orestes for the murder of his mother.

210 *One's flesh and blood:* the leader argues that, since husband and wife are not blood relations, for one to kill the other is not an offense against the blood-bond. Apollo contends that since marriage is a "consummation" (the Greek term *telos* also implies "a rite, ceremony, established

office"; see A n. 71f.) instituted by the King and Queen of Heaven, Zeus and Hera, it has a higher binding power than even ties of blood (as Christians might argue from its "sacramental" aspects).

242 Perhaps it was here, if we may credit the ancient biography of Aeschylus on this point, that the Furies had such a disturbing effect upon the Athenian audience; see Intro., pp. 88ff.

249 The Furies are wingless (54f.), an anthropomorphic trait they share with Athena (415).

250 *Outracing ships,* etc. Nautical imagery will take an auspicious course, once the storms of shipwreck are channeled into tides of joy, gentle winds and blessings by the shower. The man-of-war becomes the ship of state with Pallas at the helm; see A notes 185ff., 1004; *LB* n. 203.

270 *Hades,* god of the dead, is regarded here as the recorder of human conduct or, literally, the public examiner of officials when their term of office has expired. The metaphor from a memorandum tablet resembles the "books of life" which will be consulted on the Day of Judgment according to The Revelation of St. John (20.11ff.).

275ff *Where to speak,* etc. Even the speech of the murderer who has not been purged might contaminate the listener. The fact that Orestes may go among men without harming them is proof that he has been decontaminated. The swine was used in rites of purgation, especially those of the Eleusinian Mysteries, because it was the preferred victim of the chthonic powers. Its blood was shed over the murderer's head and was thought to absorb his bloodguilt as it flowed down his body.

289 *The Argive people,* etc. Three years before the production of the *Oresteia* in 458 B.C., this city-state had made an alliance with Athens against Sparta. Possibly Aeschylus transferred Agamemnon's capital from Mycenae (as it is in Homer) to Argos to please Athens' new allies.

291ff *Libya . . . the Giants' Plain:* an early legend localized Athena's birth at Lake Tritonis in Libya. The reference here was probably prompted by the fact that in 460 B.C. the Athenians had sent a fleet to help a Libyan leader in a revolt against his Persian overlords. The Giants' Plain is Phlegraea in northeastern Greece, the scene of the battle between the Olympians and the Giants, in which the Olympians triumphed over their more primitive enemies.

306 *Chains of song:* the chorus that follows is a kind of magical incantation intended to paralyze its victim. (A recurring refrain is typical of such spells; the anapaestic meter of the Greek implies that the chorus marched as it sang.) Such incantations are referred to as elsewhere in Greek literature, but only here—apart from the nonliterary spells of the magical papyri—do we find a full example of it. Like the witches' chorus in *Macbeth* (first performed at a time when belief in black magic was strong in England), this evil spell of the Furies must have had a powerful effect on the fifth-century Athenians, who believed in many horrific demons and ghosts—a "shriveling effect," as it is called in the refrain. For the relationship between the Furies' "chains," thought by Pythagoreans to shackle impure souls in Hell, and the torments of Orestes in this world, see Intro., pp. 74f.

308 *Art:* crafts and arts, once images, are now performed before our eyes, and will change in force from destructivity to creativity, to become the arts of behavior, justice, and society; see A n. 150, LB n. 233.

310 *To steer the lives of men,* etc. The claim is ultimately acknowledged and enlarged by Athena (942f.).

322 *Mother Night:* here Aeschylus substitutes Night for Earth (who according to another tradition was the mother of the Furies), perhaps because he had already mentioned Earth as the primeval deity of Delphi; see n. 1. Images of parenthood and fertility, perverted in A, ambivalent in effect in LB, here expand into a preoccupation with evolution—the spiritual evolution of the gods, the cultural evolution of mankind. Everything, we may say, is traced back to its origins, and these, in Aeschylus' hands, are not simply reclaimed, they are often challenged and revised, so that they may be more cherished and invigorate the poet's vision of our future; see Intro., pp. 13f., 87ff.; E 72ff., 348ff., 430ff., 468ff., 666ff., 751ff.; A n. 265, LB n. 131ff.

330f *frenzy striking frenzy,* etc. There are no verbs in this refrain, only participles which, while describing the Furies' song, make them participate in its frenzy. As Rose explains, the Furies "are not ministers of vengeance but Vengeance itself, so their charm is not a cause of madness but madness embodied in words and actions." *Ripping cross the lyre*: see A n. 995.

335 *Spun . . . the Fates*: the three sisters whose threads "run through all things"; as named by Hesiod (*Theogony* 904ff.), they are *Klôthô*, who "spins" the thread of life, *Lachesis*, who "allots" each man and woman a certain measure of it, and *Atropos*, who "cannot be turned aside" from cutting it at last—in Milton's words, the Fate "with th'abhorred shears, / [who] slits the thin-spun life"; see notes 116, 972, 1055.

351 *Pious white robes*: the gods' attire for festal occasions.

354f *Reared like a tame beast*, etc. Like Helen in the parable from A (713-32).

360 *Exempt*: perhaps a reference to the procedure by which a litigant was exempted from a legal burden he could not sustain. *No trial*, etc. The Furies would waive the *anakrisis*, the preliminary hearing.

409 *Scamander*: chief river of the plain of Troy, near which the Athenians had a colony, Sigeion, in Aeschylus' time. They claimed that it was allotted to them after the Greek victory in the Trojan war.

413 *Theseus*: the great national hero of Athens. His legends are numerous; those that inform the *Oresteia* tend to make him a contemporary figure, part myth, part fifth-century hero. His past achievements and the current aspirations of his people are joined in the historical present of the play. He too repelled the barbarian invader, he established a democratic federation and, according to Plutarch, instituted the splendid festivals—the Panathenaia and the Festival of Migration for the Metics—that consecrate the city of Athens to Athena. Aeschylus creates an analogue for each event. Theseus' ideal of democracy, recorded by Thucydides, as a society strong in individuality and order is celebrated in *E*. His invitation to all nations, also recorded by Plutarch, to participate in the benefits of democracy—"Come hither, all ye people"—may echo in the closing chorus. For the Athenians' imitation of Theseus and his achievements, see W. Robert Connor, "Theseus in Classical Athens," in *The Quest for Theseus*, ed. Anne G. Ward (London: Pall Mall Press, 1970), pp. 143-74.

415 *Cape:* the *aigis*, a magical mantle (originally a breast-plate) which was part of Athena's battle-dress.

441 *The oath:* as Headlam explains, "Either party might either offer himself to take a solemn oath or ask his opponent to do so: the oath would be to the truth of the essential facts on which the pleadings were based: if both parties agreed to have the matter decided in this way, then this was a final decision." Orestes will not take the oath because the facts are not at issue—he admits he killed his mother; the question is whether or not his action was justifiable. That is the thrust of Athena's position here, and it prepares us for one of the major themes in the play: the evolution of oaths from their ritualistic power to exonerate the criminal to their power to sanctify the evidence, hence to insure a valid trial. Perjury becomes a crime, in short, and the Furies will have jurisdiction over it; see n. 946.

455 *Ixion:* traditionally the first Greek to slay a kinsman, the equivalent of Cain in Genesis. He was granted purification by Zeus; see n. 726ff.

486f *Not even I should decide a case of murder:* perhaps it is simply not her province, or too emotional an issue, as she suggests; but it is strange, after she had killed so many men at Troy, that she should hesitate to learn what murder means. This is Athena's education in the postwar years, and she does not hesitate for long.

494 *Blights our land,* etc. As if reflecting the influence of the Mysteries on *E*, images of agriculture, perhaps more than any other pattern in the play, will grow from a negative to a positive extreme. Athena transforms the Furies' power to destroy the earth into their power to promote its harvest. She herself will cultivate the Athenians "as a gardener loves his plants" (921) and guard the fruits of culture; see 792 to the conclusion; *A* n. 517, *LB* n. 205.

514ff *We are the Furies,* etc. They had been discriminating avengers; an age of lawlessness would force them to loose an indiscriminate tide of vengeance.

528 *The house of Justice falls:* in the binding-song the Furies sought the overthrow of lawless houses; now they lament the overthrow of their own house, the house of law where victims once appealed for justice.

529 *Terror helps*: the doctrine that fear of punishment (implied in the word "deterrent," originally "terrifying away from") was necessary for the maintenance of law and order was widely held in antiquity.

531 *Suffer into truth*: see A 179.

539 *Strike the balance*: the metaphor of the balance scales of justice now will yield to a celebration of the balance of the Mean as seen in legal equity, social equality, and an equilibrium that extends from the psyche to the cosmos; see A n. 436, LB n. 61.

542 *Violence is Impiety's child*, etc. The genealogy of *hubris* that Agamemnon fatally embodied will be succeeded by legitimate prosperity; see A 744–60, and Intro., pp. 77f.

573 *Etruscan battle-trumpet*: Etruria in Italy manufactured a celebrated kind of trumpet in the fifth century B.C. It was thought to be Athena's special instrument.

588ff *The trial begins*: for some of Aeschylus' adaptations of fifth-century legal procedure, Intro., pp. 77ff., 81f. The Furies' first two questions are formulaic—*quid, quomodo*: Did you kill your mother? Yes. How? I cut her throat, Orestes answers staunchly. But the third—*quibus auxiliis*: With whose help?—reveals that Apollo has brought him to this pass, yet left him quite defenseless. He must rely on his father, though the Furies remind him Agamemnon is as dead as the mother Orestes murdered. She had to die, she killed two men at once—father and husband both— he protests ingeniously. But die she did, absolved, in effect, while he lives on for trial. The Furies' logic is ruthless. Orestes asks why they never pursued his mother. They only punish kindred murder, they say, contradicting themselves perhaps, but leading him to his most contradictory defense.

595 *Three falls*: see A n. 169ff.

628 *Zeus, you say*, etc. As the Furies waived the prosecutor's customary speech for a dramatic cross-examination of Orestes, so when Apollo plays the *sunêgoros* or public advocate, they tersely interrupt his speech for the defense.

635 The Amazons were famous as archers; see n. 697ff.

655ff *But once the dust drinks down a man's blood*, etc. The familiar theme, applied in turn against Agamemnon, Clytaemnestra and Orestes, finally recoils, as Thomson observes, "to show that the case of Orestes cannot be decided by a simple appeal to the *lex talionis*." It is a curious irony of history that Apollo emphatically denies the possibility of a resurrection in addressing the court of the Areopagus where, more than five hundred years after the performance of this trilogy, Saint Paul would make belief in the Resurrection the kernel of his appeal to the Athenians to accept the new faith.

666ff Apollo alleges that mothers are not true parents but only act as receptacles, so to speak, for the child which is already formed in the sperm of the father. The argument was of biological interest to the Greeks; it was also sociological and economic propaganda which might be used to insure the male inheritance of property in the democratic state.

682ff *A new ally*, etc. For Apollo's questionable conduct during the trial, see Intro., pp. 79f., 82. He may even end his peroration by adding insult to injury. Orestes freely offered Athena the loyalty of Argos (*E* 288–90); now Apollo dangles it before her as a bribe.

696ff *This will be the court:* Aeschylus' derivation of the Areopagus from the trial of Orestes reflects the poet's response to the democratic reforms which, during his lifetime, had curtailed the powers of the supreme court of Athens. The choice of judges, formerly a matter of aristocratic birth, had been "democratized" by the introduction of the lot; the authority of the court as a king's council that oversaw the workings of the Constitution had been eliminated; and its jurisdiction had been reduced to cases of homicide. Aeschylus may seem to support the last reform by deriving the court from a case of homicide, but his warnings against innovations (706ff.), his reference to the Areopagus as a *bouleutêrion*, a senate as well as a tribunal (696, 718), and the democratic cast which he imparts to the ancient institution at its inception may suggest that he wishes to preserve its broadest powers.

697ff An Attic legend said that the Amazons, a nation of women warriors from near the Black Sea, once invaded Athens and occupied the "Crag of Ares" (i.e., the rock of the Areopagus opposite the entrance to the Acropolis) in revenge for Theseus' attack on them and his abduction of their queen Hippolyta. The Athenians defeated the Amazons and drove them off. The Persians also used the Areopagus as a launching site for their attack on the Acropolis. Legend and history often merge in the suggestive double vision of the play; see Intro., p. 90; notes 289, 291ff., 409, 413, 696ff.

717 *Scythia's rugged steppes or Pelops' level plain:* Scythia was a district northwest of the Black Sea. Pelops' name was given to the Peloponnese (literally "the island of Pelops"). The two names are used to represent the uncivilized and civilized world.

720 *Night watch:* the image once applied to Clytaemnestra (A 257). The nightly sessions of the Areopagus, its vigilance and severity may suggest that the great court bears similarities to chthonic worship, in fact that Athena has institutionalized the Furies; see Intro., pp. 80, 85.

726ff The interchange between Apollo and the Furies may be "mythological mudslinging," as Anne Lebeck has called it. The Furies are clearly not without their threats, but Apollo's threats combine wobbly mythology with a certain moral obtuseness. Did Zeus's judgment falter, he asks, when he pardoned Ixion for manslaughter? Yes, perhaps. The man went right on sinning—he tried to seduce Hera, courting the punishment he received: perpetual rotation on a wheel. And Admetus (the son of Pheres, king of Thessaly) was less a model of piety, as Apollo claims, than simply a favorite of the god. Apollo drugged the Fates with wine, moreover, and so "persuaded" them to allow Admetus to escape his death on condition that he should find a good replacement. (His wife, Alcestis, undertook to die for him and was restored to life by the intervention of Apollo and Heracles.) There may be a question, in short, about the credibility of the gods. It may be as much to lend them support as to blunt the Furies' anger, which may indeed be valid, that Athena casts her ballot as she does; see Intro., pp. 81ff.

767 *The lots are equal:* the question of the number of the jurors and the nature of their verdict is vexed indeed. Some have argued that their number is uneven, that they vote six to five (according to the allotment of lines 726–48: two lines for each of ten jurors, three lines for an eleventh) in favor of the Furies, and that Athena casts her lot for Orestes, simultaneously creating the tie which her vote is

designed to break. "This view, however," as Thomson points out in his extensive note on the problem, "is incompatible with [806–08], where Athena, anxious to conciliate the Furies, tells them that they have not really been defeated because the votes were equal. If the votes have only been made equal by the addition of her own, she is adding insult to injury. She could only hope to appease the Furies by such an argument if the votes of the judges have been equally divided irrespective of her own." Persuaded by such internal evidence, we prefer to believe that the number of jurors is even, that they may be deadlocked five to five (allotting 726–45 into ten couplets for ten jurors, followed by the eccentric triplet which allows the jurors to return to their seats), and that Athena's ballot may simply break the tie.

"As to the grounds on which Athena bases her decision," Thomson continues, "they are stated plainly and unequivocally . . . [751–55]; and . . . they touch the vital point at issue. In the later tradition her motive is said to have been mercy . . . or, what is virtually the same thing, *filanthrôpia*. . . . In this play too her conduct throughout is expressive of these qualities, but, if Aeschylus had wished to leave her motive as indefinite as that, he would have done so; and the fact that he did not, but made her base her decision on particular reasons deduced from the hearing of the case, can only mean that she upholds the plea for the defence that the homicide was justifiable. This is not inconsistent with her attitude at [484–87], where she was merely concerned to explain why she could not decide the issue out of hand, as both parties to the dispute expected her to do; nor is it inconsistent with her assurance to the Furies at [806–08], where she contends that, since the votes of the judges were equally divided, the result cannot be regarded as dishonourable to them."

What is crucial, in other words, is that Athena conduct herself so judiciously throughout the trial that, throughout its aftermath which may be more important, she can mediate successfully between the Furies and the citizens of Athens. For beyond the question of the balloting and the number of the jurors, where internal evidence may be debated, and beyond the question of Athena's motives, where internal evidence would seem to be convincing, lies the clear, momentous result of the court proceedings in *The Eumenides*: namely, Athena's establishment of justice, not with the collaboration of her fellow Olympians—least of all with Apollo the God of Law—but with the rudimentary morality of the Furies and the indispensable, never-ending efforts of mankind; see Intro., pp. 83ff.

771 *"He lives again,"* etc. Orestes may echo Hector in the *Iliad* (6.479ff.), fulfilling in effect that father's hope that a son may live a greater life than he.

780 *We ourselves:* the royal We, perhaps, or a reference to Orestes and his father, reunited in spirit.

792 *You have ridden down,* etc. Now the Furies have been ridden down by all the gods, not simply Apollo (see 151); now they will not only attack mankind (514ff.) but devastate the earth.

816ff *By all my rights:* as the exclusive patroness of Athens. Here and in her next speech Athena institutionalizes what Clytaemnestra had offered the Furies earlier—an elaborate sacrifice appropriate to the spirits of the dead—but by accepting Athena's offer of the land's first fruits the Furies also become, in effect, the spirits of regeneration; see 110ff. and n.

838 *His lightning-bolt:* Athena was the only other Olympian empowered to use the preferred weapon of Zeus.

847 *Disgrace,* etc. What the Furies deplore is the idea that they should lose their power of roaming the earth in pursuit of the blood-guilty and be confined merely to a cave in Athens.

870 *The battle cock:* see A n. 1706.

877 *Do great things,* etc. The phrasing may transform the *lex talionis*—the law of retaliation that "the one who does the work must suffer"—into a civilized law of responsibility and reward; see A n. 1592, *LB* n. 320.

893 *Persuasion: Peitho* has finally evolved from a destructive force to its most compassionate, constructive form, the power by which one wins an opponent over by reason rather than compulsion. *Peitho* also has an institutional, political and "democratic" power especially sacred to Athens, where her worship was established by Theseus, her statue stood near the Acropolis, and her priestess enjoyed a special seat in the Theater of Dionysos; see Intro., 84f.; *E* 839, 981f.; *A* n. 378ff., *LB* n. 714.

913 *Nothing that strikes a note of brutal conquest:* "While the victory is [Athena's]," as Thomson comments, "the credit for it belongs to the Furies who have conceded it." Agamemnon's fatal concessions to Clytaemnestra have come right at last; see A 938ff.

930 *Ares:* as if to include the alternate version of the founding of the Areopagus, where Ares was exonerated for manslaughter.

941ff The fact that Athena speaks now in lyric anapaests, not in the iambics of dialogue, shows that she is deeply moved by the "conversion" of the Furies, who reply in freer lyric rhythms. This form recalls the exchange between Clytaemnestra and the elders at the end of A (1476–1605); its result, the creation of social harmony, is the opposite.

946 *The crimes of his fathers,* etc. Some believe that Aeschylus would not revert to a doctrine of hereditary guilt unless it pertained to the procedure of the Areopagus, namely, the oath which those who testified would take, "in effect a curse which they invoked," as Thomson explains, "in the event of their committing perjury, on themselves and their descendants."

955 *Pan,* etc. Pan had a shrine on the slopes of the Acropolis near the Areopagus; Earth, Hermes and Ploutos or Wealth had statues in the sanctuary of the Semnai at the base of the Areopagus.

958f *Silver:* there may be a reference to the rich silver mines at Laureion in Attica. *Secret treasure of Hermes:* who brings wealth to light, the god of lucky finds.

972 *Gods of wedlock,* etc. In the spirit of reconciliation that ends the *Oresteia,* the Olympian Zeus and Hera coalesce with the matriarchal Fates, now also known as "gods" as well as "spirits," who coalesce in turn with the Furies, their sisters by their common mother Night.

983 *Zeus Agoraios:* the god of popular assemblies where "persuasive oratory carries the day" (Rose).

1020 *The Rock King:* a way of referring to the king of the rocky Acropolis in the time of the earliest inhabitants whom the Greeks called Pelasgians.

1021 *Our guests:* literally Metics, *metoikoi.* This word, which means in general "people who change their residence," had a special meaning in Athens where the Metics comprised a special class of foreigners with certain rights and privileges (though not those of full citizenship). This enlightened policy indicated a more tolerant attitude toward foreigners than elsewhere in Greece; see A n. 63, LB n. 959. For resemblances between the conclusion of *E* and the Panathenaic Procession, the public ritual in which the Metics received their yearly recognition, see Intro., p. 86; and Walter Headlam, "The Last Scene of *The Eumenides*," *Journal of Hellenic Studies*, xxvi (1906), 268–77.

1046 *The first dark vaults of Earth:* the Furies, now to be known as the Eumenides, the Kindly Ones (1050, though the line may be disputed), were believed by the Athenians to inhabit a sacred cave on the north face of the Acropolis; as the Semnai Theai, the Awesome Goddesses, they enjoyed a similar sanctuary at the base of the Areopagus. Aeschylus is the first writer known to have made this triple identification.

1053 *Cry in triumph:* the earlier cries of vengeance echo now in cries of joy; see A n. 30, LB n. 383.

1054 *This peace:* this doubtful passage may contain a reference to the Truce of God during the Olympic Games and the Eleusinian Mysteries, a moment of harmony between mortals and immortals here perhaps made permanent at last.

1055 *Zeus and Fate:* in the archaic world the relationship between Zeus and Fate had been ambiguous—now one predominated, now the other; the *Oresteia* concludes with a balance of power between the two great forces; see Intro., pp. 87ff.

GLOSSARY

Acheron: one of the rivers of Hades.

Aegeus: a legendary king of Athens and father of Theseus.

Aegisthus: the son of Thyestes, paramour of Clytaemnestra, usurper of Agamemnon's throne.

Agamemnon: the son of Atreus, brother of Menelaus, husband of Clytaemnestra and father of Iphigeneia, Orestes and Electra; commander-in-chief of the Greek expeditionary forces sent to Troy, and king of Argos.

Althaia: the daughter of Thestios and Eurythemis, who murdered her son Meleager; see *LB* n. 587.

Amazons: a nation of women warriors from near the Black Sea, famous as archers and the invaders of Athens; see *E* n. 697ff.

Apollo: the god whose provinces include music, poetry and the arts of government and civilization, invoked in the *Oresteia* as the god of archery, roads, healing, prophecy, purification and the law; see Intro., pp. 8, 29, 52ff., 63, 71ff., 75ff., 87; A notes 107, 1218; *E* notes 65f., 726ff.

Areopagus: the supreme court of Athens, named for its location on the Crag of Ares; see *E* n. 696ff.

Ares: the god of battle and the warlike spirit.

Argos: a city on the Argive Plain and, throughout the trilogy, the seat of Agamemnon's empire, hence the name given to a district in the northeastern Peloponnese, or more generally, to Greece itself; see A introductory n.

Artemis: the sister of Apollo, goddess of the hunt, wild creatures, childbirth and fertility; see A n. 135ff.

Athena: the daughter of Zeus and patron goddess of Athens; the virgin warrioress and protectress of the city, whose provinces include the arts of government, the handicrafts of women, skills in general and wisdom; see Intro., pp. 14f., 33, 68, 75ff., 87ff.

Atreus: the son of Pelops and father of Agamemnon and Menelaus, the Atreidae.

Aulis: a district on the narrow strait between Euboea and the Greek mainland where the Greek fleets gathered before embarking for Troy and where Agamemnon sacrificed Iphigeneia.

Beacons: for locations of the stations, see A notes 281ff. through 309.

Calchas: the seer of the Greek armies.

Cassandra: daughter of Hecuba and Priam, king of Troy; priestess of Apollo, abducted to Argos by Agamemnon and murdered with him by Clytaemnestra; see Intro., pp. 5, 26ff., 45f., 62, 84; A notes 1145, 1196, 1218, 1279, 1297.

Clytaemnestra: the daughter of Leda and Tyndareos, king of Sparta; wife of Agamemnon and paramour of Aegisthus, mother of Iphigeneia, Orestes and Electra, and queen of Argos.

Daulis: a district in Phokis on the road from Thebes to Delphi; see *LB* n. 657.

Delos: the island birthplace of Apollo and one of his chief sanctuaries.

Delphic Oracle: the supreme oracular seat of Greece, originally sacred to Mother Earth but later presided over by Apollo. It is located on the southern slopes of Parnassus and towers above the Gulf of Corinth.

Delphos: the eponymous hero of Delphi.

Dionysos: the son of Semele and Zeus, god of fertility, wine and ecstasy; see Intro., pp. 8ff., 47f., 68ff., 89, 96.

Dog Star: *Sirius* (from *Seirios*, the Scorcher), the brightest star in the heavens, whose summer appearances are associated with madness and intense heat.

Electra: the daughter of Agamemnon and Clytaemnestra, sister of Orestes and Iphigeneia.

Erechtheus: an early king of Athens whose house, called the Erechtheum, was on the Acropolis.

Fates: the *Moirai* ("the Apportioners"), shadowy but potent figures who ultimately controlled men's destiny. How far their powers and those of Zeus overlapped was a major problem in Greek religion and formed part of the theme of Aeschylus' *Prometheus* trilogy: see Intro., pp. 85ff., 96; A n. 131, E notes 335, 972, 1055.

Fury: Vengeance personified; see Intro., throughout.

Geryon: a mythical giant with three bodies and three lives; see A n. 859.

Gorgon: a fabulous female monster whose glance could turn a person into stone; see LB n. 818, E n. 51ff.

Hades: the lord of the underworld and arbitrator of the dead.

Harpies: winged female demons; see E n. 51ff.

Helen: the daughter of Zeus and Leda, half-sister of Clytaemnestra; her abduction by Paris produced the war between the Greeks and Trojans.

Hephaistos: the god of fire and mechanical crafts.

Hera: the consort of Zeus, with whom she presides over marriage and its rites.

Hermes: the god of heralds in A, of messages and stratagems and the Escort of the Dead in LB; see A n. 505, LB notes 1, 126, 803; E n. 93.

Inachos: the chief river of Argos.

Iphigeneia: the daughter of Agamemnon and Clytaemnestra, sister of Orestes and Electra.

Ixion: traditionally the first Greek to slay a kinsman; see E notes 455, 726ff.

Kronos: the youngest son of Sky and Earth, leader of his brother Titans against the Olympians, and father of Zeus, deposed by him in turn.

Leda: the mother of Helen, Castor and Pollux, by Zeus, and of Clytaemnestra by Tyndareos, king of Sparta.

Menelaus: the son of Atreus, brother of Agamemnon, husband of Helen.

Mother Earth: the offspring of Chaos, husband of the Sky, mother of the Titans, and the original possessor of the shrine at Delphi.

Navelstone: the *omphalos* at Delphi, supposed to mark the center of the Earth.

Night: born of Chaos, mother of the Day and the Furies.

Odysseus: the son of Laertes, husband of Penelope, father of Telemachus, and king of Ithaca; see *A* n. 827.

Orestes: the son of Agamemnon and Clytaemnestra, brother of Iphigeneia and Electra, in exile throughout the action of *A* but later the avenger of his father, the executioner of his mother and Aegisthus, and prince of Argos.

Orpheus: the legendary musician and singer; see *A* n. 1662ff.

Paris: the son of Priam and Hecuba, prince of Troy, abductor of Helen.

Parnassus: the great mountain massif in Phokis, made sacred by the Muses and the oracle and temple of Apollo on its slopes.

Pelops: son of Tantalus, ancestor of Atreus and Agamemnon.

Pentheus: the king of Thebes who rejected Dionysos and was torn in pieces by his mother and other followers of the god; see *E* n. 24.

Persephone: the daughter of Demeter and consort of Hades; see Intro., p. 69ff., 85f.

Perseus: the legendary hero of Argos who killed the Gorgon, Medusa; see *LB* n. 818.

Phineus: a legendary king of Thrace and victim of the Harpies; see *E* n. 51ff.

Phoebe: the Titaness generally associated with the moon, the grandmother of Apollo; see *E* n. 7.

Phokis: a region in central Greece along the Gulf of Corinth.

Pleiades: a major constellation that sets in autumn; see *A* n. 8.

Pleisthenes: an unidentified figure among the ancestors of Agamemnon; see *A* n. 1634.

Pleistos: a river that rushes below the heights of Delphi.

Poseidon: the god of earthquakes, water and the sea; see Intro., pp. 95f. *E* n. 27.

Priam: the king of Troy and father of Cassandra, Paris, Hector and many others.

Pylades: the son of Strophios and prince of Phokis, comrade of Orestes.

Pythia: the priestess of Apollo at Delphi; see *E* n. 37f.

Scamander: the chief river of the Trojan Plain.

Scylla: the legendary sea-witch of the *Odyssey* (see *A* n. 1244), or the daughter of Nisos and princess of Megara (see *LB* n. 597).

Scythia: a region in South Russia inhabited by nomads who were renowned warriors and archers.

Simois: the second river of the Trojan Plain.

Strophios: a legendary king of Phokis and the father of Pylades; see *A* n. 869ff., *LB* n. 661f.

Tantalus: a Lydian king and founder of the line of Pelops, Atreus, Agamemnon, and Orestes. His Asian origin perhaps implied a streak of un-Greek brutality in him and his descendants.

Themis: Tradition, the Titaness whose province is established law and custom.

Theseus: the great national hero of Athens; see *E* n. 413.

Thrace: a mountainous region north of Greece, in the eastern half of the Balkan peninsula.

Thyestes: the son of Pelops, brother of Atreus, father of Aegisthus, and invoker of the curse upon his brother's house.

Troy: a city near the Aegean entrance to the Dardanelles, the capital of the Troad and the Trojans.

Zeus: the son of Kronos, the father of the Olympian gods, and the most powerful among them. His spheres include hospitality and the rights of guests (Zeus *Xenios*), the possessions of the house (Zeus *Ktêsios*), the public assembly (Zeus *Agoraios*), rituals and their fulfillment (Zeus *Teleios*)—especially the ritual of marriage, which he oversees with his consort, Hera—the accomplishment of justice or revenge (Zeus *Dikêphoros*), the harmonization of the Olympian gods and the spirits of the dead (Zeus *Sôter* or Third Saving Zeus), and the governance of the universe, which was controlled to some extent by Fate as well; see Intro., throughout; *A* notes 161, 245, 796; *E* notes 210, 726ff., 983, 1055.

The gold cup on the cover showing the capture of wild bulls with hunting-nets and hobbles, is from the tholos-tomb at Vaphio near Sparta, c. 1500 B.C.; now in the National Museum, Athens. The motif of the crown at the opening of each play is from a gold funerary diadem for a woman, discovered in Schliemann's grave circle within the citadel of Mycenae. The motif of the procession at the close of each play is from a gold signet ring from the lower town at Tiryns; it portrays the Great Goddess, seated, with a falcon behind her and an incense-burner before her; she extends a sacred cup toward four Ta-urt demons who approach her, bearing libations of holy water from the heavens. The other illustrations are drawn from Mycenaean ornaments and seals.

ROBERT FAGLES is Professor of Comparative Literature and Chairman of the Department at Princeton University. His translation of *The Poems of Bacchylides* was published by the Yale University Press with introduction and notes by Adam Parry and foreword by Sir Maurice Bowra. Under the direction of Maynard Mack, Mr. Fagles was one of the associate editors of The Twickenham Edition of Pope's *Iliad* and *Odyssey*. He and George Steiner edited *Homer: A Collection of Critical Essays*. Mr. Fagles' poems and translations have appeared in many journals, and *I, Vincent: Poems from the Pictures of Van Gogh* was recently published by the Princeton University Press. His complete translation of Sophocles' *Theban Plays*, written in collaboration with Bernard Knox, will soon appear.

W. B. STANFORD is Regius Professor of Greek, Emeritus, at Dublin University and Senior Fellow of Trinity College, Dublin. His several works include the acclaimed *Ulysses Theme*, definitive editions of Homer's *Odyssey* and Sophocles' *Ajax*, *Aeschylus in His Style* and pioneering studies of metaphor and ambiguity in Greek poetry, and, more recently, *The Sound of Greek* and, with J.V. Luce, *The Quest for Ulysses*. Mr. Stanford was representative of Dublin University in the Senate of the Irish Republic from 1948 to 1969 and has been Chairman of the Dublin Institute for Advanced Studies since 1972.